PRAISE FOR

The Fall of Affirmative Action

"This book stands as a brilliant reminder that the nation's struggles to overcome the tragic legacy of discrimination against African Americans cannot and should not be subject to closure. Justin Driver's insightful analysis of the Supreme Court's decision in *SFFA v. Harvard* provides much-needed hope for our future. A book critically important to this fraught moment for American higher education."

LEE C. BOLLINGER,
president emeritus of Columbia University and author of *A Legacy of Discrimination: The Essential Constitutionality of Affirmative Action*

"Justin Driver is a dazzling commentator on legal affairs who deploys prodigious knowledge and a knack for lively writing to make complex controversies accessible. This is, without exception, the single best volume in the library of books about affirmative action. It passionately advances a thesis—affirmative action is useful and ought not to have been nullified—while paying scrupulous attention to contending points of view. It is a masterful intervention that offers bracing instruction whatever your prior inclination. *The Fall of Affirmative Action* warrants reading and rereading."

RANDALL KENNEDY,
Michael R. Klein Professor of Law, Harvard Law School

"Although much has been written about affirmative action, Professor Justin Driver has written a book that is stunning in its originality and insights. He carefully shows the weaknesses in both the conservative critiques and the liberal defenses of affirmative action. Most important, he offers a concrete path forward for universities to pursue diversity while being consistent with the Supreme Court's rulings."

ERWIN CHEMERINSKY,
dean of University of California, Berkeley School of Law

"Always read Justin Driver, one of our foremost thinkers on law and education—especially now, when so much is unsettled in this enormously consequential domain of American life. This book is full of insight, trenchant analysis, and provocative questions about what the loss of affirmative action means."

EMILY BAZELON,
author of *Charged: The New Movement to Transform American Prosecution and End Mass Incarceration*

"Justin Driver wields one of America's most agile legal minds, and this important book shows it. In the face of affirmative action's demise, he does something rare: offers clear-eyed, workable ideas to help American higher education pursue its highest ideals."

FRANKLIN FOER,
author of *The Last Politician: Inside Joe Biden's White House and the Struggle for America's Future*

The Fall of
Affirmative Action

COLUMBIA GLOBAL REPORTS
NEW YORK

The Fall of Affirmative Action

Race, the Supreme Court, and the Future of Higher Education

Justin Driver

United States

The Fall of Affirmative Action
Race, the Supreme Court, and the Future of Higher Education

Copyright © 2025 by Justin Driver

Published by Columbia Global Reports
91 Claremont Avenue, Suite 515
New York, NY 10027
globalreports.columbia.edu

Library of Congress Cataloging-in-Publication Data Available Upon Request

ISBN 979-8-987053-76-8 (paperback)

Book design by Kelly Winton
Map design by Jeffrey L. Ward
Author photograph by August W. Brown

Printed in the United States of America

For Laura,
for everything

CONTENTS

Introduction

On June 15, 1963, as President Charles Odegaard looked out upon thousands of graduating students assembled for the University of Washington's commencement exercises, he surveyed the scene with a mounting sense of dismay. Odegaard should have had plenty of reasons to celebrate. For most university presidents, of course, graduation ceremonies are joyous occasions, annual opportunities to drink in the stirring bagpipes, flowing academic regalia, and beaming family members. In addition, the weather—a perpetual concern in rain-drenched Seattle—was nothing less than spectacular. One local newspaper noted that the "[b]rilliant sunlight matched exactly life's golden vista [for] graduates." More broadly, Odegaard—who had been at the helm for five years—had begun transforming the University of Washington from a solid, but essentially regional, institution into a first-rate academic hub. Even if UW would never quite realize Odegaard's aspiration of becoming "the Harvard of the West"—that laurel surely belonged to Stanford—his enthusiasm about the place and its future

attracted dazzling professors and generous funding the likes of
which the former outpost had never seen.

On that bright Saturday afternoon in June 1963, however, Odegaard found all these reasons for cheer were overshadowed by the disturbing parade that unfolded before his eyes. As throngs of new graduates from the various schools and colleges filed across the stage to claim their degrees, Odegaard noticed that virtually all of them had one thing in common: white skin. It risks little exaggeration to note that the only black at Washington's commencement exercises could be found on the academic gowns. Odegaard was sufficiently stricken by the monochromatic display that, immediately after descending the stage, he twice asked himself a simple five-word question: "Where are the black students? Where are the black students?" Odegaard's query has—in assorted guises—haunted American higher education for the last six decades.

Odegaard had received his doctoral degree from Harvard University many years earlier by training as a medievalist. He was, however, attuned to the problems afflicting modern American society. Indeed, when Odegaard delivered his address to the graduating students in 1963, he stressed the importance of refusing to permit deep learning to remain wholly an abstraction. "Wisdom is revealed in action," Odegaard insisted, "in the way in which you hold knowledge, in the way in which you select it for the determination of relevant issues, in the way in which you employ it to add value to immediate experience."

For his own part, Odegaard had determined that no more relevant, pressing issue confronted the mid-twentieth century United States than the problem of anti-Black discrimination. Upon attaining Washington's presidency in 1958, Odegaard

14   circulated a memorandum requiring that the university proceed "solely on the basis of merit of the applicants without regard to race, creed, or color." But it quickly became apparent that Odegaard's antidiscrimination policy proved insufficient to bring more than a trickle of Black students to campus.

The 1963 commencement ceremony marked a breaking point for Odegaard, sparking what he later called "a growing awareness that just an open-door" approach was inadequate to ensure that the university educated more than a trivial number of Black students. Provocatively, Odegaard argued that the nation's long, sorry history of Black suppression should now—in a certain sense—be inverted. "It is clear . . . that the history after slavery of 100 years of separate and unequal treatment will have to be matched by at least some years of separate and unequal treatment the other way, if the situation is to be remedied." In an arresting turn of phrase, Odegaard proclaimed: "*[E]quality was not enough*; . . . some more positive contribution had to be made to the resolution of this problem in American life, and something had to be done by the University of Washington." That "more positive contribution" Odegaard and his colleagues devised would soon become widely known by the term "affirmative action."

The University of Washington School of Law—at Odegaard's prompting—implemented a notably muscular form of affirmative action. The law school faculty went so far as to adopt an entirely separate admissions program geared toward boosting the enrollment of minority students. Echoing Odegaard, the admissions policy stated that "the faculty recognizes a special obligation . . . to contribute to the solution of the [racial] problem," and noted that it felt moved to do so "[b]ecause certain

ethnic groups . . . have historically been limited in their access
to the legal profession and because the resulting underrep-
resentation can affect the quality of legal services available
to . . . such groups, as well as limit their opportunity for full
participation in the governance of our communities." While
the policy avoided imposing a strict racial quota, it specified
that "the faculty . . . believes that approximately 15 to 20 percent is . . . a reasonable proportion [of racial minorities in a law
school class] if there are sufficient qualified applicants available." The law school's aggressive admissions approach would
ultimately become the Supreme Court's earliest encounter with
the legality of affirmative action in a dispute called *DeFunis v.
Odegaard*—an opinion that is now all but forgotten even among
many constitutional law mavens.

That *DeFunis v. Odegaard* has fallen into neglect is both
understandable and regrettable. It is understandable because
the *DeFunis* decision effectively amounted to a *non*decision.
By the time the dispute reached the Supreme Court in 1974, a
rejected white applicant named Marco DeFunis had not only
been ordered admitted to Washington's School of Law by a lower
court but stood only weeks shy of graduation. Accordingly, the
Supreme Court as a body declined to reach the lawsuit's merits, deeming the dispute moot in light of DeFunis's pending
graduation.

It is regrettable that *DeFunis* has now been forgotten,
though, because Justice William O. Douglas wrote a key opinion that not one of his colleagues agreed to join. Douglas argued
that the Supreme Court wrongly punted on a legal issue that
would doubtless recur. On that score, Douglas was assuredly
correct, as the Supreme Court in subsequent decades regularly

16 considered, reconsidered, and reconsidered again whether the Fourteenth Amendment's Equal Protection Clause prohibits universities from engaging in affirmative action. More significantly, Douglas's separate writing in *DeFunis* uncannily anticipated the Supreme Court's recent decision eliminating affirmative action. Douglas's obscure writing from more than a half-century ago merits renewed focus today because it augurs the shape of things to come in higher education.

On June 29, 2023—six decades to the month after President Odegaard's grim revelation—the Supreme Court of the United States killed affirmative action in a case called *Students for Fair Admissions, Inc. v. President and Fellows of Harvard College* (*SFFA*). Now that affirmative action is dead, the least we can do is ensure that it receives a proper burial.

Affirmative action, long one of the nation's most incendiary topics, succeeded in transforming American society for the better. Beginning in the late 1960s, the policy brought significant numbers of Black students to elite college campuses, integrating what had been lily white institutions and, more profoundly, assaulting the nation's basic racial hierarchy. In the face of repeated challenges, the Supreme Court upheld affirmative action's constitutionality in an unbroken series of decisions dating back to the 1970s. But a decade ago, one of the policy's central opponents—a conservative activist named Edward Blum—alighted upon a new strategy for attacking affirmative action. Rather than asserting that such policies harmed white applicants, he contended that Asian Americans were its true victims. Blum created SFFA, an organization that filed lawsuits contesting admissions policies of the nation's oldest public

college (the University of North Carolina) and oldest private
college (Harvard). That strategy reaped dividends two years ago
when a 6−3 decision—joined by all three of President Trump's
appointees—banned affirmative action.

Several observers have asserted that the Supreme Court's
elimination of affirmative action will have precious little in
the way of practical effect on Black enrollment in elite universities. In 2013, when many believed that the Supreme Court
stood poised to outlaw the policy, Professor Randall Kennedy
of Harvard Law School insisted that any such opinion was des-
tined to prove ineffectual. "[A]ffirmative action will remain
a substantial presence in American life . . . no matter how the
Supreme Court resolves [the current dispute]," Kennedy
claimed. The affirmative action principle, Kennedy maintained,
had become too venerated, too entrenched on American campuses for any judicial decision to provoke an admissions overhaul. A decade later—as the *SFFA* dispute sat pending at the
Court—legal scholar Melvin Urofsky similarly contended that
the judiciary could not banish affirmative action even if it tried.
"While affirmative action plans may change in the forthcom-
ing years," Urofsky wrote, "it does not seem that, whatever the
Supreme Court may say [in *SFFA*], they will go away."

Following *SFFA*, moreover, such predictions have continued. In one of the first major law review articles evaluating the decision, two authors contended "the *SFFA* decision
will have almost no practical effect at all," branding the opinion merely "a symbolic victory for affirmative action's conservative opponents." Surprisingly, even a jurist who dissented in
SFFA—Justice Sonia Sotomayor—appeared at times to endorse
the notion that *SFFA* would prove feckless. "[T]he [majority's]

opinion today," she asserted, "will serve only to highlight the Court's own impotence in the face of an America whose cries for equality resound." Dissenting Supreme Court Justices, of course, voice their objections, sometimes heatedly, in high-stakes cases. But they seldom assert that their colleagues' opinions should be marked dead on arrival.

Prominent opponents of affirmative action have also argued that universities will refuse to modify their admissions approaches post-*SFFA*. For example, Richard Sander—an influential scholar who has condemned affirmative action because he believes it places racial minorities in academic settings for which they are ill-prepared—suggested after *SFFA* that college campuses may collectively defy the adverse judicial decision. "[A] very plausible outcome of this [*SFFA* opinion] will be that schools will just cheat and say, 'Let's see who gets sued,'" Sander said. "The chances of an individual school getting sued are low, and the cost of suing is really high."

Sander's contention that any admissions dean or university general counsel would greet a lawsuit as just another day at the office provided an unrealistic, unduly cavalier posture in the face of litigation. As the legendary Judge Learned Hand once proclaimed, "I must say that, as a litigant, I should dread a lawsuit beyond almost anything else short of sickness and of death." Reasons abound that lawsuits are dread-inducing experiences, including—most obviously—time, energy, and expense. A less straightforward reason for hoping to avoid being sued, though, offers a powerful motivating force: litigation offers virtually innumerable opportunities for personal and institutional embarrassment. The *SFFA* lawsuit against UNC, for example, revealed UNC admissions officers discussing candidates' racial identities in raw, objectionable fashions. Among other choice comments, UNC officials stated: "[S]tellar academics for a Native Amer/African Amer kid."; "If its brown and above a 1300 [SAT] put them in for [the] merit/Excel [scholarship]."; and "I'm going through this trouble because this is a bi-racial (black/white) male."

The threat of litigation against universities in the post-*SFFA* moment is anything but theoretical. To the contrary, a veritable rogues' gallery of the conservative legal movement quickly assembled to make clear that they relish pursuing litigation against universities they believe have failed to comply with the Supreme Court's opinion. Only hours after the Court issued the decision, Blum—who not only founded the SFFA organization, but also quarterbacked the Supreme Court's evisceration of the Voting Rights Act—issued a press release declaring: "We remain vigilant and intend to initiate litigation should universities defiantly flout this clear ruling." Similarly, Stephen Miller—the adviser who in Trump's first administration played a central role in devising both the Muslim Ban and 2017's "American Carnage" inaugural address—sent a letter to every single law school accredited by the American Bar Association in his capacity as president of America First Legal, notifying them that the organization stood poised to file lawsuits. Not to be outdone, then-Senator JD Vance of Ohio fired off a letter to Federal Trade Commission Chair Lina Khan alleging illegal collusion among colleges following *SFFA*.

Today, Deputy Chief of Staff Miller and Vice President Vance possess among the most powerful voices in the second Trump administration, which quickly made clear that the federal government would use its immense authority to target

20   higher education in ways that extend well beyond the admissions office. Indeed, the Department of Education circulated a hostile notice in February 2025 notifying universities that it would wield *SFFA* as a cudgel to shape virtually every domain in higher education. "Although *SFFA* addressed admissions decisions, the Supreme Court's holding applies more broadly . . . ," the Trump administration asserted. "Federal law thus prohibits covered [universities] from using race in decisions pertaining to admissions, hiring, promotion, compensation, financial aid, scholarships, prizes, administrative support, discipline, housing, graduation ceremonies, and all other aspects of student, academic, and campus life." The letter propounded a highly dubious interpretation of *SFFA*, arguing that the opinion's sweep extended much further than it actually swept. The notice aimed primarily not to foster legal comprehension, of course, but instead to intimidate universities into acquiescing to the Trump administration's myopic legal vision.

     Speculation that *SFFA* would not meaningfully depress the enrollment of racial minorities at leading universities proved ill-founded. Due to *SFFA*, the first-year college classes who moved into their dormitory rooms on many of the nation's coveted campuses in the fall of 2024 included far fewer Black students than those who had moved into those same dorms only one year earlier. The *SFFA*-fueled decline in Black enrollment is, quite simply, staggering. Consider only a few of the many available data points, bearing in mind that Black people make up 14 percent of the United States population. At M.I.T., Black enrollment plunged from 15 percent to 5 percent. At Amherst College, an institution that justifiably prides itself on a venerable history of welcoming African American students, Black enrollment fell from 11 percent to just 3 percent. At Stanford, Black enrollment plummeted from 9 percent to only 5 percent. Furthermore, the percentage of Black students at Johns Hopkins declined by a stunning 66 percent. Three Ivy League colleges—Brown, Columbia, and Cornell—all experienced declines in Black enrollment of 40 percent or greater, as did other prominent colleges, including Carnegie Mellon, Tufts, and Pomona. The Supreme Court's calamitous decision in *SFFA* thus threatens to create a lost generation of Black students on the nation's foremost campuses.

What began on elite university campuses, of course, will not remain there. Instead, the relative paucity of Black students at prestigious institutions of higher education will have cascading consequences that in the coming decades will reverberate throughout executive suites, governmental offices, cultural institutions, experimental laboratories, and every other sector of American society. The Supreme Court has in prior decisions emphasized this link between leading universities' racial composition and the nation writ large. In an opinion upholding affirmative action at the University of Michigan Law School in 2003, for example, Justice Sandra Day O'Connor repeatedly struck this theme. "In order to cultivate a set of leaders with legitimacy in the eyes of the citizenry," O'Connor wrote, "it is necessary that the path to leadership be visibly open to talented and qualified individuals of every race and ethnicity." Leading universities must include meaningful racial diversity, Justice O'Connor reasoned, "so that all members of our heterogeneous society may participate in the educational institutions that provide the training and education necessary to succeed in America."

22   Taking these ideas seriously, however, casts the *SFFA* opinion in a harsh, unforgiving light. Justice O'Connor's opinion suggests that *SFFA*—by vastly reducing Black enrollment at many eminent colleges—not only threatens a legitimacy crisis within the United States, but also denies many Black citizens the educational opportunities needed to thrive.

Thus, even more important than *SFFA*'s reduction in Black Ivy Leaguers is what the abandonment of affirmative action signifies for the American experiment in multiracial democracy. Beginning in the 1960s, affirmative action boldly challenged and transformed the nation's dominant attitude regarding where Black people belong in American society. If the United States were a train, there can be no doubt that, from the very beginning, Black people had systematically been assigned to the caboose. Affirmative action helped to change this foundational ethos, asserting and demonstrating that Black people were not in fact "beings of an inferior order" who had been "justly and lawfully reduced to slavery for [their] benefit," as *Dred Scott v. Sandford* once insisted. Instead, the programs made clear that Black people belonged in the most rarefied segments of American society. As Professor Gerald Early recently explained: "What made affirmative action important for so many Black people, despite the fact that comparatively few directly benefited from this rather boutique social policy, was that it changed the way we thought about where Black people could be or where they belonged."

This basic sense of Black belonging represented an assault on and repudiation of American pigmentocracy. Professor Orlando Patterson of Harvard has captured this point vividly. "For all its imperfections, affirmative action has made a major difference in the lives of . . . minorities," Patterson wrote. "In utilitarian terms it is hard to find a program that has brought so much gain to so many at so little cost. It has been the single most important factor accounting for the rise of a significant Afro-American middle class." Viewed through this prism, *SFFA* dismantled a powerful engine of social mobility, as the adoption of affirmative action jump-started the Black middle and upper-middle classes. The Supreme Court's abandonment of affirmative action stalls and jeopardizes that vital progress.

SFFA demands lucid analysis because it is the most significant judicial opinion involving race and education since *Brown v. Board of Education* invalidated segregation seven decades earlier. Despite its significance, *SFFA* remains profoundly misunderstood, and those misunderstandings hold baleful consequences for all of American society. It is essential therefore to clarify what *SFFA* means, and, just as important, what *SFFA* does not mean. This book offers a panoramic view of *SFFA*—advancing fresh, provocative perspectives on the opinion, racial equality, higher education, constitutional interpretation, the Supreme Court, and even the United States itself. It challenges conservatives by demonstrating that *SFFA* will—even as viewed by their own preferred lights—create a less desirable admissions regime than the old affirmative action model it replaced. The book also challenges liberals by demonstrating that their own shopworn efforts to justify affirmative action have failed to confront powerful objections. In addition, it challenges defeatists by advancing novel proposals explaining how leading universities can avoid returning to bygone days, when Black students seldom walked the courtyards of power. The death of affirmative action therefore need not mean the demise of racial diversity in higher education. Finally, this book challenges the entire

24   nation to view *SFFA* in its larger historical and cultural moment, when white racial grievance and resentment play an outsized role in shaping modern American politics. Today, when many Americans justifiably feel deep anxiety about the nation's racial trajectory, it is incumbent upon alarmed citizens not simply to turn a blind eye to *SFFA*. Rather, we must scrutinize *SFFA* from multiple vantage points both to understand the misbegotten opinion and to understand what can be done about it.

The Conservative Case Against *SFFA v. Harvard*

In 1979, one year after the Supreme Court issued *Regents of the University of California v. Bakke*, then-Professor Antonin Scalia published a short article with a long title excoriating the decision, *The Disease as Cure: "In Order to Get Beyond Racism, We Must First Take Account of Race."* Scalia—in only eleven crisp pages—contended that the *Bakke* decision upholding the constitutionality of affirmative action marked an unwise retreat from what he deemed the Fourteenth Amendment's colorblind mandate. If race-conscious student assignment plans presented an unconstitutional malady in cases like *Brown v. Board of Education*, Scalia suggested, how could admissions policies that explicitly use racial categories somehow receive a clean bill of health in *Bakke*? In other words, how could racial classifications have been the "disease" during the Jim Crow era and then suddenly somehow morph into the "cure" in the late 1970s? Scalia asserted that *Bakke* would not only fail to help America's race relations, but would significantly harm them: "From racist principles flow racist results."

26   Scalia's article denouncing *Bakke* more than four decades ago has now largely been forgotten. But it merits renewed attention in the wake of *SFFA v. Harvard*, as Scalia's critique proved prescient along four dimensions. First, Scalia argued that affirmative action policies boost undeserving beneficiaries, advancing the most privileged racial minorities—including "the son of a prosperous and well-educated black doctor or lawyer." Second, articulating an early version of what has come to be known as mismatch theory, Scalia blamed affirmative action for promoting Black students with mediocre academic records into elite academic environments where they are ill-prepared to compete. Third, Scalia contended that affirmative action balkanized American society, paving the road to racial resentment by unjustly requiring "many white ethnic groups that came to this country . . . relatively late in its history" to sacrifice valuable opportunities as compensation for a racial debt that long predated their arrival. Making the argument in unusually personal terms, he noted: "My father came to this country when he was a teenager. Not only had he never profited from the sweat of any black man's brow, I don't think he had ever seen a black man." Finally, Scalia contended that Justice Lewis Powell's controlling opinion in *Bakke*—which made racial diversity on campuses a constitutionally permissible rationale for affirmative action—seemed almost designed to forestall meaningful judicial review. Due to Powell's opinion, Scalia lamented, affirmative action plans "will be effectively unappealable to the courts," as "[t]here's no way to establish . . . that the diversity value of New York City oboists has not been accorded its proper weight." Various justices in the *SFFA* majority echoed each of these four claims as they eliminated affirmative action.

Not surprisingly, conservatives have overwhelmingly hailed *SFFA* as among the most hallowed judicial decisions in Supreme Court history. A *Wall Street Journal* editorial titled "A Landmark for Racial Equality" saluted *SFFA* as a "watershed declaration," and deemed it "one of [the Supreme Court's] finest hours." SFFA founder Edward Blum celebrated the decision as auguring "the restoration of the colorblind legal covenant that binds together our multi-racial, multi-ethnic nation." Writing in *National Review*, Ed Whelan praised *SFFA* as—without exception—Chief Justice John Roberts's "greatest opinion in his eighteen years on the Court."

The right's initial celebration of *SFFA* may, however, yield to condemnation. Liberal law professors have, of course, roundly castigated *SFFA*. But even as assessed from the perspective of conservatives' own principles, *SFFA* ushers in a legal regime that is markedly worse than the one it replaced. Indeed, while conservatives have long believed that a decision ending affirmative action would help to alleviate what they deem America's primary racial ailments, now that *SFFA* has arrived it is becoming apparent that the decision only intensifies the disease. By conservatives' own professed lights, then, *SFFA* contains not an antidote, but a toxin.

Affirmative action's supporters too often pretend that the policy has no drawbacks whatsoever, portraying it as a first-best solution, rather than a second-best solution. Sophisticated backers of affirmative action have, however, acknowledged that it possesses costs as well as benefits. Reacting to *Bakke*, Professor Derrick Bell in 1979 emphasized that the program's supporters, including himself, "should not forget that the relief these programs provide is far from ideal," and encouraged all

28   observers to "recognize the limitations of minority admissions programs." Similarly, in 2013, Professor Randall Kennedy stated: "Some defenders of affirmative action, fearful of making any concessions, argue as if affirmative action poses no costs, entails no risks, involves no dangers. The reality is far different."

Unrecognized in the voluminous affirmative action debates, however, is that the converse point also holds: affirmative action's detractors have failed to recognize that their preferred approach raises dangers of its own. Those dangers are considerable, and even one who is dedicated to advancing conservative principles must grapple forthrightly with the serious risks *SFFA* poses to their ideological commitments. This point has been permitted to hide in plain sight because conservatives have been targeting affirmative action so ardently and for so long that they have dedicated insufficient attention to the particularities of the regime that will replace the old affirmative action model now that it has been destroyed. Following *SFFA*, however, these questions can no longer be evaded. Today, with its long-sought victory firmly in hand, the conservative legal movement may soon recognize that the opinion is actually a glorious defeat.

I wish to emphasize that I am neither a conservative nor an opponent of affirmative action. Quite the opposite: I identify as a liberal who has dedicated substantial effort to defending affirmative action and, indeed, attempting to forestall an outcome very much like the one the Supreme Court announced in *SFFA*. In this chapter, however, I do not focus on advancing my own first-order view of this contested terrain. Instead, I aim to articulate a conservative critique of *SFFA* in a manner that will be recognizable to conservatives of various stripes. That endeavor requires me to invoke some ideas, premises, and even language that I wholeheartedly reject. To take only two of the many possible examples, I am unconvinced either that a victimology mindset ranks high on the list of what ails Black Americans, or that the supposed mismatch phenomenon presents a major problem in higher education. Rather than contesting such ideas and others that enjoy widespread adherence in conservative circles, however, this chapter instead shows how accepting those conservative views should mean rejecting *SFFA*.

Before mounting the conservative case against *SFFA*, a brief overview of the written opinions that emerged from the decision is in order. The aim here is not to provide a comprehensive overview of *SFFA*. Instead, it is to lay the groundwork for demonstrating how the demise of affirmative action—one of the conservative legal movement's most intensely coveted treasures—reveals itself upon close inspection to be fool's gold.

Chief Justice Roberts wrote the majority opinion in *SFFA*. He framed the case in a straightforward manner as "involv[ing] whether a university may make admissions decisions that turn on an applicant's race." In answering the question presented in the negative, Roberts spoke in the register of colorblind absolutism: "Eliminating racial discrimination means eliminating all of it." Given that *SFFA* construed Harvard and UNC's affirmative action measures as forms of racial discrimination, those programs must fall.

But *SFFA* carved out two exceptions to its broad colorblindness decree. First, in the opinion's fourth footnote, Roberts noted that the Solicitor General's brief had emphasized the importance of affirmative action policies to the nation's military academies, and that they were not parties in *SFFA*. Therefore,

30   *SFFA* concluded that those institutions were for the time being excused from altering their race-conscious admissions programs "in light of the potentially distinct interests that military academies may present."

Second, Roberts clarified that all universities may in fact consider race during the admissions process if they received application essays exploring racial themes—at least in certain circumstances. In a highly significant passage, Roberts allowed: "[N]othing in this opinion should be construed as prohibiting universities from considering an applicant's discussion of how race affected his or her life, be it through discrimination, inspiration, or otherwise." *SFFA* warned, however, "universities may not simply establish through application essays or other means the regime we hold unlawful today." Instead, universities may provide a boost on the basis of application essays discussing race only if they addressed *individualized* experiences. "A benefit to a student who overcame racial discrimination, for example, must be tied to *that student's* courage and determination," *SFFA* explained. Roberts contended that this restricted use of race in admissions was desirable because it would prevent universities from teaching "the touchstone of an individual's identity is not challenges bested, skills built, or lessons learned but the color of their skin." These universities' fixation on race, he reasoned, had detrimental consequences for the nation.

Roberts maintained that the Harvard and UNC admissions programs were both driven by the wrongheaded belief that "there is an inherent benefit in race *qua* race—in race for race's sake." Where Harvard embraced "the pernicious stereotype that 'a black student can usually bring something that a white person cannot offer,'" he noted, UNC maintained "race in itself

'says [something] about who you are.'" Roberts made clear that
the universities had faltered by failing to identify a compelling
interest for using racial classifications in admissions. "[T]he
interests [Harvard and UNC] view as compelling cannot be subjected to meaningful judicial review," *SFFA* concluded, because
"it is unclear how courts are supposed to measure [the universities'] goals." This analytical move strongly resembled the
concern then-Professor Scalia articulated in 1979 that *Bakke*'s
rationale was "effectively unappealable to the courts" because
it was impossible to ensure "diversity value[s]" received their
"proper weight."

Justice Clarence Thomas's uncommonly rich, expansive
concurring opinion contained several significant lines of attack
condemning affirmative action. Justice Thomas had disdained
affirmative action since long before he joined the Court, and
he savored this moment, when *SFFA* effectively overruled the
Court's precedents upholding affirmative action. Notably, a trio
of Justice Thomas's central arguments in *SFFA* extended claims
ventured in then-Professor Scalia's article from more than four
decades prior.

Start with Thomas's contention that affirmative action
often promotes undeserving beneficiaries—not racial minorities who are down on their luck, but instead those whose families have already risen. Scalia raised the specter of affirmative
action boosting the children of "prosperous and well-educated
black" physicians and attorneys. Justice Thomas upped the
ante. He observed that a hypothetical Black applicant named
"Jack . . . the son of a multimillionaire industrialist," could plausibly receive a race-based admissions boost over another Black
student from humble origins because "both [applicants] are

32 black, after all." This absurdity laid bare affirmative action's shameful overinclusiveness, Thomas contended, as the policy aids "the most well-off members of minority races without meaningfully assisting those who struggle with real hardship."

Next, Thomas highlighted the mismatch argument, *i.e.*, the idea that affirmative action elevates Black and brown students into settings in which they are ill-equipped to succeed. It is essential to realize, Thomas asserted, that affirmative action does not meaningfully expand the pool of Black and brown college students. Instead, he observed: "[T]hose racial policies simply redistribute individuals among institutions of higher learning, placing some into more competitive institutions than they otherwise would have attended." While these students could well have thrived at less demanding universities, Justice Thomas continued, "[t]he resulting mismatch places many blacks and Hispanics . . . in a position where underperformance is all but inevitable because they are less academically prepared than the white and Asian students with whom they must compete."

Third, Justice Thomas emphasized that affirmative action produces racial resentment and balkanization. Where Scalia focused upon the harms he believed flowed from requiring many white immigrants to pay down a racial debt that they did not owe, Thomas highlighted the racial invective that some hopeful college applicants who receive rejection letters might direct toward admitted Black and brown students. "Applicants denied admission to certain colleges may come to believe— accurately or not—that their race was responsible for their failure to attain a life-long dream," Thomas wrote. He contended that affirmative action policies thus yield "[n]ot racial

harmony," but instead "*exactly* the kind of factionalism that the
Constitution was meant to safeguard against."

In addition, Justice Thomas's *SFFA* concurrence advanced
two linked arguments that require explication. Justice Thomas—
spotlighting a prominent conservative grievance with affirmative action—charged that such programs encourage Black and
brown students to adopt a "self-defeating" attitude that prioritizes racial "victimization." Instead of noting "the great accomplishments of black Americans, including those who succeeded
despite long odds," Thomas contended affirmative action's
defenders incorrectly insist upon "label[ing] all blacks as victims." That view was not just "irrational," but "unfathomable,"
according to Thomas: "What matters is not the barriers [Black
students] face, but how they choose to confront them. And their
race is not to blame for everything—good or bad—that happens
in their lives." He called the "racial[ly] determinis[t]" mindset
"an insult to individual achievement," one that is "cancerous to
young minds seeking to push through barriers, rather than con-
sign themselves to permanent victimhood."

Relatedly, Justice Thomas contended that affirmative
action programs heightened the salience of race on college campuses and thus marred the broader American society. "Far from
advancing the cause of improved race relations in our Nation,"
he claimed, "affirmative action highlights our racial differences
with pernicious effect." Supporting this claim, Thomas stated,
"[i]t has become clear that sorting by race does not stop at the
admissions office," as racially identifiable clubs, centers, and
even housing have proliferated on campuses in recent decades.
He suggested *Bakke* and its progeny shouldered the blame for
the "stagnat[ion]" of "racial progress on campuses," as their

34   legacy "appears to be ever increasing and strident demands for *yet more* racially oriented solutions."

Justice Neil Gorsuch's concurrence suggested that the college application processes at Harvard and UNC fueled racial obsession: "[T]he trial records show [that] applicants are prompted to tick one or more boxes to explain 'how you identify yourself.'" For Gorsuch, who has sometimes expressed libertarian inclinations, this unhealthy preoccupation with racial identity was particularly galling because the various boxes had suspect origins. "Where do these boxes come from?" he asked. "Bureaucrats. A federal interagency commission devised this scheme of [racial] classifications in the 1970s to facilitate data collection." In addition, Justice Gorsuch expressed concern that "a cottage industry" of college consultants had sprung up that helped Asian American students attempt to conceal their racial identities in an effort to maximize their chances of admission to leading universities. He suggested that indigent Asian Americans might be particularly harmed by being priced out of this industry: "[I]t is hard not to wonder whether those left paying the steepest price are those least able to afford it—children of families with no chance of hiring the kind of consultants who know how to play this game."

Justice Brett Kavanaugh dedicated his concurrence to arguing that *SFFA* in no sense marked an abandonment of the Court's affirmative action precedents. For Kavanaugh, that included the twenty-five-year extension that *Grutter v. Bollinger* granted to affirmative action in 2003, when the Court upheld the University of Michigan Law School's admissions program. Amplifying a point in Roberts's majority opinion in *SFFA*, Kavanaugh argued *Grutter*'s quarter-century expiration date for affirmative action was not a haphazard aside, but instead "an important part of [a] nuanced opinion for the Court." Justice Kavanaugh stated that he—and *SFFA*—"abide[d] by *Grutter*'s . . . temporal limit"— because the majority opinion meant that colleges were in fact permitted to use affirmative action through the admissions cycle "for the college class of 2028." Those contending that *Grutter*'s twenty-five-year timeline meant that universities should be permitted to use affirmative action through 2028, he suggested, should be understood as in effect arguing the regime extended until "the college class of 2032," which would be a full twenty-nine years post-*Grutter*.

The upshot of these opinions is that the conservative justices, in gutting affirmative action, portrayed the Harvard and UNC admissions programs as increasing racial victimization, and echoed then-Professor Scalia's concerns about mismatch theory, undeserving beneficiaries, and racial balkanization. The Court's opinion in *SFFA*, however, does not eliminate those concerns; it accentuates them. In advancing his anti-*Bakke* broadside, then-Professor Scalia argued, "There is . . . a lot of pretense or self-delusion (you can take your choice) in all that pertains to affirmative action." Perhaps. But *SFFA* demonstrates that, as we enter the post—affirmative action era, the conservative legal movement has long been harboring copious amounts of pretense or self-delusion about what that world entails.

The dissents in *SFFA* written by Justice Sonia Sotomayor and Justice Ketanji Brown Jackson, and joined by Justice Elena Kagan, launched potent lines of liberal attack against the Court's decision. The leitmotif of Justice Sotomayor's dissent lambasted *SFFA* for embracing constitutional colorblindness in a world that remains color conscious. "[T]he six unelected members

36   of today's majority," she stated, "upend the status quo based on
their policy preferences about what race in America should be
like, but is not, and their preferences for a veneer of colorblindness in a society where race has always mattered and continues
to matter in fact and in law." This approach had nothing to rec-
ommend it, she believed: "Equality requires acknowledgment of
inequality." For Sotomayor, *SFFA* marked a retreat not just from
the Court's affirmative action decisions but from *Brown v. Board
of Education* itself. The affirmative action decisions, she posited, "extended *Brown*'s transformative legacy to the context of
higher education," by "promot[ing] *Brown*'s vision of a Nation
with more inclusive schools." Justice Sotomayor dismissed the
majority's concession that universities may sometimes consider
race in application essays as "an attempt to put lipstick on a pig."

Justice Jackson's dissent sounded similar dominant
themes, as she, too, warned of the perils of *SFFA*'s premature
embrace of colorblindness. "[D]eeming race irrelevant in law
does not make it so in life," she wrote. "[U]ltimately, ignoring race just makes it matter more." Jackson also marshaled
extensive empirical evidence chronicling the "[g]ulf-sized
race-based gaps [that] exist [regarding] health, wealth, and
well-being of American citizens." In Justice Jackson's view, "the
well-documented intergenerational transmission of inequality
that still plagues our citizenry" rendered it ludicrous to assert
"that anyone is now victimized if a college considers whether
[this] legacy of discrimination has unequally advantaged its
applicants."* The Court's liberal wing thus articulated powerful

---

*Justice Jackson recused herself from participating in the resolution of the
Harvard portion of the case, meaning that as a technical matter her dissent
applied only to the UNC case. Jackson's recusal was due to her serving on

rejoinders to *SFFA*. Entirely absent from those dissents, however, were sustained arguments demonstrating that *SFFA*
undermines the very principles that conservatives themselves
have long championed.

Victimizing Essays

In *SFFA*'s most arresting feature, Chief Justice Roberts allowed
that colleges may award applicants an admissions boost if their
personal essays "discuss[] . . . how race affected his or her life,
be it through discrimination, inspiration, or otherwise." This
allowance, combined with *SFFA*'s prevention of colleges from
accessing racial boxes on applications,* seems virtually guaranteed to produce a state of affairs that conservatives will detest
even more than the system that *SFFA* replaced. Under the old
regime, Black and brown college applicants could (if they so
desired) check the relevant racial box, and then write their personal statements about their passion to study Proust, Plato,

the Harvard Board of Overseers when President Biden nominated her to the
Supreme Court.

As a private institution, Harvard is formally governed by a statute—Title
VI of the 1964 Civil Rights Act—not the Constitution's Equal Protection
Clause, which applies to public entities. But the Supreme Court in *SFFA*
framed the question as whether Harvard and the University of North
Carolina (UNC) violated the Equal Protection Clause because the statutory
and constitutional provisions have been deemed coextensive. *See SFFA*, 600
U.S. at 197–98.
* *SFFA* has been widely interpreted to prevent universities from accessing
racial boxes during the admissions process. *See, e.g.*, Jessica Cheung,
"Affirmative Action Is Over. Should Applicants Still Mention Their Race?,"
New York Times Magazine (September 4, 2023), https://www.nytimes
.com/2023/09/04/magazine/affirmative-action-race-college-admissions
.html ("This year, in response to the court's decision, many colleges will
hide the box on the Common App that indicates the applicant's race . . .").

38   differential geometry, string theory, *The Odyssey*, or anything
      else under the university's vast sun. Under the *SFFA* regime, in
      contrast, Black and brown applicants are strongly encouraged
      to produce narratives of racial woe that not only utilize the vic-
      timhood mindset that conservatives loathe, but also complicate
      the tale of America's racial progress that conservatives prize.
      College application essay writing, moreover, is a far more delib-
      erate, constitutive act than simply checking a racial box, which
      can happen quickly and without much thought at many quo-
      tidian settings—including, for example, the DMV. Exemplary
      college application essays, in contrast, require careful planning,
      sustained thought, and numerous rounds of revisions. As Black
      and brown college applicants spend an outsized amount of time
      polishing their statements of highly individualized brushes
      with racism in response to *SFFA*, they will not simply abandon
      those sentiments when they arrive at college. Instead, much
      to conservatives' chagrin, those students will lug their senses
      of racial aggrievement to campus right along with their dorm
      refrigerators. This essay-driven dynamic will surely succeed in
      heightening the salience of race at universities—and around the
      nation.

      Many prominent conservatives have denounced affirma-
      tive action's penchant for requiring racial minorities to portray
      themselves as victims. While Justice Thomas's *SFFA* concur-
      rence voiced concern that race-conscious admissions promoted
      a "self-defeating" belief in Black "victimhood," the undisputed
      urtext of racial victimization is Shelby Steele's bestselling book
      from 1990, *The Content of Our Character: A New Vision of Race
      in America*. Steele contended that a major "liability of affirma-
      tive action comes from the fact that it . . . encourages blacks to

exploit their own past victimization as a source of power and privilege." Affirmative action, Steele maintained, thus "nurtures a victim-focused identity in blacks" such that in order "to receive the benefits of preferential treatment one must, to some extent, become invested in the view of one's self as a victim." When suffering becomes a source of empowerment, Steele argued, "blacks are encouraged to expand the boundaries of what qualifies as racial oppression, a situation that can lead us to paint our victimization in vivid colors, even as we receive the benefits of preference." In a particularly evocative turn of phrase, Steele asserted: "The power to be found in victimization, like any power, is intoxicating and can lend itself to the creation of a new class of super-victims who can feel the pea of victimization under twenty mattresses."

It would be difficult to overstate how influential *The Content of Our Character*'s concern about victimization proved among conservative critics of affirmative action. Six years after Steele contended that affirmative action created hypersensitive "super-victims," legal scholar Lino Graglia similarly expressed fear that the idea of Black authenticity had become synonymous with "displaying an exceptional ability to discern and protest supposed racial slights." In 2000, John McWhorter's condemnation of race-conscious admissions in his own bestseller—*Losing the Race: Self-Sabotage in Black America*—openly acknowledged his debt to Steele. "[T]he Cult of Victimology," McWhorter asserted, "has become a keystone of cultural blackness," which wrongly "treat[s] victimhood not as a problem to be solved but as an identity to be nurtured." In 2010, Linda Chavez similarly argued: "Victimology and affirmative action go hand in hand. . . . But thinking you're a victim is a lousy way to

40   get ahead.... It's a defeatist attitude that encourages failure, not success."

The *SFFA* essay-based approach to racial diversity, however, seems almost perfectly designed to increase the disempowering sense of victimhood that conservatives have long lamented. That is because the new system invites applicants to fixate on their encounters with racism far more than the box-checking method that *SFFA* jettisoned. Admittedly, prior to *SFFA*, some racial minorities doubtless dedicated their application essays to recounting instances when racism knocked at their door. One former college admissions officer discerned a trend before *SFFA* that, in personal statements, "white students discussed their passions," and "Black students discussed their pain."

In the new post-*SFFA* era, however, even Black and brown applicants who would prefer to avoid focusing upon their racial pain now may feel compelled to do so. The *New York Times* covered a high school senior named Rayne Rivera-Forbes, who identified as Afro-Latina, and noted that *SFFA* caused her to "'just feel a bit lost.'" Rivera-Forbes's personal statement could have conceivably focused upon her time serving as a student representative on the local school board, or her desire to someday become an elected official. Indeed, she "didn't want to write her essay about race," the *Times* reported, but "now that the race box is gone, she feels she should at least mention it." Similarly, one Black high school student who hoped to study neuroscience at a leading college commented: "It's now put onto the student to display all the struggles that they went through and relive that trauma of growing up in an underprivileged community...."

In 2024, a Cornell undergraduate of color expressly told the university newspaper that if she had applied before the end of affirmative action, she would not have focused her essay on racial identity. "I would have talked more about my achievements and things I'm interested in," she said, "rather than just about how my parents came here [to America]." Feeling "limited" about what she "could talk about on the application," she regretted that "other students who weren't of color . . . could mention other aspects of [themselves in] their application[s]. . . ."

Predictably, at least some Black college students have expressed delight that they applied under the pre-*SFFA* system, and were thus able to avoid any temptation to capitalize upon their racial tribulations. On the heels of *SFFA*, a Black freshman at Duke University voiced relief that she had felt free to write her essays about her family, reality television, and recreational activities. "But if I were applying now, I think I would . . . opt for writing about things that I don't really like thinking about, like my experiences with racism or my racial trauma," the Duke student stated. "You're going to be having a lot of minority students basically telling a single story, and it's not fair because that takes away from the uniqueness of the applicant." *SFFA* thus pressures Black and brown students to cram their individual lives into a preset racial narrative, and in the process negates their individuality.

It is hardly accidental that two Black students quoted above invoked the word *trauma* in discussing the sort of material that they felt admissions offices would expect. "[T]he trauma plot," it has been argued with some force, has become the dominant narrative structure of our time, and "[t]he appetite for stories

42   about Black trauma" seems insatiable.* Nowhere is that phenomenon more pronounced than in the college application
essay. *SFFA*, of course, promises only to intensify what one high
school senior labeled "this fad of trauma dumping" in college
applications. Indeed, no less a legal authority than *Teen Vogue*
has noted that *SFFA* "puts an even harsher burden on applicants' essays," and that students now "are . . . ranking themselves
against their peers in a form of trauma Olympics."

This higher premium placed on racially traumatic experiences produces numerous undesirable consequences. Most
prominently, many college applicants will be filled with racial
resentment that they feel compelled to—in the parlance—
perform their trauma for admissions officers. Applicants who
have experienced genuinely traumatic events seem likely to
find reliving those events *ad nauseam*, well, traumatizing. As a
Harvard Crimson editorial, titled "College Essays and the Trauma
Sweet Spot," observed recently: "[T]his pressure to package
adversity into a palatable narrative can be toxic." The editorial
added: "It can make applicants, accepted or not, feel like their
admissions outcomes are tied to their most vulnerable experiences. The worst thing that ever happened to you was simply not enough, or alternatively, it was more than enough, and
now you get to struggle with traumatized-imposter syndrome."
Predictably, students who win admission to elite universities

---

* In identifying and critiquing what she labels "the trauma plot," Parul Sehgal
observes that trauma has become "a source of moral authority, even a kind
of expertise," and that "[t]rauma trumps all other identities, evacuates
personality, remakes it in its own image." Parul Sehgal, "The Key to Me,"
New Yorker, January 3, 2022, at 64–66. For a potent satire of the ravenous
appetite for Black trauma narratives, see *American Fiction* (Orion Pictures
2023) (adapted from Percival Everett, *Erasure* (2001)).

after submitting an essay emphasizing racial trauma may also
experience a distinct type of imposter syndrome, believing that
they secured their spots only because of their brushes with
misfortune.

More insidiously, the trauma premium in college application essays encourages Black and brown students who
have—mercifully—led lives relatively devoid of such painful experiences both to feel that they have been robbed of the
authentic racial experience and to comb through their pasts,
groping for that elusive "pea of victimization" buried beneath
dozens of well-insulated mattresses. On this account, applicants who have ample reason to hum a few bars of the song
"Happy" will instead feel obligated to write essays intoning
"Nobody Knows the Trouble I've Seen." *Teen Vogue*'s Trauma
Olympics thus may—for at least some applicants—be superseded by the Microaggression Olympics. Although *SFFA* surely
intended no such outcome, the opinion nevertheless effectively
discharged the starter's pistol in that ungainly contest.

Encouraging applicants to write elaborate, individualized narratives of racial aggrievement to win admission to
elite universities also clashes with a foundational conservative commitment holding that America has witnessed tremendous strides toward the goal of racial equality during the last
several decades. Whereas Professor Derrick Bell once emphasized "the *permanence* of racism," conservatives endorse almost
exactly the inverse proposition. For conservatives, racism in the
United States is a problem that has been defeated, and it makes
no sense—legal or otherwise—to obsess over what McWhorter
labeled the "remnants of racism."

44   This conservative emphasis on American racial progress animated the Roberts Court's decision in *Shelby County v.
Holder*, which invalidated the Voting Rights Act of 1965's coverage formula for preclearing electoral changes. The VRA's
onerous preclearance approach may have been justified to combat 1960s-style southern racism, *Shelby County* reasoned, but
increasing racial equality rendered that approach obsolete. "The
Voting Rights Act of 1965 employed extraordinary measures
to address an extraordinary problem," Chief Justice Roberts
wrote for the Court in *Shelby County*. But, he emphasized, "history did not end in 1965." *Shelby County* noted that the 1960s
witnessed horrific anti-Black violence in Selma, Alabama, and
Philadelphia, Mississippi. But "[t]oday both of those towns are
governed by African-American mayors," Roberts wrote, a racial
transformation that must be acknowledged, as "there is no
denying that ... our Nation has made great strides."

        Chief Justice Roberts's opinion in *SFFA*, however, encour-
ages racial minorities to minimize or even outright deny the
nation's racial progress that he touted in *Shelby County*. The
strongest, most powerful essays that Black and brown applicants can produce in the post-*SFFA* era will dwell upon—
indeed, luxuriate in—the absence of racial progress. In response
to *SFFA*, students will write essays bemoaning the police stop
that seemed like a fishing expedition, the time a fellow camper
hurled a racial epithet, the teacher who doubted whether
Advanced Placement calculus was the right fit, the store clerk
who refused to accept a polite "just browsing," and myriad other
racial indignities. Instead of being attuned to ways in which the
nation's racial situation has improved, Black and brown students will instead be rewarded for highlighting life experiences

that reveal the nation's racial progress has stalled—or perhaps even moved in reverse.

As a theoretical matter, of course, *SFFA* permits applicants to write essays exploring how race shaped their lives "through discrimination, inspiration, or otherwise." It hardly seems extravagant to maintain, though, that applicants will gorge on "discrimination," and largely abstain from "inspiration" and "otherwise." During oral argument in *SFFA*, Justice Amy Coney Barrett asked questions that sketched how an essay sounding in "inspiration" or "otherwise" might run: "What if . . . an applicant wrote an essay about how integral their racial identity was to them as a source of pride and the cultural attributes of the racial heritage were very important? Would that be okay even if it were all intimately tied up, say, with . . . the traditions of a Mexican family?"

For better or for worse, this hypothetical racial essay of pride and inspiration sounds excruciatingly dull. In modern times, an excellent personal statement—like many pieces of good writing—requires at least some friction and tension, including obstacles overcome, or, as *SFFA* itself put it, "challenges bested." Drawing inspiration from family gatherings—of whatever racial heritage—is the personal statement equivalent of exploring one's love for rainbows, ice cream sundaes, or long walks on the beach. Those essays are simply not going to get the job done in the ultracompetitive world of college admissions.

Although conservatives—including then-Professor Scalia, Chief Justice John Roberts, Justice Samuel Alito, and Justice Clarence Thomas—have often objected that affirmative action typically benefits wealthy racial minorities, it seems quite probable that *SFFA*'s new essay-driven diversity approach will

46   redound even more to the benefit of privileged Black and brown
      applicants. Here, too, *SFFA* perversely threatens to intensify the
      very problem that it sought to remedy.

      Why would *SFFA*'s newfangled essay-based regime favor
      Black and brown students from affluent backgrounds more than
      those from humble backgrounds? One might intuitively believe
      that the exact opposite dynamic would materialize. After all,
      Black and brown students from poorer backgrounds could be
      assumed to have more ugly encounters with overt racism than
      students from wealthier backgrounds, whose privilege might
      serve to insulate them from some of life's racial indignities.
      That ugliness—while searing—would nevertheless furnish
      poorer applicants with powerful material for personal state-
      ments that could well move the admissions needle.

      The trouble with this analysis, however, is that the *SFFA*
      essay-based diversity approach will most reward sophisti-
      cated applicants who know how to finesse the system. Those
      with access to circles of affluence will have much greater suc-
      cess navigating the new, murkier world created by *SFFA* than
      those lacking such access. Conservatives vociferously maligned
      the box-checking approach to college admissions because the
      attendant boost benefited the Black scion of a wealthy indus-
      trialist as well as the Black son of a struggling sanitation
      worker. But it is also true that the box-checking regime virtu-
      ally assured that all Black applicants—even the poorest ones—
      would receive the boost. All they needed to do was simply check
      the box, a straightforward step that democratized the racial
      bump.

      SFFA's novel approach means that the racial boost will be
      reserved only for those who obtain the required knowledge

to access it effectively, and poorer applicants are less likely to acquire that knowledge. Justice Gorsuch's *SFFA* concurrence made a version of this argument, though it appeared in a quite disparate context. In *SFFA*, recall, Gorsuch contended that a "cottage industry" had emerged to help Asian Americans conceal their racial identities, and that this dynamic would harm students who could not pay the freight. Surely, though, *SFFA* will foment a new "cottage industry"—if it has not already created one—that helps wealthy Black and brown applicants strike exactly the right tone in their personal statements to maximize their chances of securing admission.

The concern that *SFFA*'s essay-based approach to diversity will inflict outsized harms on underprivileged Black students is, alas, hardly hypothetical. Following *SFFA*, the *Washington Post* covered Demar Goodman's shifting college application strategy. Goodman, prior to *SFFA*, had planned his personal statement to be "about growing up Black in a poor part of Atlanta. About attending an underserved high school with a reputation for drug use. About making do with subpar materials, out-of-date technology, and people's prejudices. About how he persevered, rejoicing at every academic accolade because it disproved assumptions about who he could be and what he could achieve." Goodman's intended statement, in other words, seemed to be exactly the sort of essay that could materially improve his chances in the college admissions sweepstakes.

But *SFFA*'s intervention provoked Goodman to alter his plans dramatically. Not only did *SFFA* convince Goodman that it was no longer worth even applying to Harvard—his dream college—but he also decided against addressing race in his personal statement because he believed doing so was now useless.

48   Instead of chronicling his resilience in the face of racial adver-
      sity, Goodman's personal statement focused upon his exten-
      sive "collection of flag lapel pins." The story of how *SFFA* almost
      certainly harmed Goodman—one of the very sorts of students
      the majority portrayed itself as helping—is as evocative as it
      is dispiriting. And early returns suggest that Goodman is far
      from the only racial minority growing up in challenging circum-
      stances whose college plans suffered from the more complex
      admissions world created by *SFFA*.

      The unintended outcome of *SFFA*'s essay-based approach
      to racial diversity is that it will increase the salience of race
      on college campuses—exactly the opposite effect that con-
      servatives hoped they would achieve by dismantling affirma-
      tive action. Justice Thomas was not the only conservative voice
      in *SFFA* who blamed affirmative action for elevating the sig-
      nificance of race in university settings. During oral argument,
      SFFA's counsel—Cameron Norris—stated flatly: "[R]acial pref-
      erences on college campuses in our belief . . . have increased
      racial consciousness." Patrick Strawbridge, who represented
      SFFA in the UNC case, made a closely related remark during
      oral argument. Chief Justice Roberts also repeatedly floated the
      idea at oral argument that affirmative action policies should be
      blamed for establishing the wrong racial climate: "I'm talking
      about student groups taking [their] cue from the university and
      saying we ought to take race into account [with] whatever we're
      doing." Elsewhere, he stated: "I get the sense . . . that race per-
      meates a lot of what happens at the university." Roberts did not
      intend this as a compliment.

      Such statements in *SFFA* are only the most recent and
      most prominent of the widespread conservative anxiety that

contends race-conscious admissions systems have the pernicious effect of increasing race's salience. Lino Graglia pressed
this point memorably in 1970: "Affirmative action is a prescription for racial conflict and animosity, and the prescription
is being filled. It is the root cause of the majority of problems
plaguing American campuses today." Similarly, Carl Cohen
asserted that affirmative action delayed the day when skin
color possessed no greater significance than eye color. "Race
preference . . . obliges everyone to think early and often about
his ethnic identity," Cohen argued. "Race becomes the irritant
underlying almost every public issue, the intensifying ingredi-
ent of community controversy, and the salt in social wounds."
Cohen contended that affirmative action promotes both a sort
of racial tribalism and the lesson that race represents the core
of one's humanity: "Ethnic identification begins to saturate
everyday life. We must be able to prove *what* we are. You are an
American, yes—but an American of *which kind?*"

Yet, as should by now be clear, the Court's opinion in
SFFA—which will lead to the proliferation of racialized personal
statements—seems likely to yield even greater racial salience
on university campuses than did racial box-checking. Indeed,
the essay prompts many universities have devised in response
to *SFFA* further instill the very lesson that conservatives wish
would dissipate: the notion that racial differences define who
we are. Only six weeks after the Court issued *SFFA*, a *New York
Times* article—titled "Colleges Want to Know More About You
and Your 'Identity'"—surveyed the new college application
landscape and found: "A review of the essay prompts used this
year by more than two dozen highly selective colleges reveals
that schools are using words and phrases like 'identity' and 'life

50 experience,' and are probing aspects of a student's upbringing and background that have, in the words of a Harvard prompt, 'shaped who you are.'" Some new essay prompts overtly instruct applicants to write about race if they so wish. But even prompts that take a subtler approach—inquiring about applicants' "identity" and what has "shaped who you are"—nevertheless reinforce the paramount importance of race; they just do so in a circuitous fashion. Some of the roundabout approaches are, moreover, awfully straightforward. Consider Dartmouth College's post-*SFFA* prompt, which will win few points for subtlety: "'It's not easy being green . . .' was the frequent refrain of Kermit the Frog. How has difference been a part of your life, and how have you embraced it as part of your identity and outlook?"

This new state of college applications strongly resembles the mindset from which Chief Justice Roberts's *SFFA* opinion recoiled, including when he noted with evident disdain that a lawyer defending UNC's admissions program contended that race "'says [something] about who you are.'" Universities now—both directly and indirectly—instruct students that race says not only *something* about who they are, but something *major*, and prompt students to write lengthy testimonials exploring the centrality of race to their identity formation. How then, from a conservative perspective, did *SFFA* not inaugurate a marked decline from the prior method?

One need not be conservative, moreover, to harbor significant reservations regarding how *SFFA* encourages Black and brown applicants to conceive of race as *the* singular, dominant aspect of their identities. In his 1994 memoir, Professor Henry Louis Gates Jr.—a liberal, distinguished scholar of African American literature and history at Harvard—balked at

the notion that Black people must subscribe to the totalizing,
all-consuming vision of race that *SFFA* unintentionally promoted. "I rebel at the notion that I can't be part of other groups,
that I can't construct identities through elective affinity, that
race must be the most important thing about me," Gates wrote.
"Is that what I want on my gravestone: Here lies an African
American?"* If Gates bristled at being thrust into racially confined roles, many other liberals will doubtless chafe when they
feel themselves being eased into the racial straitjacket.

Similarly, many Black liberal intellectuals may object on
racial grounds to *SFFA*'s encouragement of Black applicants to
showcase their racial agonies. In the 1960s, Ralph Ellison published an essay protesting the dubious notion "that unrelieved
suffering is the only 'real' Negro experience." Ellison insisted
that "there is . . . an American Negro tradition which teaches one
to deflect racial provocation and to master and contain pain,"
and "which abhors as obscene any trading on one's own anguish
for gain or sympathy." Assuming Ellison's characterization is
correct, *SFFA* guarantees that college admissions offices today
confront a veritable torrent of racial obscenity.

Mismatching Students

Conservative critics of affirmative action, including then-
Professor Scalia and Justice Thomas, have often lambasted
the policy because they insist that it promotes racial minorities into academic settings for which they are underprepared. This critique—which has come to be labeled "mismatch

---

* In a fascinating twist, when Gates applied to Yale College in the 1960s, his
personal essay opened: "My grandfather was colored, my father was Negro,
and I am black." Henry Louis Gates Jr., *Colored People: A Memoir* 201 (1994).

52 theory"—predates the Court's validation of affirmative action in *Bakke*. In 1970, eight years before *Bakke*, Professor Graglia advanced the mismatch criticism in one of the earliest law review articles to wrestle with the then-novel phenomenon of affirmative action in university settings. "Special admission programs, almost by definition, operate to [e]nsure that students are placed in schools for which they are not qualified," Graglia stated. "As a result, many students fully qualified for other schools, attend institutions for which they are ill-equipped." Economist Thomas Sowell, who has profoundly influenced Justice Thomas's thought, has articulated formative versions of the mismatch idea. In an article published shortly before *Bakke* appeared, Sowell condemned affirmative action for inflicting "a disastrous and permanently scarring experience" on young racial minorities "who would normally qualify for good, non-prestigious colleges where they could succeed, [but] are instead enrolled in famous institutions where they fail."

Though respected scholars have challenged the empirical basis for mismatch theory in recent years, many conservatives nonetheless remain firmly committed to the notion's veracity—at times seeming almost to accept it as an article of faith. Justice Thomas's *SFFA* concurrence, over the vociferous objections of Justice Sotomayor, presents only one recent illustration of mismatch theory's durability within conservative circles.

Assuming arguendo that mismatch is a real phenomenon, however, it seems almost certain that *SFFA* will increase the occurrence—placing even more students into settings in which they are unlikely to flourish. *SFFA* will not, of course, extinguish the desire of universities to enroll significant numbers of Black and brown students. The diversity ethos is, as several scholars have suggested, too firmly embedded in higher education to be completely eradicated by a single judicial decision. But *SFFA* will likely inspire universities to admit more Black and brown students from very different high schools than those who were typically admitted under the old system of racial diversity. And these new students may be much less well prepared to succeed than the students who were typically admitted before *SFFA*.

Under the pre-*SFFA* regime, the Ivy League and its peer institutions often admitted Black and brown students who attended private schools and boarding schools where they compiled strong records, but finished outside the very top percentiles of graduates. Under the post-*SFFA* regime, it will be more difficult to admit such students and to justify such admissions in a litigation context. Accordingly, leading universities may respond by admitting the valedictorians and salutatorians from large, underprivileged urban high schools. Conservatives may well be tempted to cheer this transformation, contending that if any racial minorities should receive a preference in college admissions, that preference should surely go to students from nonaffluent backgrounds. The trouble with this approach, however, is that the racial minorities who conservatives often deem undeserving beneficiaries may well be the very students who are best prepared to excel at elite universities.

This claim is sure to stir considerable controversy; indeed, Justice Alito stridently attacked a version of this idea as an elitist delusion several years ago. At the outset, then, it may be helpful to offer a few notes of clarification. For one thing, it is not necessary to believe that students who attended large, urban, underprivileged public schools are not *academically* prepared for leading universities to believe that a version of the

54   mismatch idea nevertheless pertains. That is because many students who graduate from such schools will be accustomed to learning and living in thoroughly monoracial environments, leaving them *socially* unprepared to thrive in their new racially diverse environments. For another, it is important to realize that Black and brown students who attend private and boarding schools need not have been raised by wealthy parents; to the contrary, the existence of scholarships at these schools means that it is overly simplistic to assume that having attended a rarefied school means that one hails from an affluent household. Finally, no less a conservative authority than Justice Thomas has repeatedly suggested that Black students who attended non-racially diverse, underprivileged public schools are mismatched at elite universities. Thus, according to perhaps the nation's preeminent constitutional conservative, *SFFA* itself is poised to lure many Black students into alien settings where they are set up to fail.

The notion that it would be advantageous to devote special effort to admit some students of color who attended high school in racially diverse—rather than only monoracial—settings became hotly contested in 2016. In *Fisher v. University of Texas* (*Fisher II*), the Supreme Court weighed the ability of one of the nation's foremost public universities to use racial classifications in admissions. The overwhelming majority of UT's Black and brown students were admitted through the Top Ten Percent plan, whereby graduates of Texas public high schools who ranked within the top decile received automatic admission to the state's flagship university in Austin. The Top Ten Percent plan yielded significant racial diversity in Austin because many Texas high schools featured student bodies that were composed almost exclusively of Black and brown students. In addition to this formally race-neutral program, though, UT also admitted some students using racial classifications. When this race-conscious system was initially challenged in *Fisher I*, UT defended that program, in part, by noting that racial classifications allowed UT to ensure that it matriculated not exclusively students of color who graduated from urban, all-minority high schools, but also some who graduated from meaningfully integrated environments. In *Fisher I*, UT explained that students of color admitted through race-conscious means guaranteed that it could welcome, say, "[t]he African-American or Hispanic child of successful professionals in Dallas," or even "[t]he black student with high grades from Andover."

The Supreme Court in 2013 issued a narrow, technical decision in *Fisher I*, clarifying the pertinent constitutional test. When the matter returned to the Court three years later in *Fisher II*, UT no longer foregrounded its Andover defense. But when *Fisher II* resulted in the Court upholding UT's race-conscious system, Justice Alito demonstrated that he had in no sense forgotten the discarded, unorthodox justification. Rather, Justice Alito pounced on the idea, excoriating it as an unconscionable distortion of affirmative action's true aims: "UT has . . . claimed at times that the race-based component of its plan is needed because the Top Ten Percent Plan admits the *wrong kind* of African-American and Hispanic students, namely, students from poor families who attend schools in which the student body is predominantly African-American or Hispanic." He dismissed any race-based preferences for the children of Andover and the Dallas professional class as an unjust inversion, one that "turn[ed] affirmative action on its

56   head." Summarizing his incredulity, Justice Alito concluded: "[W]e are told that a program that tends to admit poor and disadvantaged minority students is inadequate because it does not work to the advantage of those who are more fortunate. This is affirmative action gone wild."

This castigation, of course, resonates with a dominant view among affirmative action's conservative critics—including then-Professor Scalia in his post-*Bakke* article and Justice Thomas in his *SFFA* concurrence—that the program too often rewards relatively privileged racial minorities. The objection that race-conscious programs reward undeserving beneficiaries has figured prominently in conservative commentary from the very beginning. In Graglia's foundational critique from 1970, for example, he charged: "Negroes may be specially admitted [under affirmative action] even though they are of middle class background, have professional parents, or otherwise appear to have had average or above average cultural opportunities." Nearly twenty-five years later, Walter Benn Michaels offered perhaps the most famous version of the critique: "When student and faculty activists struggle for cultural diversity, they are in large part battling over what skin color the rich kids should have."

Conservative opponents of affirmative action have thus vehemently advanced two lines of attack, contending that the policies promote both mismatch and undeserving beneficiaries. Conservatives have dedicated insufficient attention, however, to acknowledging that the two critiques can be viewed as existing in substantial tension with each other, and perhaps may even be irreconcilable. Those critiques are competing, that is, because the students from the least privileged backgrounds—the deserving beneficiaries—may be the very students who are most mismatched at the nation's elite campuses. One year after *Bakke*, then-Professor J. Harvie Wilkinson III acknowledged this point, when he noted that university administrators thought that "[n]othing . . . could be worse" than an admission program that targeted economic disadvantage because that approach "would . . . disqualify by definition many of the ablest minority students, those from middle-class backgrounds." Candid liberal supporters of affirmative action have sometimes made this point in reverse, noting that racial minorities from the most deprived backgrounds are likely to be over-matched at ultracompetitive universities.

Perhaps surprisingly, though, the premier advocate of the idea that students of color who attended high school in modest, monoracial circumstances may be mismatched in elite universities is Justice Thomas. But because Justice Thomas has not ventured this particular version of mismatch in his judicial writings, legal scholars have generally neglected this significant feature of his views on affirmative action. In the early 1990s, Thomas read journalist Ron Suskind's *Wall Street Journal* profile of Cedric Jennings, an ambitious high school student who was earning top marks at Ballou High School, "[t]he most troubled and violent school in the blighted southeast corner of Washington, D.C." All too predictably, Ballou educated a student body that was almost entirely Black. Justice Thomas was sufficiently impressed by the young man's efforts to achieve in the face of adversity that he extended Jennings a standing invitation to visit his Supreme Court chambers. When the momentous visit occurred several months later, Suskind accompanied Jennings and chronicled Thomas remarkably

58   warning the hopeful twelfth grader that he was about to receive
      an extended, harsh lesson in mismatch.

      After the subject of college plans arose during the visit,
      Jennings excitedly informed Justice Thomas that he was headed
      to Brown University in the fall. But "Thomas frown[ed] and
      [shook] his head," informing Jennings: "Well, that's fine, but I'm
      not sure if I would have selected an Ivy League school.... You're
      going to be up there with lots of very smart white kids, and, if
      you're not sure about who you are, you could get eaten alive."
      Understandably, Jennings seemed taken aback, but Thomas
      continued: "It's not just at the Ivies, you understand. It can
      happen at any of the good colleges where a young black man,
      who hasn't spent much time with whites, suddenly finds him-
      self among almost all whites. You can feel lost." To make sure
      that Jennings understood the enormous stakes of feeling lost,
      Justice Thomas drew upon his own college days at Holy Cross,
      telling Jennings about the "smartest black kid [he] ever knew"
      who "got confused about who he was and ended up getting
      addicted to drugs and dropping out." Thomas's raw advice to
      Jennings is, of course, an unmistakable embrace of the notion
      that racial minorities who attend monoracial high schools are
      socially mismatched at eminent universities.

      It may be tempting to dismiss Justice Thomas's advice to
      Jennings as mere off-the-cuff talk that in no way reflects his
      considered judgment. But yielding to that temptation would
      be misguided. In his memoir, *My Grandfather's Son*, Thomas
      stated in a significant passage that he witnessed several Black
      college classmates at Holy Cross in the late 1960s suffer badly
      from the mismatch of being thrust into a racially alien environ-
      ment. Black Holy Cross students who had previously attended

school in all-Black environments struggled, Thomas maintained, because "they lacked the social experience that would have made it easier for them to leave the comfort zone of segregation and move into the white world." Justice Thomas objected that Holy Cross placed these Black students in a position to fail: "Why, I asked, were these gifted young people being sacrificed on the altar of an abstract theory of social justice—and who profited from their failure?"

At first blush, *SFFA* might have been thought to quell the mismatch concern, but—upon close inspection—it instead promises only to heighten the issue. The consequences for students from marginalized backgrounds could prove dire. One can easily imagine Justice Thomas, in a moment of candor, expressing deep concern for this group of guinea pigs preparing to embark on a journey into the unknown, and also wondering: Who stands to gain from any failures in this high-stakes experiment?

Perspicacious readers may object that a tension exists between two different claims about *SFFA*'s harms. On the one hand, I argued above that students from affluent families will more readily succeed in navigating *SFFA*'s essay-based diversity regime. On the other hand, I now contend that *SFFA* will redound to the (short-term) benefit of students from underprivileged high schools. What gives?

One way to reconcile these claims is to note that *SFFA* could plausibly increase the percentages of Black and brown students from both ultra-privileged backgrounds *and* ultra-deprived backgrounds, effectively squeezing out applicants from the middle class. To the extent that the two claims still seem irreconcilable, though, that difficulty stems from conservatives'

60   multifarious, kitchen-sink-style attack on affirmative action.
        On this view, conservatives have launched a thousand arrows
        against affirmative action over the years, but they have dedicated
        inadequate energy to examining the analytical incoherence
        that bedevils their varied charges. In our new post–affirmative
        action world, though, conservatives will need to dedicate
        greater effort to contemplating the assorted trade-offs.

The Balkanizing Military Carveout

One of *SFFA*'s most surprising features appeared in its fourth
footnote, which declined to require the nation's military academies to comply with the decision. This carveout was driven by
the fear that, in the absence of overt affirmative action, those
institutions—including the United States Military Academy
at West Point and the Naval Academy in Annapolis—would be
unable to produce a racially diverse officer corps to lead a racially
diverse group of enlisted servicemembers. The consequences of
having few Black and brown officers would pose grave national
security concerns, a dynamic that infamously emerged during
the Vietnam War. In *Grutter v. Bollinger,* Justice O'Connor's
opinion for the Court invoked and relied upon an amicus brief
filed by several esteemed former military generals, who drove
home the necessity of a diverse officer corps for the military's
ability to function effectively. Whereas *Grutter* construed the
military's racial diversity needs as applicable to the larger society, *SFFA* in effect concluded that the military's needs on this
front could differentiate it from that society.

        Conservatives might be thought to abhor *SFFA*'s military
exemption for a few different reasons. Most intuitively, colorblindness proponents could believe that *SFFA* adopted a partial

remedy to a problem demanding an absolute solution. In addition, conservatives who believe that the military's unique position in American society means that it should in fact receive
greater leeway to consider race may object that *SFFA*'s carveout will prove woefully ineffective in realizing its ambitions.
Conservatives in this camp would note that the military academies produce only 19 percent of the active-duty officers, with
ROTC programs producing nearly double that percentage. In
order for the military exemption to prove effective in ensuring
a racially diverse office corps, then, *SFFA* should have afforded
civilian universities with ROTC programs at least some discretion regarding racial classifications.*

The most significant conservative objection to *SFFA*'s military exemption, however, would note that the carveout fosters
racial balkanization, promising to deepen the nation's divides.
SFFA's military exemption could have the effect of funneling
ambitious Black and brown students—who prize the status
associated with graduating from a first-rate university—into
a career in the military, even though they may hold no deep
desire to serve. But the persistence of race-conscious admissions at West Point and Annapolis—which provide a top-notch
education that is also tuition-free—will make it easier for
underrepresented minorities to gain admission to those academies than to their civilian peer institutions. Some Black and
brown twelfth graders will surely resent being forced to select

* While it may initially seem that the importance of ROTC to producing
military officers amounts to so much inside baseball, this point arose during
oral argument, with Solicitor General Elizabeth Prelogar expressly noting
"more officers come from ROTC programs" than from the academies. *See*
Transcript of Oral Argument at 150, Students for Fair Admissions, Inc. v.
Univ. of N.C., 600 U.S. 181 (2023) (No. 21-707).

62   between receiving an excellent education at a military academy and a weaker education at a nonmilitary college. Those feelings of resentment will only grow when they realize that the US military—including the academies—continues to be plagued by an unvarnished racism that would be unfathomable on many American college campuses today. More broadly, even apart from the students of color who feel coerced into entering the academies, *SFFA*'s military exemption seems likely to foster the belief in Black and brown communities that the Supreme Court offered this special dispensation intentionally to harm those communities by coopting bright young minds and placing their bodies in harm's way.

Conservatives—including then-Professor Scalia in 1979 and Justice Thomas in *SFFA*—have often contended that one of race-conscious admissions' most deleterious features is that it sows the seeds of racial discord, thereby balkanizing American society. In *Grutter*, Justice Anthony Kennedy's dissent struck this point with great force. Affirmative action's "unhappy consequence will be to perpetuate the hostilities that proper consideration of race is designed to avoid," Justice Kennedy asserted, making it harder to "bring[] . . . about the harmony and mutual respect among all citizens that our constitutional tradition has always sought."

While it is certainly true that conservatives have overwhelmingly highlighted concerns about racial balkanization when seeking to avoid feelings of white resentment, conservatives surely would not contend that the principle ignores the racialized resentments of nonwhite people. The overarching conservative commitment of the right's race jurisprudence holds that the law must not treat different racial groups in a

racially differentiated fashion. Thus, if white racial aggrieve-   63
ment can merit judicial solicitude, Black and brown racial
aggrievement can also merit judicial solicitude. And *SFFA*'s military exemption seems almost designed to foster Black resentment not just toward the military, but even toward the nation it
serves.

The notion that Black servicemembers would find *SFFA*'s
military carveout deeply alienating is hardly conjecture. After
SFFA, one West Point graduate spoke poignantly about the
lessons that the Supreme Court's opinion taught to Black
Americans:

> Affirmative action is good enough for Black folks to die on
> behalf of this country, but it's not good enough for Black
> folks to have access to becoming among the best lawyers,
> teachers, doctors, engineers, artists that this country has
> to offer. I can die for this country, but I certainly can't learn
> and instruct and save and build. And it felt like a direct slap
> in my face, and it was very disappointing and dishearten-
> ing for me. Because I asked myself, man, what was it all for?
> Why did I serve if I'm only looked at as cannon fodder?

It is hard to imagine a Supreme Court opinion in the modern era
instilling a deeper sense of racial balkanization.

Racism in the US military has a lengthy, sordid history, but
events stemming from the Vietnam War era play an outsized
role in shaping modern perceptions that the armed services
were particularly inhospitable environments for Black people.
In 2023, an academic study exploring why Black Americans support using military force less than white Americans observed:

64   "Vastly disproportionate rates of Black casualties at the begin-
      ning of the Vietnam War offended many Black Americans, and
      they did not soon forget this unequal distribution of harm."
      In 1966, long before the rise of mass mobilization against the
      Vietnam War, Huey P. Newton and Bobby Seale's Black Panther
      platform declared: "We want all Black men to be exempt from
      military service." A landmark oral history chronicling Black
      soldiers' experiences during the Vietnam War teems with
      instances of racial mistreatment. The paucity of Black officers
      in Vietnam—combined with a heavily Black group of enlisted
      soldiers—created optimal conditions for racial balkaniza-
      tion. As the amicus brief of retired military generals invoked in
      Grutter found, these disparities "heightened racial tension" and
      "the armed forces suffered increased racial polarization, perva-
      sive disciplinary problems, and racially motivated incidents in
      Vietnam and on posts around the world."

      The profound racial problems within the military are far
      from confined to the distant past. In 1988, within the seminal
      text titled "Black Steel in the Hour of Chaos," noted philoso-
      pher Chuck D memorably instructed: "[T]hey could not under-
      stand that I'm a Black man / and I could never be a veteran."
      Indeed, the modern military is marred by some of the starkest
      anti-Black racism that appears throughout American society.
      Following *SFFA*, one West Point graduate, who went on to pur-
      sue legal training at Yale, noted that the opinion "doom[s] more
      minority students to the discrimination that exists within the
      ranks of our nation's military," and that "discriminatory poli-
      cies and attitudes . . . stifle [the] success [of racial minorities]"
      in the military disproportionately. Polling data support this
      assessment, as more than half of the military's racial minorities

surveyed told the *Military Times* a few years ago that "they had seen examples of white nationalism or ideologically driven racism among their fellow troops." With President Trump's return to power in 2025, fueled in part by a resurgence in white nationalism, those figures seem certain to rise in the future.

Racial minorities make up 43 percent of the active-duty military, but the highest rungs of leadership in no way reflect that diversity. Indeed, although the nation's top military brass included more than forty commanders in 2021, only two of those were Black. In October 2020, when a photograph emerged of President Trump in the Oval Office surrounded by top admirals and four-star generals, the assemblage appeared so monochromatically white that one Black retired Army officer noted that judging by the photo's complexion, "[y]ou would have thought it was 1950." The lack of prominent Black leaders in today's military did not occur by accident. Rather, the *New York Times* recently reported that "[t]he African-Americans who do become officers are often steered to specialize in logistics and transportation rather than the marquee combat arms specialties that lead to the top jobs." Former Secretary of Defense Lloyd Austin has recalled that, as a high-ranking officer in the 82nd Airborne Division, he instructed a white servicemember to deliver briefings because he believed that those in his charge would be less likely to heed instructions coming directly from a Black man.

As recently as 2020, the West Point official intercollegiate football team's flag featured an acronym that originated in the Aryan Brotherhood of Texas prison gang. Black servicemembers, moreover, continue to be pelted with a barrage of racial epithets: some Marines routinely refer to their Black colleagues

66   as "nonswimmer[s]," and some Army Rangers routinely refer to their fellow Black servicemembers as "Night Ranger[s]." Black Navy pilots receive racist call signs, including "8-Ball," and their colleagues have referred to them collectively as "eggplants." Receiving such odious treatment could cause many Black servicemembers to resent not only their individual racist tormenters, but also the nation that permits such abuse to be directed toward those who dedicate their lives to providing it security.

In *Bakke*'s immediate wake, then-Professor Scalia allowed in 1979 that he held "grave doubts about the wisdom of where we are going in affirmative action," and that he found the jurisprudence involving race "an embarrassment to teach." Scalia deemed it an "utterly confused field," and concluded: "[I]t is increasingly difficult to pretend to one's students that the decisions of the Supreme Court are tied together by threads of logic and analysis."

Legal conservatives have, of course, long pined for affirmative action's demise. But as *SFFA* thrusts the nation into the post—affirmative action era, conservatives may once again grow to harbor deep reservations about the wisdom of where we are heading. Now that the long-sought victory has been realized, it has become apparent for several powerful reasons that conservatives will profoundly regret the legal order that *SFFA* generates. According to conservatives' own principles, then, the edifice that *SFFA* hastily erected seems far less hospitable than the one that the Supreme Court dismantled.

How *SFFA v. Harvard* Confounds Legal Liberals

The Civil War that ruptured the nation in the 1860s begat a constitutional revolution in the form of three pivotal amendments designed to make Black people full participants in the American experiment. Although the Thirteenth Amendment abolished slavery and the Fifteenth Amendment extended the franchise to Black men, what would eventually become the most celebrated and the most litigated passage of constitutional text adopted during the Reconstruction era appeared in the Fourteenth Amendment. The central passage, which appears at the very end of the Amendment's first section, prohibits states from "deny[ing] any person within its jurisdiction the equal protection of the laws." Surprisingly, when the Fourteenth Amendment was ratified in 1868, this Equal Protection Clause attracted relatively little notice, as contemporaneous observers fixated on the Amendment's other provisions. As late as the 1920s, Justice Oliver Wendell Holmes, in a majority opinion for the Supreme Court, could be found dismissing the Equal Protection Clause as "the usual last resort of constitutional arguments." Holmes

68   overstated his case, as the clause was never quite the redheaded stepchild of the Constitution that he portrayed. But it is nevertheless astonishing to observe that the Equal Protection Clause, which was initially cast as an understudy, over time assumed the starring role in our nation's constitutional drama.

For the last five decades, constitutional law scholars have contended that the Fourteenth Amendment's Equal Protection Clause contains two dueling visions. The first theory views the Clause as prohibiting the government from engaging in racial classification. The second theory, in contrast, construes the Clause as prohibiting the government from perpetuating racial subordination. In some cases, jurists traveling via these two theories would arrive at precisely the same destination. Thus, *Brown v. Board of Education* would have invalidated school segregation regardless of whether the justices subscribed to an anticlassification or an antisubordination theory of equal protection. Separate schools both treated students differently on a racial basis (that is, it *classified* them) and perpetuated racism by suggesting that Black people were inferior (that is, it *subordinated* them). The centrality of these concepts to modern constitutional law is virtually impossible to exaggerate, as they form the very axis upon which the Equal Protection Clause turns.

This theoretical debate loomed large because it held quite tangible consequences for assessing the constitutionality of affirmative action, long a combustible subject in American law and life. Whereas theories of anticlassification and antisubordination view *Brown* together as fast friends, those theories quickly become bitter, even ferocious enemies at the first sight of affirmative action. The anticlassification school—associated overwhelmingly with constitutional conservatives—holds that affirmative action violates the Constitution because the programs treat students differently based on race. But the antisubordination school—identified predominantly with legal liberals—contends that affirmative action passes constitutional muster because the programs treat no one as racially inferior. To the contrary, antisubordination theorists suggest that race-conscious admissions policies are designed to combat the racial stratification that has defined US society, with Black people forming a racialized underclass.

In 1976, Professor Owen Fiss of Yale Law School published the foundational article advancing what came to be termed the antisubordination theory. "[W]hat the Equal Protection Clause prohibits," Fiss instructed, is "the state law or practice [that] aggravates . . . or perpetuates . . . the subordinate position of a specially disadvantaged group." Fiss's timing was hardly accidental, as the Supreme Court's first, inconclusive brush with affirmative action in *DeFunis v. Odegaard* occurred two years before his article debuted, and its momentous decision in *Regents of the University of California v. Bakke* would appear two years later. Fiss made no secret that his alternative vision of the Equal Protection Clause was driven by a desire to ensure that judges did not invoke the anticlassification theory to invalidate the then-fledgling affirmative action programs.

What may have started out as an alternative theory of equal protection has become thoroughly mainstream. Prominent liberal legal scholars have, tipping their academic caps toward Fiss, articulated numerous theories elaborating upon the foundational work. Thus, to name only two major approaches, Professor Laurence Tribe offered "an antisubjugation principle," and Professor Cass Sunstein advanced "the anticaste principle."

70   In 2004, Professor Reva Siegel offered a notably crisp defini-
      tion of the antisubordination principle as "the conviction that
      it is wrong for the state to engage in practices that enforce
      the inferior social status of historically oppressed groups."
      Although these theories certainly diverge in their nuances, they
      are nonetheless united by the overarching commitment that—
      whatever the terminology—emphasizing antisubordination
      values means viewing affirmative action as constitutionally
      permissible.

          But antisubordination is a far more protean concept than
      my fellow legal liberals allow. Although liberals since the 1970s
      have overwhelmingly promoted an equal protection dichot-
      omy notable for its tidiness, the constitutional reality is messy,
      chaotic, and—perhaps above all—strange. The career of anti-
      subordination has been strange, I contend, because pledg-
      ing allegiance to antisubordination in no way requires saluting
      affirmative action. Rather, many conservatives who detest
      affirmative action have claimed that the programs themselves
      subordinate Black people. By lowering typical admissions stan-
      dards, critics argue, affirmative action policies perpetuate the
      repugnant myth of Black intellectual inferiority.

          Although arguments contending that antisubordina-
      tion values undermine rather than support affirmative action
      have been articulated in high places, traditional antisubordi-
      nation scholars have steadfastly refused to treat these argu-
      ments with the seriousness that they deserve—or even any
      seriousness at all. The dominant approach has been to acknowl-
      edge the challenge ever so briefly, and then to bat it away with
      blunt, conclusory force. Early on, Fiss exhibited the technique:
      "If the court truly believed that a state policy—even if called

'benign'—impaired the status of blacks then the policy would be invalid. But I doubt whether anyone believes that preferential admissions to law schools for blacks impairs the status of the group." Compared to some of his contemporaries, though, Fiss's treatment was downright expansive, as they often managed to shoo away the objection in a single sentence or buried it in a footnote.

Liberal antisubordination scholars' refusal to grapple in a sustained fashion with the competing arguments regarding their chief concept is deeply perplexing. Even before Fiss published his formative article, Justice Douglas's opinion in *DeFunis v. Odegaard* employed antisubordination arguments to criticize affirmative action policies. Those policies, Douglas wrote, conveyed "stigma and caste," and placed "a stamp of inferiority" on Black and brown students by suggesting they "cannot make it on their individual merit." In so arguing, Justice Douglas telegraphed arguments that Justice Thomas has repeatedly invoked against affirmative action. Many other legal luminaries have advanced similar antisubordination claims against race-conscious admissions policies, including then-Professors Richard Posner, Antonin Scalia, and J. Harvie Wilkinson III. Strikingly, several preeminent left-of-center scholars— including Professors Derrick Bell, Stephen L. Carter, and Randall Kennedy—have voiced similar critiques of affirmative action. Antisubordination, it seems, is a coat of many colors.

This chapter endeavors to embrace rather than elide antisubordination's complexity, which has, over the last few years, grown more complex still. Although interrogating antisubordination's multiple meanings is an intellectual task long overdue, the Supreme Court's decision in *SFFA v. Harvard* endows

72   the matter with even greater urgency. Fully understanding that cataclysmic legal dispute is impossible, in my view, without foregrounding antisubordination's multiplicity. SFFA's primary argument can be viewed as sounding in antisubordination logic. Although SFFA occasionally suggested that lowered admission standards tarnished Black and brown students, its primary antisubordinating argument presented a different focus. By imposing lower personal ratings on Asian Americans and artificially capping their enrollment, SFFA maintained, Harvard demeaned that racial group by construing them as nerdy, narrow, and perpetually foreign. Antisubordination served as a throughline for various Justices' opinions in *SFFA v. Harvard*, but liberals and conservatives utilized that concept in radically divergent fashions.

Before delving into these arguments, I should emphasize that nothing herein should be taken as concluding that antisubordination must be abandoned. I do believe, however, that it will no longer do for proponents of antisubordination to close their eyes to substantial claims—advanced by a wide array of formidable legal theorists—in the hopes that those complications will somehow magically disappear. That intellectual strategy seldom pays dividends. Therefore, although the bulk of this chapter explores antisubordination's deeply contested nature, I fervently hope that it sparks dialogue among traditional antisubordination theorists regarding how the concept might be defended, refined, and elaborated.

The Standard Antisubordination Account
The standard liberal view of equal protection extols celebrated decisions—including *Strauder v. West Virginia, Brown*

v. Board of Education, and *Loving v. Virginia*—as invalidating
legal approaches that subordinate Black people. The standard
account typically begins in the late nineteenth century, with the
Supreme Court's opinion in *Strauder*. There, the Court invalidated a statute that prohibited Black people from serving on
juries, reserving that honor for white citizens. Justice William
Strong, writing for the Court, utilized classic antisubordination
rhetoric, reasoning that the statute acts as "practically a brand
upon [Black people] . . . an assertion of their inferiority, and a
stimulant to that race prejudice." The Fourteenth Amendment,
Strong maintained, was fundamentally designed to prohibit
both "discriminations which are steps towards reducing [Black
people] to the condition of a subject race," and "legal discriminations, implying [their] inferiority."

While acknowledging that *Brown* certainly contained some
anticlassification reasoning, antisubordination scholars highlight the iconic decision's language condemning school segregation because it perpetuated notions of Black inferiority.
Chief Justice Earl Warren—in *Brown*'s most resonant passage—
contended: "To separate [Black students] from others of similar age and qualifications solely because of their race generates a
feeling of inferiority as to their status in the community that may
affect their hearts and minds in a way unlikely ever to be undone."

Loving's invalidation of state bans on interracial marriage
is also a canonical antisubordination decision. *Loving* embraced
antisubordinationist reasoning, the standard account holds, by
finding that statutes cannot lawfully elevate whiteness as supe-
rior. Writing for the Court in *Loving*, Chief Justice Warren found
that "[t]he fact that Virginia prohibits only interracial marriages involving white persons demonstrates that the racial

74   classifications . . . [are] measures designed to maintain White Supremacy." Virginia's statute preserved and uplifted whiteness, simultaneously lowering and demeaning nonwhiteness.

Palmer v. Thompson's legitimation of Jackson, Mississippi's decision to close its municipal swimming pools, rather than to integrate them, can be viewed as illustrating the constitutional perils that flow from refusing to apply antisubordination values. In one of the most reviled racial decisions in modern American history, Justice Hugo Black's majority opinion in *Palmer* applied a rigid anticlassification rule, framing the case as involving "whether black citizens in Jackson are being denied their constitutional rights when the city has closed the public pools to black and white alike." So framed, Justice Black had little difficulty concluding that because Jackson had not racially classified residents, it also had not violated the Equal Protection Clause.

Had *Palmer* embraced an antisubordination approach, however, it would have reached the opposite outcome, finding that Jackson's swimming pool closures were driven by a view of the Black body as undesirable, even contaminated. Justice Byron White's dissenting opinion in *Palmer* repeatedly evinced antisubordination logic. While pool closures to avert integration might treat all races equally, he observed, they also express "an . . . official policy that Negroes are unfit to associate with whites." For many liberal scholars, then, *Palmer*'s wrongheaded outcome demonstrates how constitutional interpretation goes awry when antisubordination goes missing.

Troubling the Standard Account
Liberal scholars have routinely asserted that affirmative action combats subordination. Far too frequently disregarded, however,

are the numerous arguments suggesting that affirmative action programs themselves subordinate Black people. Bringing these oft-overlooked antisubordination arguments to the fore complicates the notion that jurists concerned with caste must invariably believe that affirmative action programs pass constitutional muster.

In 1974, Justice Douglas used highly charged language in *DeFunis v. Odegaard* to invoke the legacy of *Brown v. Board of Education*, an opinion that he joined exactly two decades earlier. "A segregated admissions process creates suggestions of stigma and caste no less than a segregated classroom," Douglas wrote, "and in the end . . . may produce that result despite its contrary intentions." He further suggested that the existence of affirmative action programs could lend credence to the misguided notion "that blacks or browns cannot make it on their individual merit. That is a stamp of inferiority that a State is not permitted to place on any lawyer." In this remarkable passage, Douglas utilized many hallmarks of antisubordination language, expressing concerns about "stigma and caste," stereotyped beliefs of racial inadequacy, and, of course, the dreaded "stamp of inferiority." Although Douglas's dissent may have been the first time that a Supreme Court justice used antisubordination reasoning to question affirmative action, it was far from the last.

Indeed, four years after *DeFunis*, Justice Powell's controlling opinion in *Bakke* briefly cited and elaborated upon Justice Douglas's view entertaining how affirmative action could harm Black and brown students. In *Bakke*, Justice Powell famously cast the decisive vote in a Court split 4−1−4. He concluded that university admissions offices may in some instances consider race without violating the Constitution, but he also prohibited

76   them from implementing the sort of naked quota adopted by
University of California Davis Medical School. While Powell
refused to ban considerations of race in admissions, he nevertheless allowed that "preferential programs may only reinforce
common stereotypes holding that certain groups are unable
to achieve success without special protection." Justice Powell
did not, of course, view affirmative action's potentially subordinating effects as disqualifying, but he did concede that they
existed.

    In recent years, Justice Thomas has amplified this con-
cern that programs designed to help Black people actually
end up subordinating them. Justice Thomas's magnum opus
of antisubordination is his dissenting opinion in *Grutter v.
Bollinger*, where he excoriated the Court's decision upholding the University of Michigan Law School's race-conscious
admissions policy. "I believe blacks can achieve in every avenue
of American life without the meddling of university administrators," Thomas opined, not so subtly intimating that his colleagues in the majority believed that Black students needed
affirmative action to flourish. Justice Thomas further noted
that some Black applicants would be admitted to Michigan's
Law School even in the absence of race-conscious policies. But,
he maintained, there was no way to distinguish Black students
"who belong[ed]" at Michigan on the merits and those who
gained admission due to the boost of affirmative action. "The
majority of blacks are admitted to the Law School because of
discrimination, and because of this policy all are tarred as undeserving," he wrote. Thomas contended that the ghost of affirmative action haunts virtually all of Black achievement. "When
blacks take positions in the highest places of government,

industry, or academia, it is an open question today whether their
skin color played a part in their advancement," he vented. "The
question itself is the stigma—because either racial discrimination did play a role . . . or it did not, in which case asking the
question itself unfairly marks those blacks who would succeed
without discrimination." In this ardent passage, Justice Thomas
thus availed himself of quintessential antisubordination logic,
asserting that affirmative action "tar[s]," "stigmat[izes]," and
"marks" Black people as substandard, and therefore violates the
Equal Protection Clause.

In the Supreme Court's first encounter with the University
of Texas's undergraduate admissions program, Justice Thomas
returned to this antisubordination melody. *Fisher v. University of
Texas* (*Fisher I*) considered whether admissions officers could—
after accepting the overwhelming majority of the incoming
class with students whose academic records placed them within
a top percentile of their high schools—use explicit racial classifications in rounding out the class. Although *Fisher I* declined
to determine whether Texas's express racial classifications violated the Equal Protection Clause, Justice Thomas wrote a separate opinion warning of the "insidious consequences" that result
from "racial engineering." Anticipating the formation of SFFA,
Justice Thomas noted the University's policy "injures . . . Asian
applicants who are denied admission because of their race."

Justice Thomas reserved his greatest concern, however, for
Black and brown students, who he believed were harmed most by
affirmative action. Not only did the underrepresented minorities who were admitted with express racial classifications have
their achievements "taint[ed]," but, Thomas insisted, the taint
applied to every member of those racial groups at Texas. "In this

78   case," he contended, "most blacks and Hispanics attending the University were admitted without discrimination under the Top Ten Percent plan, but no one can distinguish those students from the ones whose race played a role in their admission." No matter how accomplished Black and brown students were in high school—Thomas intimates—valedictorians, National Merit Scholars, and United States Presidential Scholars alike walk around the Austin campus with "a badge of inferiority" pinned to their chests solely as a result of their skin color. In this sense, receiving a letter offering admission to the flagship university in Texas becomes ineluctably transformed into a booby prize—at least for Black and brown students. If that is not racial subordination, one can almost hear Thomas asking rhetorically, then tell me: What is?

Although justices who support affirmative action and justices who oppose affirmative action both invoke antisubordination rationales to bolster their competing positions, liberal and conservative justices talk right past each other when doing so— even when they are using the rationale (though not the label) within the same legal dispute. This phenomenon appeared most clearly in *Schuette v. Coalition to Defend Affirmative Action*. That case considered whether the Equal Protection Clause prohibited states from banning affirmative action in education. The Court, in a 6–2 decision written by Justice Kennedy, held that states could do so without running afoul of the Constitution. In an impassioned dissent, Justice Sotomayor castigated her colleagues in the majority for ignoring that "[r]ace matters" in myriad ways, including the nation's "racial caste" system, and the "persistent racial inequality in [American] society." Justice Sotomayor also tweaked Chief Justice Roberts by reformulating

the most famous sentence that he has ever written, when he
intoned: "The way to stop discrimination on the basis of race is
to stop discriminating on the basis of race." Justice Sotomayor
retorted: "The way to stop discrimination on the basis of race is
to speak openly and candidly on the subject of race, and to apply
the Constitution with eyes open to the unfortunate effects of
centuries of racial discrimination."

Chief Justice Roberts felt compelled to write a brief concurring opinion in *Schuette* that responded to Justice Sotomayor's
critique by saying, in effect: *just so*. Roberts, that is, fought antisubordination with antisubordination, reasoning that one significant reason that Black and brown students might doubt
whether they "belong" at an elite college is due to affirmative
action itself. "[I]t is not 'out of touch with reality' to conclude
that racial preferences may themselves have the debilitating
effect of reinforcing precisely that doubt, and—if so—that the
preferences do more harm than good," he explained. Chief Justice
Roberts, with perhaps a nod to Justice Thomas, suggested that
affirmative action programs exacerbate racial inequality rather
than remediate it by teaching the lesson that Black and brown
students are not quite up to snuff. If Sotomayor appreciated the
import of Roberts's antisubordination rejoinder, her opinion
gave no such indication.

Conservative Complications
Beyond the Supreme Court, conservative voices have often condemned affirmative action by arguing that the policy tarnishes
racial minorities. These critics do not explicitly invoke the
antisubordination theory of the Equal Protection Clause, but it
is not difficult to grasp how their criticisms militate in favor of

80   invalidating affirmative action programs on that basis. Critics
      expressing this viewpoint are in no way obscure. Rather, con-
      servatives writing in this vein include many eminent nonlawyer
      public intellectuals, prominent law professors, and a few legal
      scholars who would go on to become revered jurists. The prev-
      alence of these beliefs renders the relatively modest imprint of
      the conservative antisubordination arguments in legal scholar-
      ship all the more confounding.

      Even before the Supreme Court decided *Bakke* in 1978, con-
      servatives contended that affirmative action harmed the very
      racial groups that it was designed to help. In 1970, Professor
      Lino Graglia cautioned law schools against adjusting their
      admissions standards with an eye toward producing a cadre of
      Black and brown lawyers. Law students who lacked the stan-
      dard qualifications, Graglia warned, will "in the long run rein-
      force stereotypes of incompetence." Clients who sought "a *real*
      lawyer," Graglia wrote, would conclude they needed a white
      attorney. Economist Thomas Sowell, whom Justice Thomas has
      lavishly praised, voiced similar concerns to Graglia's in a book
      published in 1972. "'What all the arguments and campaigns for
      quotas are really saying, loud and clear, is that *black people just
      don't have it*," Sowell maintained, "and that they will have to be
      given something."

      Following *Bakke*'s invalidation of UC Davis Medical School's
      admissions program, moreover, Judge Richard Posner debuted a
      critique that would become a staple of conservative argumen-
      tation: the specter of being a patient treated by a physician who
      had been admitted to medical school under an affirmative action
      program. "[S]ince people feel a natural anxiety about the qualifi-
      cations of the doctors who treat them, the idea of an 'affirmative

action' doctor is particularly troubling," Posner stated. By placing a spotlight on Black physicians, Judge Posner emphasized
that affirmative action degrades the accomplishments of even
the nation's most esteemed Black professionals.

Then-Professor Scalia's post-*Bakke* article also explored
the plight of the Black physician. Scalia contended that affirmative action, rather than counteracting the myth of Black
intellectual ineptitude, guaranteed its perpetuation by "establish[ing] a second-class, 'minority' degree." Highlighting that
racial minorities who were admitted to UC Davis Medical
School earned significantly lower grades and standardized test
scores than their white colleagues, Scalia wrote, "To put the
issue . . . in its starkest form: If you must select your brain sur-
geon from among recent graduates of Davis Medical School and
have nothing to go on but . . . pictures, would you not be well
advised—playing the odds—to eliminate all minority group
members?"*

Justice Clarence Thomas has long stressed in interviews
that affirmative action subjugated Black people. Thomas used
deeply personal terms to inform one interviewer in the 1980s
that he detested preferential treatment because "it assumes
that I am not the equal of someone else, and if I'm not equal,

---

* The anxiety surrounding the topic of Black physicians and affirmative action
appeared in an episode of comedian Larry David's *Curb Your Enthusiasm*.
In the episode, titled simply "Affirmative Action," David and his friend
Richard Lewis run into Lewis's dermatologist, who happens to be Black.
When Lewis introduces the two men, David—in, he insists, a misguided
attempt at affability—questions why Lewis would see a Black doctor in light
of "the whole affirmative action thing." Predictably, the remark generates
profound irritation, rather than the laugh that David sought. *See Curb Your
Enthusiasm*: "Affirmative Action" (HBO, December 10, 2000).

82   then I'm inferior." Thomas contended that his experiences as
a Black student at Yale Law School in the 1970s afforded him
intimate, painful familiarity with people doubting his cogni-
tive capacities due to affirmative action. "You had to prove yourself every day [as a Black student] because the presumption was
that you were dumb and didn't deserve to be there on merit," he
stated in 1980. "Every time you walked into a law class at Yale,
it was like having a monkey jump down on your back from the
Gothic arches."

Some readers may attempt to dismiss the foregoing statements that feature affirmative action's subordinating effects as
simply insincere efforts to muddy the waters. On this theory,
conservatives despise affirmative action, and they would use
any available tool to attack the policy. If they could challenge
affirmative action by contending that its supposedly greatest
virtue (Black uplift) was in fact a hideous vice (Black descent),
well, then, so much the better.

But that explanation must be dramatically incomplete.
After all, it fails to explain why many liberals—even those who
support affirmative action from both constitutional and political perspectives—nevertheless have suggested that the policy
can plausibly be viewed as communicating a message of Black
inferiority. It is thus to liberal acknowledgment of affirmative
action's subordinating effects that we next turn.

Liberal Complications

Perhaps the foremost left-of-center theorist who has contended that affirmative action amounts to Black subordination is none other than Professor Derrick Bell, a founder of
critical race theory. In 1970, not long after the nation's leading

universities adopted affirmative action programs, Bell immediately identified this feature. Anticipating criticisms that would be leveled by then-Professors Scalia and Wilkinson (among others), Bell contended: "[Black students] are, by reason of the altered admissions criteria, denied the signal of their competence which students admitted under traditional qualifications receive." Over time, Bell advanced this subjugating critique with even greater intensity. Following the Court's decision in *Bakke*, Bell contended that affirmative action "envelop[ed] minority applicants in a cloud of suspected incompetency." Bell, prefiguring Thomas Sowell and Justice Thomas, expressed further misgivings about affirmative action because it made even accomplished Black students—"the recipient class"—seem as though they were receiving a handout: "[Affirmative action] sounds in *noblesse oblige*, not legal duty, and suggests the giving of charity rather than the granting of relief." Bell went so far as to conclude that affirmative action programs may contain anti-Black racism.

In *Reflections of an Affirmative Action Baby*, Professor Stephen L. Carter defended affirmative action, but he also took great pains to acknowledge that the policy often has destructive, subordinating effects. Indeed, Black subordination formed the focal point in Carter's book. "To be black and an intellectual in America is to live in a box," Carter opened. "So I live in a box, not of my own making, and on the box [are] label[s], not of my own choosing." The labels affixed to Carter's box included, most ominously: "WARNING! AFFIRMATIVE ACTION BABY! DO NOT ASSUME THAT THIS INDIVIDUAL IS QUALIFIED!" In a passage that vividly embodied Justice Thomas's concern that no Black person—no matter how accomplished—could fully

84   escape the yoke of affirmative action, Carter made the matter personal: "Affirmative action has been with me always.... [N]o matter what my accomplishments, I have had trouble escaping an assumption that ... black people cannot compete intellectually with white people."

Professor Randall Kennedy has endorsed a similar position, supporting some forms of affirmative action while simultaneously acknowledging the policy's potential for Black subordination. One of affirmative action's "weighty" dangers, Kennedy suggested, "is that affirmative action cripplingly stigmatizes its beneficiaries and, indeed, anyone affiliated with groups that are perceived as eligible for affirmative action assistance." Kennedy observed that numerous affirmative action beneficiaries—both real and imagined—have noted "their sense of being diminished, underestimated, devalued, or condescended to at least in part because" of the policy. "Perhaps the most poignant reflection of the affirmative action stigma is the indignation with which some beneficiaries (or merely perceived beneficiaries) respond when identified as recipients, or even potential recipients, of affirmative action assistance," Kennedy contended. "A black student at the University of California in the early 1990s complained: 'I feel like I have AFFIRMATIVE ACTION stamped on my forehead.'"

Antisubordination in *SFFA v. Harvard*

The antisubordination concept forms the skeletal key for understanding *SFFA v. Harvard*, as it shaped the briefing, the oral arguments, and the opinions themselves in that momentous case. Before analyzing *SFFA* in earnest, though, it is helpful to provide some historical context for how allegations that

elite universities subordinated Asian Americans emerged over
time. Claims of subordination against Asian Americans are not
identical to those against Black and brown people. But ignoring
them as a species of antisubordination claims—with its own
distinct backstory—is profoundly misguided.

The Backstory
The notion that Asian Americans were the Model Minority
became prevalent in the mid-1960s. That timing was, of course,
hardly coincidental. When many Black citizens began violently
rebelling against racism in urban areas—including in the Watts
section of Los Angeles in 1965—it became essential to establish
that being a racial minority in the United States did not invariably yield alienation and impoverishment. A spate of newspaper articles soon appeared praising people hailing from various
Asian nations—most commonly China and Japan—who had
managed to overcome racial discrimination by dint of hard work
and sound values to realize success in America.

Lest the implication be missed, these articles often jux-
taposed the industrious Asian American with the shift-
less African American. Thus, for example, *U.S. News & World
Report* in 1966 observed: "At a time when it is being proposed
that hundreds of billions be spent to uplift Negroes . . . , the
nation's 300,000 Chinese-Americans are moving ahead on
their own—with no help from anyone else." Unlike the lessons being delivered in Black households, *U.S. News* explained,
"[s]till being taught in Chinatown is the old idea that people
should depend on their own efforts—not a welfare check—in
order to reach America's 'promised land.'" Chinese Americans
are a "law-abiding and industrious people" who are "ambitious

86   to make progress on their own," and have thereby overcome "hardship and discrimination to become a model of self-respect and achievement in today's America."

In the mid-1980s, the Model Minority notion made its way onto college campuses, as the media simultaneously chronicled—and entrenched—the stereotype of Asian Americans not just as intensely hardworking, but also as incandescently brilliant. In April 1984, two different newsmagazines published substantial articles chronicling this new breed of super-students. *U.S. News & World Report* called Asian Americans "Academic Marvels," observing that "Asians are . . . flocking to top colleges," and that "ethnic Asians have been steadily marching into the ranks of the educational elite." The article depicted Asian Americans as a relentlessly ambitious people: "Nowhere is the strong ambition of Asians more evident than in the classroom." *U.S. News* rounded out this portrait of monomaniacal Asian American excellence with the most stereotypical quotations imaginable, including from one sixteen-year-old of Taiwanese descent: "My mother pushes me tremendously. I'm worried because my grades are in the low-to-mid 90s. If I'm not at the top at this school, how can I be on top in an Ivy League School? If I went to any other school, my mother would kill me."

But the ne plus ultra of Asian American student stereotyping appeared in a *Newsweek on Campus* cover story titled "Asian Americans: The Drive to Excel." "They say that Asian-American students are brilliant," the article noted. "They say that Asian Americans behave as a model minority, that they dominate mathematics, engineering, and science courses—that they are grinds who are so dedicated to getting ahead that they never have any fun." While one might think that this language erects the stereotype with an eye toward demolishing it, the bulk of the article in fact seems designed to cement the stereotype's accuracy. Asian Americans "do flock to the sciences," *Newsweek on Campus* explained, and "frighten many other students with their academic interests and prowess." Students are so intimidated by Asian American brainpower, the article asserted, that "[o]ther students speak of dropping courses if they walk into a classroom and see too many Oriental faces." It further noted: "On one issue, no one disagrees—the willingness of Asian-American students to pay almost any price to get ahead."

The article bolstered this claim with breathless quotations from professors at leading universities attesting to Asian Americans' superhuman capacity for work. One Georgetown physics professor attested: "They'll work you into the ground. They aren't out on Saturday night getting drunk—they're hitting the books." Not to be outdone, a Johns Hopkins chemistry professor stated: "A large percentage of our Asian students are much more serious, more goal-oriented, more unidimensional than our other students."

Newsweek did allow that Asian Americans not only dominate the classroom; they also dominate the concert hall. "If practice were sure to make perfect," *Newsweek* explained, "the concert stage might soon be dominated by Asian-American musicians." The article featured an accompanying quotation from Juilliard's director of admissions, who stated flatly: "Asian students are willing to work harder from a very early age."

Predictably, some Asian American college students repudiated *Newsweek*'s blatant stereotyping. Writing in the *Harvard Crimson*, Vincent Chang and Amy Han, in an article titled "*Newsweek*'s Asian American Stereotypes," condemned the

88   "one-dimensional, technical supermen" that the magazine cre-
     ated. "Such blanket generalizations are belied by the far more
     complex reality," Chang and Han wrote. "Asians, no more than any
     other race, are not a monolithic group and cannot be character-
     ized by facile, sweeping generalities." Rather than acknowledging
     the diversity among the Asian American community—includ-
     ing "the poverty of the Chinatowns and other Asian ghettoes"—
     Newsweek contented itself with "invit[ing] resentment against
     the supposed domination of universities and technical fields by
     Asian-Americans," Chang and Han wrote.

     By the late 1980s, allegations that elite universities were
     artificially capping the percentage of Asian American students
     received widespread media attention. In 1987, an article in the
     New York Times reported Professor Ling-Chi Wang of Berkeley
     contending that "[a]s soon as admissions of Asian students
     began reaching 10 or 12 percent, suddenly a red light went on,"
     and that since 1983 "at Berkeley, Stanford, M.I.T., Yale, in fact
     all the Ivy League schools, admission of Asian-Americans has
     either stabilized or gone down." Wang also suggested that just
     as the nation's leading universities suddenly "realized they had
     what used to be called a 'Jewish problem,'" prompting them to
     limit the enrollment of Jewish students, they now realized they
     had what might be termed an Asian American problem, "and
     they began to look for ways of slowing down the admissions of
     Asians." These allegations were nothing less than incendiary.
     Indeed, shortly after the *Times* article appeared, the four leading
     news networks all contacted Wang for interviews.*

     ---

     * For many observers, Harvard's personal ratings—which scored Asian
     American applicants lower than applicants from other races—strongly
     resembled the antisemitic "character" assessments that Ivy League

Also in 1987, Professors John Bunzel and Jeffrey Au published an article in *The Public Interest* supporting the notion that
elite universities discriminated against Asian American applicants. In a series of interviews, university officials trafficked in
subordinating racial stereotypes about Asian American students, which the authors suggested could lead to reduced
admission rates. "One would think industriousness would be
regarded favorably in the college admissions process," Bunzel
and Au wrote. "However, this might not be the case for Asian
Americans. When asked what personality traits might account
for lower admission rates among Asian Americans, one admissions officer responded that they tend to be 'driven.'" The
authors also detected a series of other stereotypes that targeted
Asian American applicants:

> One admissions director, for example, expressed the
> view that Asian Americans are "taught to be humble and
> obedient" at home. An official from another institution
> stated that the university was concerned about admitting

schools wielded in the early twentieth century to depress the enrollment
of Jewish students. *See* Jerome Karabel, *The Chosen: The Hidden History of
Admission and Exclusion at Harvard, Yale, and Princeton*, 500–05, 130–31
(2005) (discussing the adoption of nonacademic criteria in admissions
by Harvard, Yale, and Princeton, and noting "[t]he key code word here was
'character'—a quality thought to be frequently lacking among Jews but
present almost congenitally among high-status Protestants"). For a claim
that the Jewish quotas at elite universities perpetuated the stereotype of
Jewish hyperintelligence, see Carl Cohen & James P. Sterba, *Affirmative
Action and Racial Preference: A Debate*, 125 n.169 (2003) ("Not long ago, the
quota for Jewish students . . . was tiny; those who made the cut had to be
exceedingly able. The myth of the Jews as supersmart was given support by
the rational inference, then, that any Jew enrolled at Harvard, or Columbia,
must indeed have been very brainy!").

90   students who had greater interests in "public service." He
          speculated that this might be inconsistent with Asian
          cultural values. . . . Another common stereotype is that
          because of cultural reasons, Asian Americans tend to be
          interested only in science and technical fields and lack an
          appreciation for a "well-rounded liberal education."

If admissions officers were willing to engage in such overt
stereotyping in public, one could only imagine how such stereotypes operated behind closed doors.

The Briefs

Affirmative action's defenders and opponents both advanced
antisubordination arguments in their briefs filed at the
Supreme Court in *SFFA*, but they did so in dramatically divergent fashions. Those defending Harvard's and UNC's admissions policies suggested that universities had not violated the
Equal Protection Clause because, unlike racial segregation,
their actions were in no sense predicated on a notion of Black
inferiority. That defense, of course, espoused the standard
scholarly account of antisubordination. Affirmative action's
opponents, in contrast, primarily contended that the universities' policies subordinated a different racial minority—Asian
Americans. In so arguing, the opponents challenged the standard antisubordination account, and suggested, in effect, that
regardless of whether one embraces an anticlassification or an
antisubordination theory of the Fourteenth Amendment, affirmative action policies must fall. Thus, although both sides
spoke of racial subordination, they failed to recognize the
commonality—and the divergence.

Briefly consider how affirmative action's defenders invoked antisubordination. Harvard's brief, for example, framed its defense by rejecting SFFA's efforts to equate race-conscious admissions with the bad old days of Jim Crow. Such comparisons were "utterly inapt," Harvard contended, because "[t]he laws in *Plessy* [*v. Ferguson*] and *Brown* excluded and separated African Americans solely on the basis of race, relegating them to an inferior caste for no reason other than race." The Solicitor General's amicus brief articulated this same anticaste view. "[N]othing in *Brown's* condemnation of laws segregating the races to perpetuate a caste system calls into question admissions policies adopted to promote greater integration and diversity," the brief asserted. "And [SFFA]'s persistent attempts to equate this case with *Brown* trivialize the grievous legal and moral wrongs of segregation."

While SFFA's brief certainly invoked anticlassification principles, it is important to appreciate that a leitmotif contended that university admissions policies (especially at Harvard) subordinated Asian American applicants. SFFA emphasized that Asian Americans have been subjected to overt, brutal racial discrimination within the United States, and that animus directed toward the group is hardly a thing of the past. To the contrary, SFFA insisted that modern admissions policies that artificially depress Asian American acceptance rates are driven by racist tropes. Asian Americans are, SFFA maintained, "stereotyped as timid, quiet, shy, passive, withdrawn, one-dimensional, hard workers, perpetual foreigners, and 'model minorities.'" In the admissions process, this "anti-Asian stereotyping" holds that students of Asian descent "are interested only in math and science." Rather than construing affirmative action as a program

92 *elevating* Black and brown applicants, SFFA suggested that the program should be viewed as *lowering* Asian American applicants, as "race [works] *against* Asian Americans—putting the lie to the notion that this discrimination is somehow 'benign.'"

The effects of these subordinating attitudes directed toward Asian Americans, SFFA argued, warped the entire admissions process. At the application stage, the "discrimination" facing "Asian-American high-schoolers" has given rise to "[a]n entire industry . . . help[ing] them appear 'less Asian' on their college applications." *Princeton Review*, the brief noted, has admonished "[i]f you are an Asian American . . . you need to be careful about what you do and don't say in your application," explicitly instructing "[d]on't say you want to be a doctor," "don't say you want to major in math or the sciences," and even "don't attach a photograph." Such advice to "de-Asian" applications was prudent, SFFA observed, because of the penalty imposed upon applicants of Asian descent.

At the recruitment stage, SFFA noted that Harvard required Asian American high school students living in certain states to earn higher standardized test scores than students from other racial groups in order to receive targeted outreach soliciting an application. Harvard implemented this racialized recruitment approach in areas where it typically received few applications, regions that Harvard dubbed "sparse country." When Harvard's Dean of Admissions William Fitzsimmons sought to explain the racial discrepancy, SFFA noted, he trafficked in "a stereotype" that Asian American students may have lived in sparse country for only "a year or two," whereas white students presumably "lived [in sparse country] for their entire lives." This subordinating stereotype, SFFA suggested, otherizes Asian Americans, construing them as forever foreign, no matter how long they (and their ancestors) have called the United States home.

Finally, at the admissions decision stage, SFFA observed that Harvard assigned Asian American applicants substantially lower personal ratings than it did applicants from other racial backgrounds. Through its personal rating, the Harvard admissions office purported to measure applicants' "self-confidence," "likeability," "leadership," and "kindness," among other attributes. The diminished personal ratings of Asian American students, SFFA argued, were driven by vicious "anti-Asian stereotypes" construing that ethnic group as possessing less appealing personalities. "Why does Harvard assign Asian-American applicants significantly lower personal ratings?," SFFA queried. "Either Asian Americans really do lack 'integrity,' 'courage,' 'kindness,' and 'empathy.' Or Harvard is discriminating against them. Because the first conclusion is racist and false, the second must be true." An amicus brief filed on behalf of an Asian American advocacy group drove home this subordinating point in even starker language. Contending that Harvard's personal rating system "demeans and dehumanizes members of this ethnic group by labelling them as somehow deficient in character," this amicus brief asserted that the practice "reinforces negative stereotypes that were historically used to justify discrimination and even violence against the Asian American community."

The Oral Argument
Discussions of antisubordination also figured prominently throughout the *SFFA* oral arguments. But, once again, critics and supporters of affirmative action invoked the concept in

94   sharply competing manners. Moreover, attorneys and justices alike at times seemed to experience profound difficulty apprehending even basic implications of the varied claims sounding in antisubordination.

Cameron Norris—who represented SFFA in the lawsuit against Harvard—invoked antisubordination from soup to nuts. He did so, that is, immediately after opening with the traditional "May it please the Court" at the tail end of his rebuttal and frequently in between. Although the Supreme Court had previously found that the status of being a racial minority would be exclusively a plus factor in admissions decisions, Norris began that "race is a minus for Asians, a group that continues to face immense racial discrimination in this country." Norris focused primarily on the subordinating effects of affirmative action on Asian American applicants. But he also noted the policy can subjugate even Black and brown students who are admitted. "[Affirmative action programs] stigmatize their intended beneficiaries," Norris stated.

Norris's peroration—what nowadays might be termed a mic drop—observed that the very terminology used to describe Asian American students during the foregoing oral argument succeeded in subordinating that group, furthering the notion that they are somehow not fully American, but instead remain forever foreign. "[W]e keep saying Asians," Norris said, his voice slightly rising with emotion. "These are not Asians. They're not from Asia. These are people who are Americans. They were born in Texas, California, Ohio, Tennessee. . . . They were born in 2005, the people who are applying to college now. They should not be the victims of Harvard's racial experimentation. Thank you." For those who may be skeptical that truncating "Asian

Americans" to "Asians" is troublesome, and connotes foreign-
ness, take a moment to contemplate the outrage that would
ensue if a jurist or an attorney shortened "African Americans" to
simply "Africans."

Conservative Justices embraced these antisubordination
claims to undermine affirmative action during oral argument.
When Patrick Strawbridge—who represented SFFA opposite
UNC—suggested that it was permissible for a student of Asian
descent to write an application essay about visiting, say, his
grandmother's native country, Chief Justice Roberts interjected
that such an essay would betray a stunning lack of sophisti-
cation. After all, he noted that topic would reveal a "not very
savvy applicant . . . [b]ecause the one thing his essay is going
to show is that he's Asian American, and those are the people who are discriminated against." Similarly, while question-
ing Harvard attorney Seth Waxman, Justice Alito focused upon
the fact that Harvard inflicted "the lowest personal scores" upon
Asian American applicants. "What accounts for that?" Justice
Alito asked, as he echoed SFFA's brief in strikingly similar language. "[I]t has to be one of two things. It has to be that [Asian
Americans] really do lack integrity, courage, kindness, and
empathy to the same degree as students of other races, or there
has to be something wrong with this personal score."

For their part, the attorneys defending affirmative action
also invoked notions of subordination. In contrast to their conservative counterparts, though, they emphasized that *Brown*
was designed to eradicate African American subordination,
and that affirmative action programs were meant to advance
that same mission. "There is a world of difference between the
situation this Court confronted in *Brown*," Solicitor General

96   Elizabeth Prelogar told the Court, "[as] the separate but equal
       doctrine . . . was designed to exclude African Americans based
       on notions of racial inferiority and subjugate them . . . and the
       university policies at issue in this case, which are . . . designed to
       bring individuals of all races together so that they can all learn."

       Perhaps the most intriguing moments of oral argument
       occurred, however, when those attempting to bolster affirmative
       action appeared to struggle grasping fully how antisubordina-
       tion could be wielded to destroy the admissions programs. One
       such moment arose when Waxman sought to answer Justice
       Alito's question regarding why Harvard assigned lower personal
       ratings to Asian American applicants. This dreaded question—
       from the perspective of affirmative action's supporters—must
       have occupied a significant percentage of Waxman's time pre-
       paring for oral argument. Here is how Waxman responded:

>   The fact that Asian Americans got a marginally—on aver-
>   age, a marginally lower personal rating score is no more
>   evidence of discrimination against them than the fact
>   that they got a marginally higher rating . . . on academics
>   and extracurriculars. It doesn't mean that they're either
>   smarter or people think they're smarter.

       Waxman liked this answer enough to offer a slightly modified
       version of it elsewhere during oral argument.

       The problem with this evidently well-rehearsed talking
       point is that Waxman's rebuttal can easily be construed as fur-
       ther entrenching ugly stereotypes about Asian Americans. Just
       as the lower personal ratings can be attributed to stereotypes
       holding that Asian Americans lack winning personalities, the

higher extracurricular and academic ratings can be viewed as the opposite side of that same coin. On this objectionable, sub-ordinating theory, the very reason that Asian Americans do not possess lively personalities is because they are too busy grind-ing away at schoolwork and extracurriculars. One intent on por-traying Harvard as discriminating against Asian Americans would view these disparate ratings as being driven by the grand unified theory of the violin-playing, exam-crushing Asian American nerd, a person seldom perceived as the most charm-ing student in school. Thus, while Waxman contended that the higher ratings in some categories for Asian Americans served to exonerate Harvard against charges that it discriminated, from at least one antisubordination perspective, those elevated ratings ended up making matters worse.

Relatedly, Justice Sotomayor posed a question during oral argument that, from the vantage point of affirmative action's conservative antagonists, could undermine the program's constitutionality. "Sometimes race does correlate to some experiences. . . . If you're black, you're more likely to be in an underresourced school. . . . You're more likely to be viewed as less academic—as having less academic potential." But as should by now be evident, many antisubordinationists would contend that affirmative action itself plays a large role in instill-ing the misguided notion that Black people have diminished intellectual capacities. For these antisubordinationists, of course, one of the most pressing steps to uprooting this wrong-headed notion is to abolish affirmative action.

98 **The Opinions**

Antisubordinating language pervaded the Court's various opinions. Chief Justice Roberts's opinion for the Court in *SFFA* has been broadly understood as imposing constitutional color-blindness in college admissions. Abundant language certainly supports that reading of *SFFA*. The majority opinion, for example, summarized the cases as addressing "whether a university may make admissions decisions that turn on an applicant's race." By responding with a resounding no, the Court can be viewed as vindicating anticlassification considerations. The Court's most resonant sentence, moreover, speaks in the color-blindness register. "Eliminating racial discrimination means eliminating all of it," Chief Justice Roberts wrote.

SFFA's embrace of anticlassification was, however, considerably more equivocal than such sweeping language suggests. As discussed above, Roberts's majority opinion in *SFFA* both excused the nation's military academies from complying with its holding, and noted that universities could reward applicants for essays that centered on race.

More significant for present purposes, however, Roberts's majority opinion in *SFFA* also repeatedly used language and concepts that are compatible with antisubordination. For example, *SFFA* construed a 1950 Supreme Court opinion as rejecting Jim Crow conditions in graduate school courses because such arrangements "worked to subordinate the afflicted [Black] students." And while Harvard and UNC preferred to view themselves as offering a "plus" to applicants from underrepresented racial backgrounds, Chief Justice Roberts reasoned, the admissions systems must fall because they "fail to comply with the twin commands of the Equal Protection Clause that race may never be used as a 'negative' and . . . may not operate as a stereotype." These "twin commands" were so significant that *SFFA* employed noticeably similar language regarding the Fourteenth Amendment's prohibitions on negative racial treatment and racial stereotyping in multiple other instances.

So, who did the admissions programs, on racial grounds, penalize and stereotype? The lower courts declined to find that the universities had in fact discriminated against Asian American applicants. *SFFA* was careful to avoid declaring that the courts below erred in that determination. Yet, *SFFA* nevertheless also made plain that the universities' treatment of Asian Americans stood top of mind. Chief Justice Roberts heaped disapproval on what he deemed the universities' comically capacious "Asian" category, as both Harvard and UNC "are apparently uninterested in whether *South* Asian or *East* Asian students are adequately represented, so long as there is enough of one to compensate for a lack of the other." *SFFA* emphasized that even the US Court of Appeals for the First Circuit, which upheld Harvard's admission program, allowed that "consideration of race has led to an 11.1% decrease in the number of Asian-Americans admitted." Along similar lines, *SFFA* noted that at Harvard: "[A]n African American [student] in [the fourth lowest academic] decile has a higher chance of admission (12.8%) than an Asian American in the *top* decile (12.7%)." While *SFFA* stated that "[t]he universities' main response . . . is, essentially, 'trust us,'" it also made plain that their treatment of Asian American applicants warranted deep distrust.

Justice Gorsuch's concurring opinion also prominently featured arguments contending that the admissions programs subordinated Asian Americans. The universities' policies,

100   Gorsuch noted, were driven by "incoherent," "irrational stereotypes" attached to "the 'Asian' category." Extending a point
raised by the majority opinion regarding the expansiveness of
the Asian American category, he observed: "[O]ne [plausible]
effect of lumping so many people of so many disparate backgrounds into the 'Asian' category is that many colleges consider
'Asians' to be 'overrepresented' in their admission pools." This
racial misconception would, of course, incentivize universities
to cull the Asian American herd. For Gorsuch, the bottom line
was that, despite talk of benign racial preferences, "Harvard and
UNC choose to treat some students worse than others in part
because of race," and that "[t]o suggest otherwise . . . is to deny
reality."

No judicial opinion of our modern constitutional era better exemplifies antisubordination's strange career than Justice
Thomas's concurrence in *SFFA*. On its face, Thomas's concurring opinion concerned itself with first confronting and
then repudiating antisubordination as a viable theory of the
Equal Protection Clause. Justice Thomas identified antisubordination as the handiwork of Professors Owen Fiss and
Reva Siegel, and suggested that Justice Sotomayor's dissent
in *SFFA* carried water for this misguided understanding of the
Fourteenth Amendment—one that he portrayed as providing an impoverished substitute for his beloved colorblind constitutionalism. Yet, even as Thomas styled himself as coming
to bury antisubordination, he nonetheless ended up praising antisubordination—or at least utilizing it. This turn for
antisubordination—cast as the villain, but somehow appearing in a heroic light within the course of a single opinion—is its
most improbable turn of all.

Justice Thomas portrayed anticaste theories of the Equal Protection Clause as an alarming fad, like parachute pants or rap metal bands, as he contended "it appears increasingly in vogue to embrace an 'antisubordination' view of the Fourteenth Amendment: that the Amendment forbids only laws that hurt, but not help, blacks." Surprisingly, this sentence marked the first time that a Supreme Court opinion had ever used the term "antisubordination," and only the second time that a federal court at any level had done so in a published opinion. But "antisubordination" would not have long to absorb its initial moment in the sun. After introducing the term to the *U.S. Reports*, Justice Thomas quickly lambasted it. Justice Sotomayor was profoundly mistaken, Justice Thomas insisted, to believe "that the Fourteenth Amendment was contemporaneously understood to permit differential treatment based on race, prohibiting only caste legislation while authorizing antisubordination measures."

Despite these expressed doubts about antisubordination, Justice Thomas—as he has so often done previously—also claimed in *SFFA* that race-conscious measures work to subordinate racial minorities. In this sense, he can be understood as arguing in the alternative; that is, even if jurists subscribe to antisubordination, Thomas suggests that they should nonetheless find affirmative action programs unconstitutional. Though supporters of race-conscious admissions policies contend that the programs "accomplish positive social goals," Thomas insisted that "what initially seems like aid may in reality be a burden, including for the very people it seeks to assist." Remixing some of his greatest hits on affirmative action, Thomas noted that, even when Black and brown

102   college students "succeed academically," race-conscious policies "stamp [Blacks and Hispanics] with a badge of inferiority"
and "tain[t] the accomplishments of all" such students. Thomas
stressed that he did not believe that Black students needed
the help of affirmative action to achieve intellectually because
those programs were produced by nothing less than racial bigotry. "[M]eritocratic systems have long refuted bigoted misper-
ceptions of what black students can accomplish," he contended.

    In addition to subordinating Black and brown students,
Justice Thomas further insisted that Harvard and UNC subordinated Asian American students. "How . . . [can affirmative
action supporters] explain the need for race-based preferences to the Chinese student who has worked hard his whole
life, only to be denied college admission in part because of his
skin color?" Thomas asked. "If such a burden would seem difficult to impose on a bright-eyed young person, that's because
it should be." There can be no doubt, he maintained, that Asian
Americans are forced to "make sacrifices . . . for this new phase
of racial subordination." Thomas suggested that this neosubor-
dination of Asian Americans was particularly noxious because
that group had deep familiarity with the older phase of racial
subordination. To clinch the point that "Asian Americans can
hardly be described as the beneficiaries of historical racial
advantages," Thomas invoked the Supreme Court's own sordid
decisions validating governmental actions that oppressed people of Asian descent.

    For her part, Justice Sotomayor's dissent advanced the
most full-throated view of the Equal Protection Clause as prohibiting subordination ever to appear in a Supreme Court opinion. She began by noting that "a foundational pillar of slavery

was the racist notion that Black people are a subordinate class with intellectual inferiority," and that "[a]bolition alone could not repair centuries of racial subjugation." Next, Sotomayor insisted that "the Fourteenth Amendment was intended to undo the effects of a world where laws systematically subordinated Black people and created a racial caste system." *Brown v. Board of Education*, she wrote, embodied this vision of the Fourteenth Amendment, as it demonstrated awareness "of the harmful effects of entrenched racial subordination on racial minorities and American democracy," and "recognized the constitutional necessity of a racially integrated system of schools where education is available to all on equal terms." Completing this constitutional picture, Sotomayor contended that the Court's preceding affirmative action jurisprudence in the "*Bakke, Grutter,* and *Fisher* [decisions] . . . exten[d] . . . *Brown*'s legacy" to higher education.

In addition to an elaborate embrace of antisubordination, Justice Sotomayor took sharp exception to Justice Thomas's claims that the affirmative action programs under review racially subordinated anyone. Regarding Black and brown students, Sotomayor contended that her colleague "cit[ed] nothing but his own long-held belief . . . that racial preferences in college admissions stamp [Black and Latino students] with a badge of inferiority." Supporting her general claim, Justice Sotomayor turned personal, emphasizing "the most obvious data point available" to the Supreme Court about affirmative action: "The three Justices of color on this Court graduated from elite universities and law schools with race-conscious admissions programs, and achieved successful legal careers, despite having different educational backgrounds than their peers."

104   Justice Sotomayor further contended that Justice Thomas "cit[ed] no evidence ... suggest[ing] that race-conscious admissions programs discriminate against Asian American students." While it is true that SFFA asserted that universities adversely treated Asian American applicants, Sotomayor stated, "a lengthy trial to test those allegations [occurred], which SFFA lost." Harvard's hotly contested personal rating was "a facially race-*neutral* component" of its admissions policy, she insisted, and therefore strict scrutiny should not even apply. Underscoring the centrality of antisubordination to her jurisprudential framework, Sotomayor sought to reframe affirmative action as working to counteract the vicious racial stereotypes that plague Asian Americans. "There is no question that the Asian American community continues to struggle against potent and dehumanizing stereotypes in our society," she noted. "It is precisely because racial discrimination persists in our society, however, that the use of race in college admissions to achieve racially diverse classes is critical to improving cross-racial understanding and breaking down racial stereotypes."

Justice Jackson dedicated much of her dissent to challenging the wisdom of constitutional colorblindness in a world suffused with color-consciousness. In the most memorable sentences that she produced during her first term, Justice Jackson contended, "With let-them-eat-cake obliviousness, today, the majority ... announces 'colorblindness for all' by legal fiat. But deeming race irrelevant in law does not make it so in life."* In

---

*Justice Jackson's invocation of Marie Antoinette calls to mind an exchange that occurred during *Bakke*'s oral argument in 1977. Justice Marshall asked the attorney opposing UC Davis's race-conscious admissions program: "You are talking about your client's rights. Don't these underprivileged

addition to critiquing anticlassification, Jackson also intimated that affirmative action programs could be squared with
antisubordination, as she contended that the nation's history
of caste had effects in the present. "Given the lengthy history
of state-sponsored race-based preferences [for white people]
in America," she wrote, "to say that anyone is now victimized
if a college considers whether that legacy of discrimination has
unequally advantaged its applicants fails to acknowledge the
well-documented intergenerational transmission of inequality
that still plagues our citizenry." Today's affirmative action programs, she insisted, do not subordinate anyone. Instead, Justice
Jackson maintained that "ensuring a diverse student body in
higher education helps *everyone*, not just those who, due to their
race, have directly inherited distinct disadvantages with respect
to their health, wealth, and well-being."

The Ghost of Justice Harlan

The oddest commonality of various *SFFA* opinions was their
spirited, competing, and relentless efforts to claim that Justice
John Marshall Harlan's dissent in *Plessy v. Ferguson* supported
their preferred outcomes. Justice Harlan loomed so large in
SFFA that he was invoked by name no fewer than *twenty-nine*
times across five different opinions. Even in a distended set
of opinions running some 230 pages, that rate of invocation is
staggering. But perhaps even more remarkable than the sheer

people have some rights?" When the attorney began to respond, "They
certainly have the right to . . . ," Justice Marshall interjected with obvious
disdain: "To eat cake." Transcript of Oral Argument at 66, Regents of Univ.
of Cal. v. Bakke, 438 U.S. 265 (1978) (No. 76-811). Although Justice Jackson
did not expressly cite the first Black Supreme Court Justice's bon mot, it
seems plausible that she was paying homage to her heroic predecessor.

number of citations to Justice Harlan's *Plessy* dissent is how discordant those citations were given that the gravamen of the underlying dispute involved discrimination against people of Asian descent.

It should arrive as no surprise that conservative and liberal Justices invoked differing portions of Justice Harlan's iconic solo dissent, which would have invalidated Louisiana's nineteenth-century law mandating racially separate railcars. Where conservatives tended to focus on anticlassification aspects of the *Plessy* dissent, liberals elevated its antisubordination elements. Thus, in one of Justice Thomas's many Harlan quotations regarding anticlassification, he wrote in heroic terms: "Only one Member of the Court adhered to the equality principle; Justice Harlan, standing alone in dissent, wrote: 'Our constitution is color-blind. . . .'"

In contrast, Justice Sotomayor rejected such distillations of Harlan's dissent as hopelessly misleading: "It distorts the dissent in *Plessy* to advance a colorblindness theory." The genuine insight in Harlan's *Plessy* dissent, Sotomayor contended, was its antisubordination understanding that racial segregation "perpetuated a 'caste' system," one animated by a belief that "'colored citizens are so inferior and degraded that they cannot be allowed to sit in public coaches occupied by white citizens.'"

The battle for Justice Harlan's soul became so intense that Justice Jackson's dissent at one point stated: "Justice Harlan knew better."* In response, Chief Justice Roberts's majority opinion quoted his colleague's dissent for that proposition, and

* To be sure, Justice Jackson's dissent in *SFFA* here invoked Justice Harlan's opinion in the *Civil Rights Cases*, 109 U.S. 3 (1883), rather than his opinion in *Plessy*. Nevertheless, the perceived need to claim the mantle of Justice

then stated: "Indeed he did," and proceeded to excerpt Harlan's
Plessy dissent, including both its anticlassification and antisubordination sections.

Evidently overlooked amid the blizzard of competing Harlan citations was a basic, antecedent question: Did the *Plessy* dissent actually merit claiming? While the dissenting view in *Plessy* certainly has a good deal more to commend it than the majority position upholding Jim Crow, I have for many years contended that it is the most over-celebrated Supreme Court opinion throughout the institution's long history and—far from incidentally—the most misconstrued. When one places Harlan's opinion in its nineteenth-century context, it was not the absolutist, ringing condemnation of racial segregation that many modern readers perceive. Instead, Justice Harlan advanced a comparatively modest claim, consistent with the fragmented understanding of the Fourteenth Amendment's Equal Protection Clause that dominated at the time.

Even more troublingly, Harlan's much ballyhooed *Plessy* dissent featured not only overt white supremacy, but also unvarnished hostility toward people of Asian descent. As to the former, Justice Harlan contended that "[t]he white race" was quite correct "deem[ing] itself to be the dominant race in this country," and he asserted that white dominance would "continue to be for all time." As to the latter, Justice Harlan noted "the Chinese race" is "so different from our own that we do not permit those belonging to it to become citizens of the United States." Justice Harlan approved of these bans on US

Harlan's legacy today surely stems in no small part from the halo that hovers above Harlan's *Plessy* dissent.

108   citizenship, and then noted with dismay that the Court's decision in *Plessy* meant that Black people could be excluded from Louisiana's white railcars, even though "a Chinaman can ride in the same passenger coach with white citizens of the United States." Harlan's views thus plainly reinforced anti-Asian subordination.

It has long been past time to retire Justice Harlan's dissent in *Plessy*. While he viewed the matter in a more attractive light than did his colleagues, that dissent was in no sense a progenitor of modern racial attitudes. At least, we should all pray it was not. But *SFFA* has succeeded, if in nothing else, at dimming prospects for the opinion being interred anytime soon. After all, if Harlan's dissent—with its animus hurled at the exotic "Chinaman"—was invoked even in a case where one of the plaintiff's central claims alleged that Asian Americans are treated as "perpetual foreigners," it would seem that virtually all such hopes are lost. That *SFFA* would rely on the *Plessy* dissent—which employed standard issue Asian-as-foreigner tropes—is yet another odd turn in the exceedingly strange career of antisubordination.

The Diversity Rationale Revisited

Accepting that antisubordination contains far greater indeterminacy than its liberal supporters typically concede does not require believing that affirmative action programs are constitutionally indefensible. Scholars drawn to the antisubordination approach could conceivably respond to critics and explain why their objections should still not carry the day. Another possibility, though, is that affirmative action programs could be supported by an alternate theoretical justification. Surprisingly,

one promising justification for affirmative action is the widely
reviled diversity rationale.

When the Supreme Court upheld affirmative action in 1978, Justice Powell's controlling opinion in *Bakke* prohibited universities from attempting to enroll underrepresented racial minorities as a corrective to historical or ongoing racial discrimination. Instead, Powell authorized universities to implement affirmative action only in the pursuit of racial diversity. Powell's diversity rationale immediately drew scorn. Then-Professor Robert Bork of Yale Law School set the early terms of debate in the *Wall Street Journal*. "[T]he solution may seem statesmanlike," Bork allowed, "but as constitutional argument, it leaves you hungry an hour later." Then-Professor Scalia derided the diversity rationale in similar terms. "Justice Powell's opinion . . . strikes me as an excellent compromise between two committees of the American Bar Association on some insignificant legislative proposal," Scalia charged. "But it is thoroughly unconvincing as an honest, hardminded, reasoned analysis of an important provision of the Constitution."

The passage of time has in no sense eliminated criticism of the diversity rationale, as commentators across the political spectrum have often disparaged Powell's justification for affirmative action. On the right, Shelby Steele has excoriated the diversity rationale as "an unexamined kitsch that whites (especially administrators and executives) use to dignify their use of racial preferences as they . . . engineer . . . a *look* of racial parity." On the left, Professor Orlando Patterson asserted that "[u]sing diversity as a rationale for affirmative action . . . distorts [its] aims" and noted that the diversity rationale was weaker compared to "[t]he original, morally incontestable goal of . . . the

110   integration of African-Americans in all important areas . . . from
       which they had been historically excluded."

       Critics of affirmative action and the diversity rationale
often object that considering race in admissions programs is
wrong because it deviates from the American meritocratic
ideal. Universities' obsession with racial diversity, on this
account, means that more-qualified applicants are rejected in
favor of less-qualified applicants—an anomaly that warps the
high-stakes college admissions process.

       This meritocracy objection, however, suffers from major
frailties. First, as numerous scholars have emphasized, the
notion of who should be deemed the most meritorious applicants is fiercely disputed. The traditional measures of high
academic achievement, commentators suggest, are too often
attributable not primarily to an individual applicant's hard
work or native intellect, but to the accidents of birth. When
accounting for relative disadvantage, moreover, it might be possible to claim that an applicant who attends an underperforming urban high school and manages 1200 on the SAT actually
exhibited greater merit than the archetypal St. Grottlesex product who "earns" 1600.*

       Second, even assuming that admissions officers could
objectively ascertain merit, it would nevertheless remain true
that colleges routinely decline to admit only the top academic
applicants. Many colleges are interested not only in welcom-
ing academic all-stars, but in fielding athletic teams, staffing
various bands, and landing the scions of both the donor class

       *"St. Grottlesex" is a standard portmanteau of several particularly tony
American boarding schools: St. George's School, St. Mark's School, St.
Paul's School, Groton School, and Middlesex School.

and their own graduates. In making such calculations, universities can be construed as jettisoning academic meritocracy. Accepting the meritocratic frame, in other words, nevertheless requires acknowledging that universities habitually depart from it, and they enjoy the latitude to do so. Rather than viewing the pre-*SFFA* affirmative action system as a fanatical repudiation of American tradition, it seems more accurate to view it as something akin to standard operating procedure—Tuesday in the admissions office. Even after *SFFA*, of course, colleges continue to receive wide leeway to form what they believe will make the strongest incoming overall class of students, which is quite distinct from merely assembling individual academic all-stars. *SFFA* should thus in no way be misconstrued as a restoration of American meritocracy.

Furthermore, those drawn to meritocratic critiques should not have been so quick to assert that the existence of affirmative action justified any presumption that Black and brown candidates were invariably admitted to elite universities solely because of that program. Justice Thomas, as discussed above, has repeatedly argued that affirmative action brands all underrepresented minorities as undeserving admitted students—regardless of how sterling their credentials. This presumption of nonmeritoriousness applies, Justice Thomas has insisted, because even though *some* Black and brown students would be admitted absent affirmative action, race is the dispositive factor for many admitted students, and it is impossible to distinguish "merit" admits from "non-merit" admits. Justice Thomas is not alone in contending that affirmative action reinforces what might be termed *the presumption of Black and brown incompetence*. In the 1980s, a white undergraduate at UC Berkeley

112   revealed: "Every time I see a black person, not an Asian, but any other person of color walk by, I think, affirmative action. It's like that's your first instinct. It's not, maybe that person was smart; it's gotta be Affirmative Action. They don't even belong here."

While that is certainly one possible perspective, there are other, more cogent ways of approaching the matter. Instead of establishing a racial default rule of Black and brown intellectual incompetence, this default rule should be inverted. After all, given that some Black and brown students would be admitted to every major academic institution even under the most stringently applied traditional criteria, why should the presumption not run that all students belong on campus—at least until confronted with strong evidence that the presumption of belonging is unwarranted? As is so often the case, in law as well as in life, the question here becomes: How do we want to be wrong? Should Black and brown students who would have obtained admission in the absence of racial considerations be wrongly presumed recipients of a diversity-driven boost? Or should Black and brown students who actually received a diversity-driven boost be wrongly presumed to have satisfied the standard admissions criteria?

In my view, presuming Black and brown *competence* is the wiser course and better advances the cause of racial egalitarianism. The contrary presumption—as articulated by the Berkeley undergraduate—seems not just incompatible with racial egalitarianism, but, well, downright racist. Given the hoary presumption of Black intellectual inferiority that has existed for centuries, it seems to me that incorrectly believing (in the absence of any evidence) that all Black students on

campus—including strangers—lack the intellectual goods is a
grave mistake.*

Perhaps the most important criticism of the diversity rationale, though, is that it is simply impossible to measure. In 2024,
John McWhorter writing in the *New York Times* articulated a version of this immeasurability critique: "[T]here is no real evidence that diversity enhances a good ... education. No reasonable
person is seeking lily-white campuses. But the idea that diversity means, specifically, better learning has turned out to be difficult to prove." In 2016, noted economist Thomas Sowell voiced
a particularly acerbic version of this skepticism: "Nothing so
epitomizes the politically correct gullibility of our times as the
magic word 'diversity.' The wonders of diversity are proclaimed
from the media ... and confirmed in the august chambers of the
Supreme Court of the United States. But have you ever seen
one speck of hard evidence to support the lofty claims?" Even
some supporters of affirmative action have doubted the quality of empirical evidence that has been marshaled to support
the diversity rationale. For example, Professor Randall Kennedy,

*While I believe that this presumption of competence should apply in
all academic settings, it seems to me that it holds overpowering force in
settings like the *Fisher* cases, which involved the University of Texas at
Austin. In that pair of cases, recall that the Supreme Court presumed that
the vast majority of underrepresented racial minorities were admitted
through a meritorious system (*i.e.*, the Top Ten Percent plan), while a
comparatively small percentage of underrepresented racial minorities were
admitted through a system that involved overt racial classifications. Even
when confronted with that regime, however, Justice Thomas nevertheless
continued to insist that students would be justified in believing that *all*
Black and brown students had been admitted through what he would deem
the back door of race-conscious admissions. But even if one were simply
playing the probabilities, that presumption of incompetence would have
been overwhelmingly incorrect.

114 in the course of defending affirmative action, nevertheless felt compelled to concede: "I remain doubtful about social scientific 'proof' of diversity's values; much of that [research] seems exaggerated and pre-determined with litigation in mind."

Conservative jurists have repeatedly endorsed similar critiques. Chief Justice Roberts's majority opinion invalidating affirmative action in *SFFA* contended that the goals of racial diversity are fundamentally elusive and immeasurable. "[I]t is unclear how courts are supposed to measure any of these [diversity] goals," Roberts complained. "How is a court to know whether leaders have been adequately 'train[ed]'; whether the exchange of ideas is 'robust'; or whether 'new knowledge' is being developed?" In 2016, moreover, Justice Alito dissented in an opinion upholding affirmative action at the University of Texas at Austin. In so doing, Justice Alito expressed frustration that those "invoking 'the educational benefits of diversity'" had "not identif[ied] any metric that would allow a court to" assess whether the purported benefits were being realized.

Contrary to conventional wisdom in both academic and judicial circles, however, persuasive empirical evidence demonstrates the positive effects of diversity in higher education. This evidence suggests that *SFFA* was incorrect to dismiss diversity as an inherently immeasurable goal. In a study published in the *Columbia Law Review*, I—along with some empirically sophisticated coauthors—investigated whether the citations to articles that a given law review publishes increase or decrease after the adoption of a diversity policy for selecting editors.

Perhaps improbably, law reviews' internal practices garnered major headlines almost two decades ago when then-Senator Barack Obama began his bid for the White House. In 1990,

Obama became the first Black person elected to lead the *Harvard*
Law Review in its century-long history. That event generated a
tremendous amount of celebratory media coverage at the time.
But eighteen years later, some observers suggested that Obama
had presided over a notoriously weak volume of legal scholarship. One commenter on a legal blog counted the total number
of citations to Obama's volume and to the adjacent volumes and
concluded that "Obama's [Volume] 104 is the least-cited volume of the *Harvard Law Review* in the last 20 years." Another
commenter went further, stating that Obama "presided over a
general 'dumbing down'" of the *Review*'s standards. Though it
went unstated, the subtext of these remarks was unmistakable: in selecting a Black student as president of the *Harvard Law
Review*, the editors who ran that journal had sacrificed quality at
the altar of diversity.

A decade later, similar accusations resurfaced, this time
in the form of a lawsuit. In 2018, groups of students, faculty,
and alumni filed lawsuits against the *Harvard Law Review* and
the *New York University Law Review* opposing practices that,
they claimed, had "subordinated academic merit to diversity
considerations."

These anti-affirmative action lawsuits offered an ideal
setting in which to examine the influence of racial diversity
on group performance in higher education. The work of law
review editors involves core higher-education functions: students work together in a group to select and edit a few articles to publish from thousands of submissions. The articles
that student-run law reviews publish have the advantage of
presenting a publicly observable outcome: article impact, as
measured by citations. We compiled a dataset of the citations

116   to the nearly 13,000 articles published by leading law reviews since 1960, assessing changes in the citations of articles published from the five years before a change in a journal's diversity policy relative to the five years afterward. We found that law review membership diversity policies increased median article citations by roughly 25 percent. This statistically significant finding emerges from law reviews that adopted racial diversity policies across a wide range of different times, and it suggests that Justice Powell's diversity rationale cannot be dismissed as so frivolous after all.

These findings have implications that extend well beyond the law review setting. If diverse groups of student editors perform better than nondiverse groups, it lends credibility to the idea that diverse student bodies, diverse student organizations, diverse faculties, diverse teams of attorneys, and diverse teams of employees generally could perform better than nondiverse teams. These results thus place empirical heft behind Justice Powell's much-derided diversity rationale from *Bakke*, and complicate the Trump administration's ongoing crusade against diversity initiatives.

In 1991, more than three decades ago now, Professor Stephen L. Carter observed that "it is hard to hold an honest conversation about affirmative action," and that "[i]t may be harder still to hold an honest conversation about the reasons why it is hard to hold an honest conversation" about the inflammatory subject. The intervening thirty-four years have not rendered that conversation much easier. Within legal circles, a severely underappreciated reason for the difficulty of that conversation stems from the fact that liberal supporters of affirmative action believe

that the programs alleviate racial subordination, and conservative critics believe that the programs perpetuate racial subordination. The two competing sides seem not even to appreciate
that they are using the same concept to arrive at diametrically
opposed conclusions. By identifying long-standing—though
unacknowledged—commonality regarding the importance of
antisubordination to affirmative action debates, this chapter
endeavors to make conversations about that heated issue, the
Equal Protection Clause, and our larger constitutional order a
little easier.

Action After
Affirmative Action

In *SFFA*'s wake, the overarching watchword among university officers reacting to the decision was *uncertainty*. A former Ivy League admissions dean stated *SFFA* had introduced "tremendous uncertainty." Echoing this sentiment, a Williams College official lamented "ongoing uncertainty" about the Supreme Court's decision, a period that persisted even after President Joe Biden's Department of Justice and Department of Education issued guidance. *The Chronicle of Higher Education* even dubbed the post-*SFFA* season "a summer of uncertainty." Similarly, the *New York Times* noted that *SFFA* introduced a "swirl of uncertainty, confusion and misinformation about an admissions process that has suddenly been made more opaque and bewildering."

Following *SFFA*, overpowering uncertainty engulfed even the most basic questions for admissions officers regarding how the opinion shifted the governing legal terrain. Well after *SFFA*'s dust settled, a *New York Times* reporter asked Amherst College admissions director Matthew McGann about evaluating an applicant who listed, as one of her extracurricular activities,

membership in her high school's Black Student Union. Here is
McGann's response:

> "That cannot be put in the context of"—he stopped him-
> self, pausing for 10 seconds. "I think the—so understand-
> ing a student's participation in an activity through a lens
> of racial status is something that at the very least can-
> not be as easily done anymore. We are still working on our
> training and guideline language on how the admissions
> staff should approach these questions."

It is hard to envision a more quotidian post-*SFFA* admissions
scenario than applicants identifying themselves as members
of a Black student group. If even that straightforward question
suffices to tie admissions officers in knots, imagine their difficulties grappling with more intricate questions.

The point here is decidedly not to single out Amherst for
being derelict in its efforts to divine *SFFA*'s meaning. The same
sort of hesitation that McGann evinced has doubtless been felt
by admissions officers around the country—even if it seldom
unfolds in the pages of the Gray Lady. A central reason that universities have struggled to discern *SFFA*'s meaning is that they
are doing so in utter isolation from one another. The universities are siloed from one another because they fear that collaboration will expose them to antitrust litigation. Those fears are
well founded, as then-Senator JD Vance's letter to FTC Chair
Khan attests. The universities' utter isolation following *SFFA* is
vividly captured by an anonymous college administrator, who
told the *Chronicle of Higher Education*: "[W]e've got plans, but
we're not going to broadcast them and put a target on our back."

120   Some initial reactions to the post-*SFFA* universe have admittedly been less than inspired. At Columbia Law School, for example, the admissions webpage posted a striking statement directed toward prospective students. "All applicants will be required to submit a short video, no longer than 90 seconds, addressing a question chosen at random," the webpage instructed. "The video statement will allow applicants to provide the Admissions Committee with additional insight into their personal strengths." The requested video's extreme brevity and the fact that this policy was adopted on *SFFA*'s heels immediately raised hackles. Columbia's actual ambition was less to furnish the admissions office "with additional insight into . . . [applicants'] personal strengths," critics suggested, but instead to uncover applicants' racial identities. After a conservative publication questioned Columbia about its newfangled policy, the law school beat a hasty retreat, insisting that the video requirement had somehow inadvertently been posted. Columbia's rapid turnabout on the video requirement illustrates how university officials have been bedeviled in their efforts to confront the post-*SFFA* era.

Even some of the advice provided in *SFFA*'s dissenting opinions appears unlikely to provide much help in countering the decision's effects. In Justice Sotomayor's dissent, for example, she recommended that "[u]niversities should continue to use . . . tools as best they can to recruit and admit students from different backgrounds," including offering admissions boosts to applicants "who speak multiple languages." A language-based admissions preference would certainly pass constitutional muster.

But universities ought to reflect carefully before changing their admissions schemes to seek applicants "who speak multiple languages." So phrased, universities would almost certainly experience an influx of privileged white students who grew up speaking English in their homes, but also managed to ace the Advanced Placement French test. That cannot be what Justice Sotomayor had in mind to combat *SFFA*. Instead, she should have recommended that universities seek applicants "who grew up speaking English as a second language." That admissions preference specifies a nonracial category—and would be constitutionally permissible. But it may also help to boost universities' racial diversity. The lack of precision in Sotomayor's multilingual recommendation is, alas, emblematic of the undertheorization that currently besets efforts to avoid *SFFA*'s catastrophic effects.

Only minutes after the Supreme Court issued *SFFA*, President Biden directed officials from the Department of Justice and the Department of Education to formulate explicit guidance instructing universities on how they could remain committed to achieving racial diversity without violating the decision. When that guidance emerged roughly six weeks later, it proclaimed: "These resources will help colleges and universities as they work to lawfully pursue efforts to achieve a student body that is diverse across a range of factors, including race and ethnicity." In fact, however, the government provided university leaders little in the way of actionable guidance, issuing a document long on bromides and short on concrete solutions. University leaders, who eagerly awaited the guidance, received desultory, bureaucratic boilerplate that failed to meet

122   the challenging moment. The guidance urged universities to: conduct an "Evaluation of Admissions Policies"; adopt "Outreach, Recruitment, and Pathway Programs"; assess "Student Yield and Retention Strategies and Programs"; and—in a nod to every bureaucrat's favorite pastime—order the "Collection of Demographic Data."

Not surprisingly, the uncertainty regarding the altered admissions reality brought about by *SFFA* deeply afflicts college applicants and their parents. Many Black high school students—and the adults who support them—are aware that the Supreme Court recently issued a major decision affecting college admissions. But the particularities of what *SFFA* actually entails remain mysterious, as few citizens possess either the inclination or the appetite to digest *SFFA*'s voluminous opinions. This uncertainty has, of course, bred misinformation among many college applicants. Some high school seniors—including Demar Goodman, the ambitious young Black man from a rough part of Atlanta—have operated under the misimpression that should their applications dare to mention their racial identities, then the college will penalize them for doing so. But not even the most expansive conservative legal interpreters of *SFFA* can credibly assert that the opinion renders applicants' mentioning their race somehow verboten. Instead, Chief Justice Roberts's majority opinion in *SFFA* expressly entertained the notion that applicants' essays will address race, and even provided that—in some circumstances—universities may construe those essays as advancing the case for admission.

Examining "Race *Qua* Race"

This chapter endeavors to shed light on *SFFA*'s central meaning, which remains shrouded in a thick fog of legal and intellectual haziness. Universities should not operate under the inaccurate view that *SFFA* forbids them from engaging in *all* racial considerations. If *SFFA* cannot accurately be construed as banning all considerations of race, then, what does that all-important opinion actually forbid? Although this point has been severely overlooked, the best reading of the decision is that it prohibits university admission officers from considering what it terms "race *qua* race—[or,] race for race's sake." Chief Justice Roberts, elaborating upon what *SFFA* sought to forbid with this language, explained that universities cannot broadly "allocate [admissions] preference[s] to those who may have little in common with one another but the color of their skin." He continued: "The entire point of the Equal Protection Clause is that treating someone differently because of their skin color is not like treating them differently because they are from a city or from a suburb, or because they play the violin poorly or well." Over the coming decades, classrooms, boardrooms, and courtrooms will witness boundless efforts to decipher, with precision, what *SFFA* means by "race *qua* race."

Those exertions, fortunately, will not occur on a blank slate. Rather, several respected legal minds have explored the phenomenon of how universities can constitutionally seek to obtain meaningful racial diversity in the modern era without resorting to the forbidden "race *qua* race," even if they have not deployed that starched formulation. The good news on this score is that numerous distinguished critics of affirmative action have appreciated that the end of affirmative action does

124 not necessarily mean that elite universities will include only a trivial number of Black students.

The most influential jurist of the last five decades is, in my estimation, Justice Antonin Scalia. Whoever comes in second place to Justice Scalia, moreover, arrives as a distant runner-up. I am far from the only liberal to view Scalia as preeminent. Consider now-Justice Elena Kagan's appraisal of Scalia when she served as dean of Harvard Law School in the 2000s. "[Scalia's] views on textualism and originalism, his views on the role of judges in our society, on the practice of judging, have really transformed the terms of legal debate in this country," Kagan stated. "He is the justice who has had the most important impact over the years on how we think and talk about law." Since Justice Scalia's death in 2016, his already outsized reputation has, if anything, grown larger still. Indeed, in high-profile cases that divide conservative justices among themselves on the current Court, the competing sides sometimes engage in intramural sparring over who can more faithfully claim to have held fast to the teachings of Justice Scalia. One current justice has gone so far as to label Scalia a "role model" and even a "hero."

Given Scalia's hold on the conservative legal imagination, his views of the post–affirmative action path forward should receive considerable attention. Intriguingly, Scalia set out his views most fully on what *SFFA*'s "race *qua* race" would entail not when he sat on the judge's bench, but instead when he sat in the professor's armchair. In 1979, then-Professor Scalia's article castigating *Bakke* included a remarkable passage that could go a long way toward illuminating what *SFFA* will ultimately mean. "I do not . . . oppose—indeed, I strongly favor—what might be called (but for the coloration that the term has acquired in the

context of its past use) 'affirmative action programs' of many
types of help for the poor and disadvantaged," Scalia explained.
"It may well be that many, or even most, of those benefited by
such programs would be members of minority races that the
existing programs exclusively favor. I would not care if *all* of
them were. The unacceptable vice is simply selecting or rejecting them *on the basis of their race.*" (The emphasis is Scalia's,
highlighting the importance of this passage.)

This statement makes clear that Justice Scalia believed universities could accord admission preferences on the basis of
non-racial criteria even if they disproportionately—indeed,
even if those preferences *exclusively*—redounded to the benefit of Black applicants. These remarks were hardly cavalier.
Instead, Scalia repeatedly invoked this idea, noting that "many"
Black citizens would be eligible to receive admissions boosts.
"I am entirely in favor of according the poor inner-city child,
who happens to be black, advantages and preferences," Scalia
stated. "But I am not willing to prefer the son of a prosperous and well-educated black doctor or lawyer—*solely because
of his race*—to the son of a recent refugee from Eastern Europe
who is working as a manual laborer to get his family ahead." On
Scalia's studied account, then, the constitutional understanding that *SFFA* termed "race *qua* race" should prevent admissions
officers from offering boosts to, say, all Black applicants due to
racial box-checking, but it should in no way forbid universities
from considering other, nonracial criteria that would aid Black
applicants.

Scalia's understanding of strategies that would remain
available to universities in a post—affirmative action world
strongly resembles the vision that the generally liberal Justice

126   Douglas sketched five years earlier in his *DeFunis v. Odegaard* solo opinion. Douglas's *DeFunis* opinion merits extended scrutiny here because it further clarifies what *SFFA*'s "race *qua* race" language both forbids and permits.

Justice Douglas emphasized that universities cannot "accord[ ] a preference solely on the basis of race," but instead must "mak[e] decisions on the basis of individual attributes" and "consider[ ] . . . each application in a racially neutral way." But racial neutrality, for Douglas, in no sense required admissions committees to turn a blind eye toward challenging racial realities. "The Equal Protection Clause . . . does [not] prohibit law schools from evaluating an applicant's prior achievements in light of the barriers that he had to overcome," Douglas wrote. "A black applicant who pulled himself out of the ghetto into a junior college may thereby demonstrate a level of motivation, perseverance, and ability that would lead a fairminded admissions committee to conclude that he shows more promise for law study than the son of a rich alumnus who achieved better grades at Harvard." Justice Douglas further explained:

> That applicant would be offered admission not because he is black, but because as an individual he has shown he has the potential, while the Harvard man may have taken less advantage of the vastly superior opportunities offered him. Because of the weight of the prior handicaps, that black applicant may not realize his full potential in the first year of law school, or even in the full three years, but in the long pull of a legal career his achievements may far outstrip those of his classmates whose earlier records appeared superior by conventional criteria.

Douglas repeatedly voiced this theme that universities may legitimately consider an individual applicant's disadvantage. "There is . . . no bar to considering an individual's prior achievements in light of the racial discrimination that barred his way, as a factor in attempting to assess his true potential for a successful legal career," he noted. Douglas's emphasis on the racial challenges and racial prospects of particular individuals—rather than entire groups—anticipated the line that *SFFA* ultimately adopted, a feature that came through most clearly in Chief Justice Roberts's discussion of individualized essays.

When the US Court of Appeals for the Fifth Circuit took it upon itself to, in effect, invalidate affirmative action for all universities within its jurisdiction in 1996, that court's opinion in *Hopwood v. Texas* similarly made clear that universities retained a large amount of admissions discretion. Closely anticipating *SFFA*'s "race *qua* race" language, *Hopwood* employed a cognate Latin phrase, noting that the decision forbade admissions officers from relying upon "race *per se*." "While the use of race *per se* is proscribed," *Hopwood* explained, "state-supported schools may reasonably consider a host of factors—*some of which may have some correlation with race*—in making admissions decisions." Not only could universities consider applicants' abilities to "play the cello, make a downfield tackle, or understand chaos theory," *Hopwood* noted: "[Universities] may even consider factors such as whether an applicant's parents attended college or the applicant's economic and social background." Even though first-generation college attendance and socio-economic disadvantage may be more common among racial minorities, *Hopwood* understood that such preferences should not be deemed considerations of race *per se*.

128   This realization that *SFFA*, properly understood, prohibits admissions officers only from considering "race *qua* race" means that universities continue to possess countless constitutionally permissible mechanisms that could help to ensure that the enrollment of Black, brown, and Native students does not plummet. To be clear, I do not subscribe to the notion that *SFFA* represented in any sense a welcome development. Rather, I believe that the decision constitutes a veritable catastrophe not just in higher education but in our larger national life, and that the pre-*SFFA* affirmative action regime was preferable to anything that will arise in its wake. That statement holds because a mountain of existing evidence suggests that race-explicit methods produce greater amounts of racial diversity in the elite educational world than methods that avoid racial classifications. Nonetheless, it is essential to realize at this critical juncture that all hope is not lost. Racial egalitarians must therefore highlight both the limited purview that "race *qua* race" encompasses and what action after affirmative action demands.

Slavery's Descendants

A promising idea for universities to consider adopting after *SFFA* would offer an admissions preference to all applicants who identify as the descendants of slaves. This approach remains constitutionally viable even after *SFFA* because the descendants of slaves is decidedly not a category that employs "race *qua* race." Yes, many Black people could place themselves in that category. But many, many Black people in the United States today would, of course, not fall into that category. Black people who are not descended from slaves would include the bulk of immigrants, or the children and grandchildren of immigrants from various

African nations after 1965, when the United States liberalized
its immigration policies. If many Black people fall on both sides
of an admissions line, that line cannot plausibly be viewed as
"race *qua* race." Recall that Justice Scalia was convinced that it
would not violate the Constitution even if *everyone* in a preferred admissions category were Black, provided that the category itself was nonracial.

Perhaps surprisingly, the method of constitutional interpretation championed by Justice Scalia—and embraced
by the majority of current justices—would seem to place
the descendants-of-slaves category on terra firma. Justice
Scalia refined and promoted *originalism*, the notion that the
Constitution must be interpreted according to its original public meaning. Originalism, once an exotic theory, has
over the last four decades become the dominant interpretive mode among conservatives. Chief Justice Roberts is the
only Republican-appointed member of the Supreme Court
who does not march behind an originalist banner, so it should
hardly astonish that *SFFA*'s majority opinion did not employ
the methodology. Originalist considerations nonetheless arose
at various points of the *SFFA* dispute. Counterintuitively, the
originalist Justices' concerted efforts to eliminate affirmative action worked to solidify the constitutionality of the
descendants-of-slaves category.

For originalists who also oppose affirmative action, *SFFA*
raised an excruciating question: How does one make sense of
the Freedmen's Bureau? That Reconstruction-era entity is tra-
ditionally understood as an instance where Congress dedicated resources to assisting Black people in various ways as
they navigated the fraught pathway from slavery to citizenship.

130   The Freedmen's Bureau thus presents a befuddling, glaringly inconvenient development for originalists bent on ending affirmative action. Why? Because the Bureau's existence suggests that the Framers of the Fourteenth Amendment's Equal Protection Clause deemed it constitutionally permissible to take account of race if the program in question was designed to benefit Black people. That contemporaneous piece of evidence about the Equal Protection Clause's meaning should loom large for anyone who styles themselves an originalist. And the most straightforward understanding would construe today's affirmative action policies as but modern analogues of the Freedmen's Bureau of 1865 in that the creators of both programs were driven by a basic desire to aid Black people.

Justice Thomas took on this question frontally in *SFFA*, endeavoring to explain how this troublesome interpretive square might be circled. The Freedmen's Bureau, Thomas creatively insisted, was not in fact a race-based program. Instead, Thomas averred that, as its name attests, the Bureau was geared not toward all Black people but instead at those who had been enslaved, *i.e.*, those who were unfree. The Bureau "applied to *freedmen* (and refugees), a formally race-neutral category, not blacks writ large," Thomas explained. "And, because not all blacks in the United States were former slaves, *freedman* was a decidedly under-inclusive proxy for race."

This interpretive move to reconcile the Freedmen's Bureau with opposition to affirmative action might seem artificial, if not downright bizarre. In this vein, decorated commentators have condemned Thomas's reading as insufficiently rooted in the pertinent history. Eric Foner, the nation's preeminent historian of Reconstruction, gave Justice Thomas's *SFFA* history a

failing mark. "['F]reedman[']' was widely used as a synonym for
Black," Foner commented after *SFFA*. "Ninety percent of Blacks
were slaves in 1860, and everyone knew whom the Freedmen's
Bureau Act was meant to assist." Writing in the *Atlantic*, Adam
Serwer went further, labeling Thomas's claim "the most baffling
argument a Supreme Court Justice has ever made."

Regardless of that claim's accuracy, it is too often overlooked that Thomas's position gives universities a green light to
offer preferences to descendants of slaves. After all, if a Bureau
that was designed to help former slaves is not a race-based
mechanism, neither is a program that is designed to help slavery's descendants. At *SFFA*'s oral argument, Justice Kavanaugh
pressed exactly this point. When the originalist's affirmative action dilemma arose, Kavanaugh asserted that "a benefit to descendants of slaves would not be race-based" if the
Freedmen's Bureau was not a race-based program. In response,
SFFA's attorney sought to resist that framing. But Kavanaugh
would have none of it, as he doubled down: "[Y]ou said . . . that
the benefit for former slaves was not race-based. If that's correct, then the benefit for descendants of former slaves is also
not race-based."

Several respected conservative scholars have already
embraced the idea that preferences for the descendants of slavery could withstand constitutional scrutiny. Most prominently, Professor Michael McConnell of Stanford—a Federalist
Society stalwart and former federal judge appointed by
President George W. Bush—has expressly suggested that the
Freedmen's Bureau militates in constitutional favor of admissions preferences for slavery's descendants. "[A] preference for descendants of slaves is much easier to defend [than

132   affirmative action]," McConnell stated, "and there are lots of
people for whom their Black race is not a proxy for having been
descendants of slaves, including all the numerous fairly recent
immigrants from Africa whom I understand . . . constitute a
surprisingly large subset of the Black beneficiaries of affirmative action." Viewing the Freedmen's Bureau as an analogue to
the descendants-of-slavery category, McConnell added, would
constitute compelling evidence for originalists because of its
"historical grounding."

Similarly, Professor David Bernstein, an ardent critic of
affirmative action who filed a major amicus brief supporting
SFFA, has elsewhere contended that admissions preferences for
slavery's descendants should be deemed constitutional. While
the "status [is] correlated with racial classification [it is] primarily [a] political and historical rather than racial categor[y],"
Bernstein wrote. "Using [that] classification[] . . . would get the
government out of the business of rewarding and penalizing
individuals' racial identity. Universities could be 'color-blind,'
while retaining the ability to redress the lingering harms
from state-sponsored racism without [violating] . . . the 14th
Amendment."Relatedly, if less emphatically, Professor Ilya Somin
wrote on *The Volokh Conspiracy*—a widely read conservative- and
libertarian-inflected website—that preferences for slavery's
descendants offered"a significant improvement over [affirmative
action] policies," and suggested that courts would uphold such
preferences if they were challenged because they would not be
subjected to the most demanding level of scrutiny that is applied
to programs featuring explicit racial classifications.

Many leading universities may feel particularly motivated to offer admissions preferences to slavery's descendants

because of growing awareness that their own histories and their own current fortunes are profoundly, inextricably connected to the peculiar institution. In 2003, President Ruth Simmons of Brown University—the first Black Ivy League head—announced a broad initiative to examine her institution's elaborate connections to slavery.

Simmons, the great-granddaughter of slaves, was the last of twelve children born to a family of sharecroppers in Grapeland, Texas, in 1945, eight decades after slavery's abolition. The family eked out the impoverished existence of sharecroppers all over the South—living in what she called "a shanty," subsisting on an inadequate diet, and holding no prospects of acquiring their own assets. Simmons's youth in Grapeland, moreover, was marred by the unmistakable, naked disdain with which white people had viewed Black people since the days of slavery. The vile notion that Black people were beasts continued to infect Grapeland's everyday lexicon. "The gathering site for Blacks was called 'buzzards' roost,'" Simmons wrote. "To many white people in Grapeland, we were a bunch of crude Blacks who reminded them of a flock of buzzards, gathering to feed on leavings and detritus. We swooped in, circled, came down for a feeding, and, once we had our fill, moved on until the next feeding."

Given this history, it hardly seems accidental that Simmons became the first university president to task a committee with investigating her institution's links to slavery. Simmons called the group a Steering Committee on Slavery and Justice. Such committees have now become prevalent, with numerous Ivy League institutions issuing their own major reports examining institutional ties to slavery during the last few years. While the committee's formation garnered headlines two decades ago,

134   higher education leaders overwhelmingly greeted the news with stunned silence. "[T]here wasn't a single peep from another university," stated the historian who oversaw Brown's undertaking. Within even left-leaning Brown, Simmons encountered resistance, as some observers accused her of dredging up distant unpleasantness that was best left in the past. Her opponents found at least some representation on the Brown committee, as a respected professor of American history stated he had encountered "no evidence" suggesting that the university should be singled out: "Brown, like a great many other people in the late 18th century, was indirectly a beneficiary on a very very small scale of the fact that slavery was a source of wealth in this country." This criticism seems belied by the fact that numerous, prominent Brown benefactors engaged in the slave trade.

When Simmons announced the committee's formation, she allowed, "It certainly didn't escape me, my own past in relationship to [slavery]." Simmons acknowledged that the subject of slavery—and reparations—could often seem daunting. "How does one repair a kind of social breach in human rights so that people are not just coming back to it periodically and demanding apologies," Simmons said, "so that society learns from it, acknowledges what has taken place and then moves on. What I'm trying to do, you see, in a country that wants to move on, I'm trying to understand as a descendant of slaves how to feel good about moving on." Simmons expressed high hopes that the group would propose concrete steps for how Brown might acknowledge and rectify its debt to human bondage: "If the committee comes back and says, 'Oh[,] it's been lovely and we've learned a lot,' but there's nothing in particular that they think Brown can do or should do, I will be very disappointed."

Brown's ensuing report ultimately led to the creation of a center on slavery and the installation of a memorial on campus. It did not, however, lead Brown to confer admissions preferences on slavery's descendants. The Brown report initiated an important conversation in higher education regarding slavery, however, and during the last two decades, presidents of the nation's foremost academic institutions have slowly followed Simmons's lead. Columbia, Georgetown, Harvard, Princeton, the University of Virginia, William & Mary, and Yale—among many others—have all researched and produced extensive reports exploring how slavery played a foundational role in shaping those institutions. In announcing Harvard's findings in 2016, President Drew Faust stated: "Harvard was directly complicit in America's system of racial bondage from the College's earliest days in the 17th century until slavery in Massachusetts ended in 1783, and Harvard continued to be indirectly involved through extensive financial and other ties to the slave South up to the time of emancipation." Faust's statement could, of course, be applied to many of our nation's oldest, most esteemed universities. As one scholar has memorably advanced this argument: "The academy never stood apart from American slavery—in fact, it stood beside church and state as the third pillar of a civilization built on bondage."

Implementing admissions preferences for slavery's descendants could also have significant, positive consequences for the broader American society. Even today, several years after the *New York Times*'s 1619 Project appeared, the United States routinely suffers a sort of historical amnesia about the harms of

136   slavery, preferring not to linger too long on that atrocity. In comparison with how Germany has openly and forthrightly grappled with the evils of its Nazi regime, American wrestling with the tolls of slavery remains in its infancy. Although it is tempting to believe that the aversion to acknowledging slavery applies exclusively to white Americans and predominantly white institutions, that aversion is in truth far from confined to those of lighter hues. For many Black Americans, one's familial connections to slavery are a painful, even shameful topic, one best left for another day that somehow never arrives. Admissions preferences for slavery's descendants would therefore play a tangible role in encouraging American society generally to deepen its engagement with a subject that too often remains taboo.

When the Supreme Court considered *Bakke* in 1978, Justice Thurgood Marshall dared to break this taboo by linking slavery's wounds to the case for affirmative action programs. "Three hundred and fifty years ago, the Negro was dragged to this country in chains to be sold into slavery," Marshall wrote. "Uprooted from his homeland and thrust into bondage for forced labor, the slave was deprived of all legal rights. It was unlawful to teach him to read; he could be sold away from his family and friends at the whim of his master; and killing or maiming him was not a crime." Nearly five decades ago now, Justice Marshall aimed to spark a national dialogue about slavery's shadow, and that effort largely fizzled. Adopting admissions preferences for slavery's descendants could play a vital role in furthering that much-needed conversation.

Introducing admissions preferences for slavery's descendants would also contain a delicious irony. When *Bakke* was decided in 1978, UC Davis Medical School and its supporters

offered several justifications for affirmative action, including efforts to counter both "historic deficit[s]" and "the effects
of societal discrimination." But Justice Powell's controlling
opinion summarily rebuffed these justifications for affirmative action, rejecting what he termed "amorphous concept[s] of
injury that may be ageless in its reach into the past." Powell's
opinion upholding affirmative action's constitutionality (relying on the diversity rationale) thus sought to slam the door on
history. Although *SFFA* criticized Powell's opinion in *Bakke* and
ended affirmative action as we have known it, admissions preferences for slavery's descendants would have the improbable
effect of reopening history's door.

Adopting preferences for slavery's descendants could be
viewed as raising significant implementation questions. Some
readers might question how universities could verify that applicants who indicated enslaved ancestry did not do so fraudulently.
On this view, it would be impractical—not to mention just plain
creepy—for university admission offices to establish research
units dedicated to rifling through applicants' genealogies.

But the import of this criticism ought not be overstated.
First, the pre-*SFFA* approach, where applicants checked racial
boxes, was by no means free of verification concerns. If one
ticked the "Black/African American" box before *SFFA*, in other
words, universities did not then seek to ascertain whether the
racial assertion actually held water. The absence of such inqui-
ries means that a preference for slavery's descendants that
superseded the old affirmative action model would not somehow represent the *creation* of verification issues but rather their
continuation.

138   Second, each passing year renders it increasingly possible for slavery's descendants—along with everyone else—to uncover the identities of their eighteenth- and nineteenth-century forebears. Even a decade ago, it seemed miraculous that Henry Louis Gates Jr., and his crack team of PBS researchers, could uncover celebrities' lost lineages for his television show *Finding Your Roots*. But the revolution of genealogical discoveries has now been at least somewhat democratized. As the *New York Times* noted in 2022: "Handwritten government records from the aftermath of Emancipation are now available for free online. Distant relatives whose ancestors were forced apart by slavery can be reached with a few mouse clicks. And the descendants of people who profited from slavery are digitizing crucial records long buried in attics and basements." Thus, even if universities felt queasy about the slavery verification question, they could nevertheless contemplate encouraging, or even requiring, applicants who seek the slavery preference to provide documentation supporting the claim. While serious obstacles doubtless remain today, technological innovation seems likely to address many of those difficulties in the not-so-distant future.

Introducing a preference for slavery's descendants would also raise major questions regarding the preferential *scope*: Who, exactly, would universities deem eligible to receive an admissions boost? Must applicants be descended from those enslaved within the United States? Or, more broadly, must they be descended from those enslaved within the Americas? In addition, should universities extend the preference to *all* descendants of slavery (however the term "slavery" is cabined), or should they limit the preference to those who can

demonstrate that the university in question benefited directly
from the bondage of that particular applicant's ancestors?

It is important to realize that granting admissions preferences to slavery's descendants would be nothing new in American higher education. In 2016, Georgetown University announced that it would provide admissions boosts to the descendants of 272 slaves that the institution owned and eventually sold, through its connection to the Maryland Province of Jesuits. Georgetown's President John DeGioia has commented: "We live, every day, with the legacies of enslavement."

Georgetown deserves commendation for taking a valuable first step on this front. But there are nevertheless compelling reasons to impugn Georgetown's program for adopting an excessively parsimonious scope. For starters, a paltry number of slavery's descendants have availed themselves of Georgetown's preference. In 2023, seven years after Georgetown enacted the program, it revealed that a total of only twenty students had been admitted—not *enrolled*, but *admitted*—who were eligible for the preference. If Georgetown aims to atone for its slave-owning past, I am surely far from alone in believing that admitting twenty students—or a little less than three per year—does little to realize the goal of atonement.

More broadly, though, Georgetown's approach to the descendants' preference seems to misapprehend the fundamental nature of chattel slavery's deep entanglement with the American economy. Slavery spread its tentacles into virtually every economic sector of nineteenth-century America, as the nation's economy became increasingly interconnected. Determining where one university's involvement with slavery started and where it ended creates bedeviling problems.

140   Suppose that one's ancestor was owned by a major donor to Georgetown University. Alternately, suppose that Georgetown invested in a Georgia plantation where one's ancestor toiled. Finally, suppose that one's ancestor picked cotton on a plantation that distributed its wares to a textile magnate whose own heirs donated lavishly to Georgetown. Should any of those descendants of slavery really be excluded from Georgetown's preference? Fixating on which university owned whose ancestors seems beside the point because one of slavery's central horrors was that it degraded individual souls and transformed them into fungible commodities. It hardly seems immoderate to maintain that the universities who are truly committed to addressing this stark injustice should now extend that fungibility presumption to slavery's descendants.

I hasten to add that reasonable minds may well differ regarding the proper scope for preferences regarding slavery's descendants. Universities could therefore draw their respective lines of demarcation in divergent fashions. Such disagreements should, however, not be suppressed but heartily welcomed. Those differences would signal that multiple universities are engaging deeply not only with slavery's past, but also with how that odious past obligates universities in the modern day. How universities resolve those abiding questions will play a significant role in forging the future of American higher education.

Some opponents of extending admissions preferences for slavery's descendants may object that adopting the policy would ignite a civil war within Black America. On this account, immigrant families from, say, Ghana, Kenya, and Nigeria also encounter racism within the United States, and their being denied admissions preferences would not only ignore that reality but would foment intra-Black resentment and alienation.* Racial minorities outside of the Black community would resent being excluded from the preference. Professor Josh Blackman—a conservative, diehard critic of affirmative action—has offered a notably florid version of this argument. Adopting a preference for slavery's descendants "would create internecine DEI strife on campuses nationwide," Blackman cautioned. "Hispanics, American Indians, and other groups would be left out. The technicolor intersectional pyramid would become a monochromatic obelisk, with only one racial beneficiary."

This criticism's full force, though, is derived from its presumption that the admissions preference for slavery's descendants would be the *sole* admissions preference that would redound to the benefit of various racial minorities. But nothing would prevent universities from simultaneously introducing an entire suite of admissions preferences designed to ensure that *SFFA* does not radically diminish racial diversity on campuses. Rather, given both the uncertainty and the urgency created by *SFFA*, announcing a wide array of admissions preferences in one fell swoop has much to commend it. That approach would, among other virtues, prevent opponents of meaningful racial diversity in higher education from attacking a single measure in isolation, and thus diminish the utility of the painfully familiar divide-and-conquer tactic. In addition, the multifaceted posture would enable universities to experiment and explore, sorting what preferences work from those that do not. At this early stage in our post-*SFFA* world, testing ideas—even

---

*I will set aside the question of whether such objections are predicated on overly sanguine views regarding the current state of Black unity.

142   if they ultimately fail to yield fruit—is among the more valuable efforts that universities can undertake.

Preferences for Immigrants

Universities could adopt preferences for immigrants without violating *SFFA*'s prohibition on considering "race *qua* race." Drawing a line preferring immigrants in no sense can be mistaken for drawing a line on the basis of race. But due to US immigration's modern racial demographics, this preference could nevertheless materially enhance racial diversity on leading college campuses. In 2018, white people accounted for less than one in five immigrants to the United States, a figure that is consistent with a long-term trend. In the higher education domain, the racial demographics are even more stark: first- and second-generation immigrants account for 10 percent of white college students; 28 percent of Black college students; 68 percent of Latino college students; and 88 percent of Asian American students. These figures suggest that an immigration-based preference could play some role in ameliorating the effects of *SFFA*.

Notably, the concept of affording admissions preferences for immigrant families arose twice during *SFFA*'s oral argument. In both instances, the conservative justices who posed the questions and the conservative attorneys who fielded the questions intimated that such preferences could withstand challenges. In one instance, Justice Kavanaugh asked Patrick Strawbridge, SFFA's attorney in the UNC case, whether universities could legally "give a plus to applicants whose parents were immigrants to this country?" After clarifying that these hypothetical boosts would apply to "immigrants regardless of country" and "regardless of their racial [descent]," Strawbridge registered no objections to such a plan. In a related vein, Justice Alito asked Strawbridge the following:

> Suppose that a student is an immigrant from Africa and moves to a rural area in western North Carolina where the population is overwhelmingly white. And the student in an [application] essay . . . say[s] . . . I was [not] subjected to any kind of overt discrimination, but I did have to deal with huge cultural differences, I had to find a way of relating to my classmates who came from very different backgrounds. Would that be permissible [to credit in admissions]?

Strawbridge responded, "I think that that would generally be permissible because the . . . preference in that case is not being based upon the race but upon the cultural experiences or the ability to adapt or the fact of encountering a new language in a new . . . environment."

Admissions preferences for immigrants would have numerous expressive benefits. First, affording preferences to people hailing from various African nations could help to lower the potential for intra-racial tensions within America's Black community that may arise after implementing admissions preferences for slavery's descendants. Some Black people who might otherwise feel tempted to oppose those preferences, in other words, could become less irritated by realizing that they, too, would be eligible for an admissions boost on the basis of immigration. Second, awarding this admissions preference to students who immigrated from various Asian nations could erode the

144   perception that the college admissions sweepstakes are stacked against Asian American applicants. SFFA premised its attack on Harvard's admission system by propounding this claim, and it generated extensive media attention. Offering admissions preferences to applicants who hail from Asian nations would serve to undercut the notion that elite universities wish to keep their institutions relatively free of students with Asian roots.

More broadly, universities announcing that they welcome immigrants onto campus could serve as a powerful, salient countermeasure to the neo-nativist politics that have become ascendant within the United States. In early 2025, neo-nativism informed some of the more startling moments of President Trump's second term—an epoch that overflowed with startling developments. Most ostentatiously, on his very first day in the Oval Office, President Trump signed an executive order that purported to eliminate birthright citizenship for certain people, even though the Fourteenth Amendment's plain language protects that right. This measure, which contravened longstanding legal principles, was driven by a racialized belief that the United States extends citizenship to too many undesirables. If there is any doubt that President Trump conceives of citizenship in racialized terms, note that he blamed immigration policies for a terrorist attack in New Orleans committed by Shamsud-Din Jabbar—even though he was born a United States citizen. By counteracting such neo-nativism, universities could underscore that many Americans continue to believe that immigration is a vital source of strength for our system of higher education and for the nation more broadly.

Predictably, some opponents of affirmative action—utilizing the divide-and-conquer playbook—have repudiated

admissions preferences for immigrants by claiming that they
would harm both slavery's descendants and Native Americans.
For example, Steven A. Camarota of the Center for Immigration
Studies has made precisely this group-based argument, explaining further: "There has always been a conflict between immigration and affirmative action[] . . . , but this would be the ultimate
turning that on its head and turning affirmative action almost
against the group it was originally designed to help." As with
the slavery's descendants preference, though, the correct way
to think about this critique is not to fold up shop, but instead
to explore what can also be done for Native American students.

Preferences for Tribal Membership
In another type of American historical amnesia, writing
about race in general—and affirmative action in particular—
seldom contemplates the challenges Native Americans students encounter regarding elite college enrollment. That over-
sight exists not because Native American students have avoided
the plunging enrollment rates that face their Black and brown
counterparts in jurisdictions that have eliminated affirmative
action. At Berkeley and UCLA, for example, affirmative action's
end in California eventually dropped Native American enrollment to 0.37 percent and 0.68 percent, respectively, whereas in
the 1990s those figures amounted to 1.82 percent and 1.22 percent. These declining enrollment numbers all-too-accurately
foretold what would occur on a national level following *SFFA*.
In the decision's aftermath, Amherst, Cornell, M.I.T., and the
University of Virginia all reported that their first-year numbers of Native students decreased by approximately 50 percent.
Admittedly, the overall enrollment figures of Native American

146   students at most elite universities were quite modest even prior
       to affirmative action's end. But those relatively small num-
       bers do not mean that enrollment concerns should simply van-
       ish. Instead, the modest initial numbers coupled with the steep
       post–affirmative action decline make addressing the issue only
       more acute.

       Judges would almost certainly invalidate an explicit admis-
       sions preference for Native American students, as they would
       find that policy violates *SFFA*'s prohibition on treating "race
       qua race." That litigation reality does not mean, however, that
       universities lack useful, pertinent tools at their disposal.
       Long-standing legal authority holds that courts will uphold the
       constitutionality of admissions preferences on the basis of offi-
       cial tribal membership rather than Native American status. In
       Morton v. Mancari, the Supreme Court in 1974—in a unanimous
       decision issued only weeks after it decided *DeFunis v. Odegaard*—
       reasoned as follows in an employment case: "The [tribal hiring]
       preference is not directed towards a 'racial' group consisting of
       'Indians'; instead, it applies only to members of 'federally rec-
       ognized' tribes. This operates to exclude many individuals who
       are racially to be classified as 'Indians.' In this sense, the prefer-
       ence is political rather than racial in nature." In harmony with
       SFFA's "race *qua* race" language, *Mancari* concluded that because
       drawing a tribal membership line both includes and excludes
       many Native Americans, it should not be construed as involving
       a racial classification at all. In 1978, Justice Powell's controlling
       opinion in *Bakke* both acknowledged this dimension of *Mancari*
       and left undisturbed its determination that a tribal membership
       criterion differed from a racial designation. The Supreme Court
       has repeatedly affirmed *Mancari*'s proposition that preferences

based on tribal membership do not violate equal protection values, with Justice Gorsuch in 2023 even declaring it a "bedrock principle that [tribal] status is a 'political rather than racial' classification."

It will arrive as no surprise that liberal scholars overwhelmingly support the constitutionality of governmental programs that offer preferences for tribal membership. But conservative scholars, too, have pledged allegiance to *Mancari*'s rule—even in the controversial context of university admissions. Not long after California voters banned affirmative action, Professor Eugene Volokh published a law review article interpreting the new measure. While "[c]lassifications based only on being an Indian . . . are racial," Volokh explained, "[i]t . . . seems proper [for California] to follow the federal constitutional example, and view classifications based on Indian-tribe membership as not being based on race. . . ."

Some observers will enthusiastically support a university application process that acknowledges official tribal memberships and thus abandons the system that relied upon applicants checking a Native American box. First, focusing upon one's individual tribal membership would enable universities to seek tribal diversity within the larger Native American community. In addition, requiring applicants to furnish tribal credentials would decrease the ability of applicants to knowingly or unknowingly assert Native American heritage when they actually possess no such thing. The racial fraudulence concern among college applicants reaches its apex in the Native American context. In 1992, the *Detroit News* published an extensive article examining the phenomenon, concluding: "Thousands of students misrepresent themselves

148   to gain entrance and scholarships to US universities, costing real American Indians access to higher education." Shifting to tribal membership's political identity and away from Native Americans' racial identity would curtail this sort of fraudulence. And it would enable giddy conservatives to proclaim that they have—at long last—solved what they deem the Elizabeth Warren problem.

Preferences for Low-Opportunity Origins

For a long season, prominent critics of racial affirmative action have asserted that the policy should be replaced by a system that focuses on preferences for students from modest economic backgrounds. Such a class-based affirmative action system would be preferable, this claim runs, because elite universities are overrun with students from privileged backgrounds, with even the racial minorities springing from relatively well-to-do circumstances. The class-based admissions system, supporters insist, would help poor Black, brown, and Native students who are most deserving of a leg up in the college admissions sweepstakes, given the obstacles that they surely have overcome. Emphasizing economic disadvantage would, moreover, address a conspicuous question that haunts approaches utilizing express racial classifications: Why should the children of two Black Harvard Law School graduates—call them the Obama daughters—receive a break in college admissions when a break is denied to the poor sons and daughters of Appalachia?

At first blush, a sheer economic preference program in admissions holds undeniable appeal. It taps into a defining feature of the American self-image as a land of upward mobility. *Ragged Dick* may have been published more than 150 years ago,

but Horatio Alger's tales continue to exercise a vise grip on the
American imagination. That grip holds today even as the actual
upward mobility rates in the United States have been outstripped by some European nations in recent decades. But as the
path to prosperity has narrowed, the American ethos nevertheless continues to cherish the ideal.

Upon careful inspection, though, simply swapping class
preferences for racial preferences in college admissions would
almost certainly have adverse consequences for the enrollment of Black students in leading universities. Yes, African
Americans are *disproportionately* poor. But given the nation's
racial demographics it is important to appreciate that America
has more poor white people than poor Black people in absolute numbers. Moreover, poor white applicants, for a variety of
reasons, more often obtain the standard academic credentials
that attract leading universities compared to their Black counterparts. Supporters of a crude class-based affirmative action
model to the exclusion of other preference programs have—
either wittingly or unwittingly—paved the road toward diminished Black enrollment in our foremost universities.

This understanding of the class-race tradeoff is not exactly
a new revelation. In 1979, one year after *Bakke*, then-Professor
J. Harvie Wilkinson III explained in detail why substitut-
ing class affirmative action for racial affirmative action would
work to increase white enrollment. "While a high percentage of
blacks were doubtless disadvantaged, almost two-thirds of the
nation's poor were white," he wrote. "And because low income
whites outscored low income blacks, adoption of a truly racially
neutral disadvantaged approach would do little more than substitute less-affluent whites for more-affluent whites." Two

150   decades later, William Bowen and Derek Bok—in their magis-
terial exploration of affirmative action's effects titled *The Shape
of the River*—further drove home this point. "[C]lass-based
preferences cannot be substituted for race-based policies if the
objective is to enroll a class that is both academically excellent
and diverse," they concluded. "[T]here are almost six times as
many white students as black students who both come from
low-[socio-economic status] families and have test scores that
are above the threshold for gaining admission to an academically selective college or university."

In recent years, some scholars have offered a creative twist
on class-based affirmative action by encouraging universities
to concentrate their efforts on college applicants who emerge
from socio-economically challenged areas of the country. In
2014, Professor Sheryll Cashin of Georgetown Law published
a prominent version of this idea in a book evocatively titled
Place, Not Race. Cashin suggested focusing upon whether applicants encountered poverty in their residential or educational
experiences.

This twist holds promise. Yet if universities offered applicants an undifferentiated low-opportunity preference, it seems
quite likely that the preference would overwhelmingly benefit
members of the white working class (as with the class-based
preference), and thereby fail to advance the goal of enrolling meaningful numbers of racial minorities from modest
backgrounds.

To address this concern, universities drawn to the low-
opportunity origin approach ought to consider placing two
additional specifications on the program. First, universities should contemplate setting a goal—or even a quota—of a

certain percentage of applicants who would be admitted under
the program. (Readers seized by the word "quota" would do well
to remember that the Supreme Court's opinion in *Bakke* invalidated *racial* quotas, not all admissions quotas. Indeed, many
admissions offices annually utilize a type of quota to ensure that
they can field a lacrosse team.) For ease of exposition, presume
that universities set aside 10 percent of each admitted class for
students from low-opportunity areas.

Next, the second, critical step that universities should
consider taking is to provide that of those admitted under
the preference, 80 percent will be drawn from urban areas and
20 percent will be drawn from rural areas. Those percentages
map onto the Census Bureau's own 2020 estimates of where the
American population resides, with 79.6 percent living in urban
areas and 20.4 percent living in rural areas. Given that Black
America is disproportionately urban and white America is disproportionately rural, this two-step approach would enable
universities to realize greater amounts of racial diversity than
a one-size-fits-all approach. Indeed, universities could even
monitor the particular low-opportunity areas where applicants are from in an effort to ensure that they are drawing students from a range of urban and rural environments. Different
parts of various cities, for example, present distinct challenges,
and nothing should prevent universities from pursuing a broad
cross-section of such environments.

This low-opportunity origin preference would be consistent with *SFFA*'s requirement that universities avoid treating
"race *qua* race." The effects of the preference may disproportionately favor racial minorities, but that does not mean that courts
interpreting *SFFA* would invalidate the admissions preference.

To the contrary, Roberts's majority opinion declared, "The entire point of the Equal Protection Clause is that treating someone differently because of their skin color is *not* like treating them differently because they are from a city or from a suburb. . . ." It is hard to imagine much clearer judicial authorization for universities to experiment with preferences based on applicants' neighborhoods.

Some proponents of the geographically driven version of affirmative action suggest focusing upon an applicant's postal zip code. But zip codes vary dramatically in their size, sometimes grouping more than 100,000 residents in one five-digit number. Zip codes in urban areas, moreover, often awkwardly group households living under highly variegated financial circumstances. My own zip code, 06511, includes not just Yale University, but the grand old mansions lining St. Ronan Street alongside tiny dwellings in some of New Haven's struggling neighborhoods.

Rather than relying upon the applicant's zip code, then, low-opportunity origin preferences should instead focus on the applicant's relevant census tract. These zones are both far more compact and far more uniform than zip codes, as census tracts aim to include approximately 4,000 residents and max out at about 8,000 residents. Given the shameful, stubborn persistence of racial isolation in housing, focusing upon urban low-opportunity census tracts could form a viable path for pursuing racial diversity in higher education. As one scholar has explained, as evaluated by "comprehensive measures of neighborhood disadvantage . . . 78% of Blacks live in 'high disadvantage' neighborhoods, compared with just 5% of Whites." These figures are stark and depressing, but this is one instance where today's racialized American ghettos actually present an opportunity.

A team of economists led by Raj Chetty and John Friedman have developed a particularly promising tool along these lines called the Opportunity Atlas. This publicly available system draws upon a massive dataset to identify neighborhoods where children's success in adulthood is a longshot, where such success is the norm, and everywhere between those two polarities. Informed by US Census data, the Atlas projects the widely varying opportunities available in neighborhoods by considering a multitude of factors—including parental income, incarceration rates, and teen birth rates. The Atlas can be viewed as being driven by the core insight that, as the maxim holds: "Talent is everywhere, but opportunity is not." With the Atlas's data-driven understandings, universities can help to ensure that opportunities for upward mobility in the United States become more prevalent.

Following *SFFA v. Harvard*, Yale College started consulting the Opportunity Atlas as one part of its admissions process. Unlike far too many of its peer institutions, Yale avoided the plunging enrollments of Black and brown students in their initial post-*SFFA* class. Yale's relative success in matriculating Black and brown students could have, of course, been driven by a variety of factors. But it seems eminently sensible to suggest that more universities should follow suit, and use the Opportunity Atlas in the hopes of identifying the many academic stars hidden in our urban and rural skies.

If universities do insist on implementing sheer class-based preferences, it would be wise for them to focus not on familial *income*, but instead on familial *wealth*. While the Black-white

154 income gap persists and remains significant, the much larger disparity arises from racial discrepancies in net worth. In 2022, the average wealth of white families reached nearly $1.4 million, whereas the average wealth of Black families barely cracked $200,000. If universities established a sliding scale of preferences based on net wealth, it could play a helpful role in boosting Black enrollment. As David Leonhardt has noted in the *New York Times*, for example, universities might consider "an admissions policy that gave extra consideration to a student who grew up in a family with a net worth of less than $30,000 [because] [m]ost Black households fall into that category; only a small share of white households do." This paucity of Black net wealth stems from the cumulative, intergenerational economic effects of racial animus in both the public and private sectors. The persistent backers of class-based affirmative action—who have sometimes been tagged with the motto "class not race"— should now adopt a new mantra: "wealth not income."

Preferences for Local Schools

Another promising, constitutionally valid method for leading universities to pursue racial diversity post-*SFFA* is to form sustained partnerships with local high schools that lack a strong track record of sending students to their region's academic powerhouse. The looming ivory towers of our nation's elite universities often cast long shadows on Black and brown neighborhoods. Even a partial listing of this phenomenon includes: Columbia's Washington Heights, the University of Chicago's South Side, Georgetown's Anacostia, Harvard's Roxbury, Johns Hopkins's West Baltimore, the University of Pennsylvania's North Philadelphia, and Stanford's East Palo Alto. The best public high school students from those neighborhoods, alas, have seldom realized the dream of matriculating just down the road. If these wealthy universities dedicated significant resources to identifying, preparing, and recruiting the most talented students who attend some of the public high schools located just beneath their nostrils, that strategy could play a modest, but nevertheless helpful role in remedying *SFFA*'s effects. Even setting aside the racial benefits of this strategy, moreover, universities should attempt to deepen such partnerships because they would help to bridge the yawning chasm that too often separates glitzy gowns from un-ritzy towns.

There is a long, if not always glorious, tradition of leading universities forging tight bonds with particular secondary schools. Phillips Academy, located in Andover, Massachusetts, for example, long sent a fleet of its most able students to Yale College. The Boston Latin School, which was founded in 1635, has sent droves of students to Harvard College, which was founded one year later. As one of Boston Latin's college counselors told the *Harvard Crimson* not long ago: "There's a joke that Harvard was started a year after our school as a place for our students to go." Not everyone, of course, finds that joke amusing, as it tidily encapsulates how outsized opportunity traverses the corridors of only select American high schools. In 2013, fully 5 percent of Harvard College's entering class graduated from one of just seven high schools. For some context, roughly 20,000 public and private high schools exist in the United States.*

---

*Of the seven Harvard super-feeder high schools, four were located in Massachusetts (Andover, Boston Latin, Lexington, and Noble and Greenough School), two were located in Manhattan (Stuyvesant and Trinity), and one was located in New Hampshire (Exeter).

156   Fostering university partnerships with a distinct set of our nation's high schools would not therefore represent an affront to American higher education. Rather, these partnerships sketched above would simply serve to democratize a privilege that has overwhelmingly been reserved for the upper crust.

Happily, some prestigious universities today seek meaningful partnerships with local high schools whose student bodies have—for generations—been largely untapped resources. In 2024, for example, Yale College announced that its incoming class included twenty-one students who attended New Haven public schools—the largest total in its more than three centuries of existence. Relatedly, the University of Virginia announced that it had identified forty high schools located in eight distinct areas of the Commonwealth that had paltry records of sending students to Charlottesville. Graduates of those forty targeted schools, UVA determined, would receive particular solicitude in the admissions process. One UVA study found that a significant part of the problem stemmed from the fact that students who attended struggling schools seldom even applied to the flagship university, perhaps viewing it as hopelessly out of reach. More universities ought to follow the inspired leads of Yale and UVA by redoubling efforts to land the talented minds in their own backyards who did not enjoy the good fortune of attending a traditional feeder high school.

The local partnership strategy runs no risk of violating *SFFA*. Targeting local, historically disadvantaged schools for admissions preferences cannot be viewed as using "race *qua* race." Conservatives have long bemoaned that affirmative action helped privileged racial minorities who already had the benefit of attending the nation's Andovers. But the local partnership

program, without resorting to forbidden individual racial classifications, could largely aid Black and brown students at the
bottom rungs of our socio-economic ladder.

One hardly needs to be a wild-eyed leftist to believe that the
Constitution permits local partnerships. In *SFFA*'s wake, Professor
McConnell—a pillar of the conservative legal community—
stated that an "applicant [who] is coming from . . . one of
these . . . catastrophically underperforming public schools
[a]nd . . . who excels coming from those schools . . . should get a
very significant boost." Amen.

The Fall and Rise of Box-checking

SFFA has been broadly interpreted as prohibiting admissions
offices from consulting the racial boxes that once adorned college applications. In anticipation of affirmative action's end, the
Common Application—which serves as a sort of college applications clearinghouse—preemptively announced that universities would be given the ability to conceal the racial boxes even
before the Supreme Court rendered its decision. Chief Justice
Roberts's *SFFA* opinion, as a formal matter, did not expressly
prohibit racial boxes. But, given the ominous cloud of litigation now polluting university air, it is understandable—if not
downright prudent—that admissions offices have opted to wall
themselves off from viewing racial boxes during the selection
process.

The decline of *racial* boxes post-*SFFA* does not mean, however, that universities are banned from considering any boxes
altogether. Colleges continue to access gender boxes on applications, and sometimes their admissions decisions even turn on
the desire to retain roughly equivalent percentages of male and

female students. But post-*SFFA*, universities might consider adding several new boxes that are correlated with both disadvantage and underrepresented racial populations at the nation's leading universities.

The box-checking approach would address a major concern that has arisen regarding the transformed admissions landscape created by the Supreme Court's decision. Many universities have responded to *SFFA* by adding supplementary essays to their applications, seeking to elicit encounters with racial hardship. But, as emphasized in chapter one, many applicants would surely chafe at being both commanded to perform their racial trauma, and inhibited from defining themselves however they deem fit. In addition, these supplementary essay prompts impose time-intensive labor on students who may well decide to reduce their number of applications rather than draft and refine yet another batch of individualized essays. Checking boxes, though, is a relatively quick, painless way for universities to obtain a treasure trove of potentially valuable information. The rise of a new sort of box-checking could thus form a valuable tool—one that imposes fewer burdens on students from marginalized backgrounds—as universities attempt to minimize the damage wrought by *SFFA*.

What sorts of boxes might universities now consider adding to their applications? Consider a few illustrative possibilities. Was the applicant born to unwed parents? Was the applicant raised primarily in a single-parent household? Does the applicant's family rent, rather than own, their residence? Does the applicant have a close family member (*i.e.*, parent or sibling) who is or has been incarcerated? Answers in the affirmative to any of these queries (let alone all four) are disproportionately

found among high schoolers who not only have led lives of relative hardship, but also have a Black or brown racial identity.
Universities could over time amass the answers to these sorts
of questions—and many others besides—thereby determining how to navigate higher education's new choppy waters most
effectively.

The Future Equal Protection Clause

The proposals outlined above, as I have repeatedly noted, pass
the constitutional test announced in *SFFA*. I do not suffer from
the delusion, however, that *SFFA* will somehow become the
Supreme Court's final word on race and admissions in higher
education. That contentious issue has been and will, in various
forms, doubtless remain an evergreen in the forest of American
constitutionalism. *SFFA* can thus be viewed not only as clos-
ing a major chapter in that saga, but also opening a crucial new
chapter.

It is possible some proposals that are perfectly constitutional today will, many years down the line, be deemed patently
unconstitutional. Such an eventuality would hardly be a startling turn of events in our constitutional order. Indeed, the
overarching narrative of the Fourteenth Amendment's Equal
Protection Clause is the story of the Supreme Court moving the doctrinal goalposts. Such moves are sometimes desirable. In 1896, the Supreme Court in *Plessy v. Ferguson* ruled that
measures requiring racially segregated railcars did not violate
equal protection principles. Fifty-eight years later, the Supreme
Court in *Brown v. Board of Education* retreated from that decision, declaring the *Plessy* regime "inherently unequal." *Brown*
transformed the nation's constitutional understanding of what

160   equality demands. But *SFFA*'s repudiation of *Bakke*, *Grutter*, and *Fisher* also transformed the nation's constitutional understanding of equality. While I regard *Brown* as a zenith and *SFFA* as a nadir, the basic, oft-overlooked point here is that, since the Equal Protection Clause was ratified more than a century and a half ago, its only constant has been change.

When—not if, but *when*—the Supreme Court eventually modifies the Equal Protection Clause's meaning post-*SFFA*, it could well further restrict the ability of universities to pursue Black, brown, and Native students. Right-wing efforts to move the contemporary goalposts of constitutionality began many years ago. Some conservative scholars, for instance, have long argued that the Fourteenth Amendment, properly understood, prohibits universities from implementing admissions approaches that seek to promote racial diversity, even if those approaches are racially neutral on their faces. The most familiar such admissions program is the University of Texas's Top Ten Percent plan, which avoids racially classifying individual students, but was adopted in an effort to boost Black and brown enrollment. In the past, the Supreme Court has repeatedly taken it for granted that the Top Ten Percent plan and its ilk pass constitutional muster.

The assumptions of yore, however, may eventually erode. Indeed, in 2024, some conservative justices indicated that they wished to reevaluate the constitutionality of race-neutral admissions approaches that seek diversity when the jurists sought to invalidate a new admissions model adopted by Thomas Jefferson High School in Fairfax County, Virginia. Thomas Jefferson, a nationally renowned magnet school, abandoned its traditional standardized test in favor of an approach that prioritized drawing students from a broader range of middle schools, including those educating large percentages of indigent students. The new admissions model succeeded in increasing Black and brown enrollment. Not surprisingly, given the high stakes of elite magnet school admissions, the Thomas Jefferson controversy generated a lawsuit and enormous media coverage. It did not, however, generate enough support at the Supreme Court to even hear the case, let alone to modify the prevailing constitutional order.

The Court's inaction did not prevent the Trump administration's Department of Education from circulating a letter in February 2025 asserting *SFFA* prohibits universities from generally pursuing racial diversity, even if they used race-neutral mechanisms in that pursuit. The explosive letter contended that universities could not shift their admissions approaches in any way if those shifts were motivated by a desire to enhance racial diversity. The letter stated, for example, that universities could not abandon standardized testing in admissions if such decisions were driven by diversity considerations. This reading of *SFFA* would also prohibit universities from, say, courting students from low-opportunity census tracts, or prioritizing students from underprivileged local schools—if they did so seeking to increase Black and brown enrollment. But *SFFA* did not in fact outlaw the goal of racial diversity; rather, it simply curtailed the means by which universities might pursue that goal, namely reliance upon racial classifications. Even SFFA founder Edward Blum conceded that the Trump administration had interpreted the opinion's meaning in a slipshod fashion. "There are race-neutral factors that will be perfectly legal, as well as fair, in admissions decisions," Blum allowed.

In all events, universities ought not get too far out in front of anticipating what moves the current right-wing Supreme Court will next impose. Diffidence in this arena will have regrettable consequences in the nation's ongoing march toward racial justice. In *SFFA*'s aftermath, one university official suggested that a curtain of undue caution had quickly descended over higher education, as university leaders exhibited a "tremendous lack of courage," and excessive retreat: "We are watching people start to cut off their arms before anybody tells them you need to cut off your arms. . . . They're volunteering to do it." Rather than battening down the hatches in anticipation of a deluge that may or may not materialize, university leaders should dedicate themselves to exploring the many channels that remain viable.

If the Supreme Court ultimately invalidates some admissions plans that arise in response to *SFFA*, moreover, those events should not overshadow the good that those plans can achieve in the interim. Litigation often takes considerable time, especially in legal disputes arising at the intersection of race and university admissions. The period stretching from SFFA's initial lawsuit against Harvard on November 17, 2014, through the Supreme Court's final decision on June 29, 2023, lasted more than eight and a half years. Similarly, the *Fisher* litigation against the University of Texas lasted more than eight years, and the *Grutter* litigation against the University of Michigan lasted more than five and a half years. Even the *Bakke* litigation against UC Davis, back in the 1970s, spanned more than four years. Those figures suggest that, even if a newly adopted university policy immediately draws litigation that eventually results in an adverse Supreme Court ruling, many, many underrepresented students of color would in the meantime be able to obtain an

elite education who otherwise would have been denied one. The
effects of those horizon-broadening admissions decisions will
assuredly reverberate across generations.

I wish to be very clear here, though, that I in no way encourage universities to defy the Supreme Court's decision in *SFFA*.
If an admissions office, say, scoured applicants' social media
accounts attempting to verify racial identities, that approach
would blatantly violate *SFFA*. Similarly, if admissions officers boosted an applicant because they believed the applicant's
name almost certainly belonged to a Black person (*e.g.,* Khalil
Greene), or lowered an applicant because they believed that
the applicant's name almost certainly belonged to a white person (*e.g.,* Troy O'Leary), those moves would also plainly violate
SFFA's mandate.*

I therefore unreservedly denounce any such defiance of *SFFA*.
I understand that many university officials detest the Supreme
Court's decision and believe that they—not the justices—
reside on the right side of history. But I also understand well
that previous, deeply committed actors believed that the
Supreme Court erred grievously when it issued *Brown v. Board*.
Their subsequent demonstrations of outright defiance against
Brown marked a searing cautionary tale in American history. We

---

* The names I have selected are drawn from former Major League Baseball
players. Their racial identities, though, are exactly the opposite of what
many readers would suppose. Khalil Greene, who played shortstop for the
San Diego Padres, is white; Troy O'Leary, an outfielder for the Boston Red
Sox in the 1990s, is Black. For related analysis, see Bill Simmons, "Mail Call
for Sports Guy," *ESPN* (May 9, 2002), https://www.espn.com/espn/page2
/story?page=simmons/020509 (describing the "Reggie Cleveland Group," as
the phenomenon where "you think a random baseball player is black and
they turn out to be white, or vice versa").

164   should be in no hurry to repeat such subversions, even in pursuit of a cause believed to be righteous. Adherence to the rule of
law cannot descend into a fair-weather sport.

Of course, even readers who are sympathetic to this chapter's broad aims may nevertheless object to these proposals on
varied grounds of overinclusivity and underinclusivity. The
preferences, that is, may simultaneously sweep in some applicants who should be left out and leave out other applicants who
should be swept in. On the overinclusive terrain, for example, what if a white college applicant—whose well-educated
bohemian parents opt to reside in an impoverished urban
area—qualifies for a low-opportunity preference? Or what if
a different white student who lives in a privileged neighborhood elects to attend an elite college's new partnership school
and wins admission? Conversely, on the underinclusive terrain, what about a college applicant who is a third-generation
Mexican American and who therefore would not qualify for an
immigrant preference? Or why should a Native American who
happens to lack card-carrying proof of her Lakota tribal status
be ineligible to receive an admissions bump? Additional, compelling examples on both fronts might easily be adduced.

Responses to these objections could follow a couple of different paths. As a first cut, the theoretically overinclusive preference recipients might be construed not as blatant vices, but
instead as subtle virtues. White students who either grew up in
blighted portions of cities or attended underperforming urban
high schools are a rarity on elite college campuses today, and
these policies could help to change that. Those students, moreover, may bring important insights and perspectives that their
classmates would otherwise lack. Even if sophisticated, wealthy

white parents seek to manipulate some of the new preferences, those manipulations could nevertheless bring desirable,
second-order benefits for the larger society. Those parents, now
that they have some skin in the game, may use their comparative
affluence and influence to advocate for systemic improvements
to destitute neighborhoods and dilapidated high schools.

The second, more discerning response, readily concedes
that these policies imperfectly realize their objectives. But that
statement applies to *all* policies. The aim here is not to solve
every problem that *SFFA* created, but rather to produce a system
that is better than the ones that many universities now employ
after *SFFA*. Critics who would permit occasional policy mis-
fires to scuttle entire plans are the very same people who battle hunger pains but refuse to settle for a half-loaf of bread when
a full loaf is nowhere on the horizon. Many years ago, Professor
Charles Black of Yale Law School offered an eloquent version of
this idea in a quite distinct context: "When we are faced with
difficulties of 'how much,' it is often helpful to step back and
think small, and to ask not 'What is the whole extent of what we
are bound to do?' but rather 'What is the clearest thing we ought
to do first?'" This chapter has aimed to identify some of those
initial, but often elusive first steps.

Lessons
and Legacies

The affirmative action wars have been raging for several decades, dating back to the period immediately following the policy's widespread adoption in the late 1960s. But *SFFA* provides a major inflection point in those wars. Yes, the Supreme Court has repeatedly issued decisions involving affirmative action. But those prior opinions can all be viewed as providing minor variations on the same major theme: the Court has routinely found that affirmative action passes constitutional muster— provided universities do not consider race in too mechanical a fashion. *SFFA*'s elimination of affirmative action represents a sea change, and the opinion will provide a focal point for years and even decades to come, as society will continually struggle with the legal decision's implications.

Consider only two momentous events that occurred one year after the Court issued *SFFA*. First, in September 2024, SFFA issued litigation hold letters to Duke, Princeton, and Yale, contending that the racial compositions of their newly admitted classes reveal that they have flouted *SFFA*'s requirements. The

student bodies at those universities did not experience a stark
contraction in Black enrollment, and reported a decline among
Asian Americans. SFFA President Edward Blum sent virtually
identical letters to all three revered universities stating, "SFFA is
deeply concerned that you are not complying with [the Court's
opinion]," and demanding that they "[p]reserve all potentially relevant documents and communications," and caution-
ing: "You are now on notice." The *Wall Street Journal* editorial
page noted this development under a headline reading: "Racial
Preferences on the Sly?" Professor John Yoo of Berkeley—a conservative legal luminary—went much further, nakedly asserting that some of the nation's premier universities have simply
defied the Supreme Court: "They're cheating. Everyone knows
they're cheating. They know they're cheating. What they are
trying to do is cheat in a way that doesn't get them caught in
court." Professor Richard Sander similarly asserted: "If [uni-
versities'] race numbers really don't change, I think that means
that they're looking for any evidence they can find that a student is African American or Black, and they're admitting them
under the same criteria they were before." These disputes will
likely take a long time to wend their way through the legal system, and that guarantees that arguments about *SFFA*'s meaning
will not abate anytime soon.

Second, seeking to extend the Supreme Court's decision
to all educational contexts, SFFA filed a lawsuit against the US
Naval Academy, contending that it, too, should be required to
embrace constitutional colorblindness. In December 2024, a
federal judge in Baltimore, Maryland, rejected that claim, reasoning that the Roberts Court set aside the nation's military
academies in *SFFA*'s fourth footnote with good reason, and

168   therefore that they could continue using affirmative action programs. Blum immediately announced that SFFA would appeal that decision, and the matter could quite plausibly someday return to the Supreme Court.

Although *SFFA* remains in its infancy, it is not too early to identify and evaluate some of the early legacies and lessons that emerge from examining the opinion and placing it in a broader context. *SFFA* throws fresh light on the Supreme Court's role in American society, the efficacy of legal opinions, egalitarian ideals in higher education, and the abhorrent politics animating the conservative movement's attack on racial diversity.

After the Court issued *SFFA* in June 2023, as former President Donald Trump's ultimately successful bid to reclaim the Oval Office gained steam, he took to Truth Social and celebrated the decision as "a great day for America." Trump—who had installed three Supreme Court Justices, all of whom joined the majority—further noted: "Our greatest minds must be cherished and that's what this wonderful day has brought." Suggesting that *SFFA* fit snugly with his promise to Make America Great Again, Trump stated: "People with extraordinary ability and everything else necessary for success, including future greatness for our Country, are finally being rewarded." A spokesperson for MAGA, Inc., similarly noted: "President Donald Trump made today's historic decision to end the racist college admissions process possible because he delivered on his promise to appoint constitutionalist justices."

In Arlington, Virginia, SFFA founder Edward Blum took a victory lap, as he had been actively plotting affirmative action's demise for more than a decade. Blum had orchestrated two prior

Supreme Court decisions that sought to eliminate affirmative action at his alma mater, the University of Texas. But twice
the Supreme Court rebuffed his advances. Blum's third effort,
with SFFA, proved to be the charm. Blum issued a press release,
extolling *SFFA* as a signal triumph. But he also issued a stern
warning: "We remain vigilant and intend to initiate litigation
should universities defiantly flout this clear ruling and the dic-
tates of . . . the Equal Protection Clause." In an adulatory *Wall
Street Journal* profile titled "Edward Blum, the Man Who Killed
Affirmative Action," he reiterated that he had not yet begun the
legal fight. "I will continue to bring challenges to other areas of
our public policies that are racially discriminatory," Blum promised. "These cases mark the end of the beginning, not the beginning of the end."

Those relatively sober statements, though, failed to capture
fully Blum's sense of elation. Blum imbued *SFFA* with something approaching divine authority. "[W]e're blessed to have
this Supreme Court opinion," he said. Indeed, when he heard
Chief Justice Roberts intone the opinion's most memorable
line—"Eliminating racial discrimination means eliminating all
of it"—Blum leapt from his chair with unbridled joy.

Where Blum was jubilant at his long-anticipated outcome,
just down the road in Baltimore, Maryland, Karsonya Wise
Whitehead had exactly the opposite reaction. Upon hearing the
news, she was so shaken, so despondent that she felt compelled
to sit down to contemplate "the type of history being made at
that moment." Whitehead's disquietude following *SFFA* was
far from isolated within Black America. NAACP Legal Defense
Fund President Janai Nelson lambasted *SFFA* as a betrayal of her
organization's greatest victory. "We roundly condemn . . . the

170   Supreme Court's decision . . . [for] distorting the legacy of the seminal decision in *Brown v. Board of Education*—which held that society must not turn a blind eye to racial inequality and can take necessary measures to address it," Nelson said. "We know that race still unquestionably matters in our society— particularly for Black people and others whose race has shaped their lived experiences in a country rooted in a history and current reality of racial injustice."

The Congressional Black Caucus called *SFFA* "so radical" an opinion that "the Supreme Court has thrown into question its own legitimacy." The CBC portrayed the decision as part of a racial "backlash" undertaken by "extremists [seeking] to turn back the clock on progress." Former President Barack Obama lamented the demise of affirmative action because it allowed "generations of students who had been systematically excluded from most of America's key institutions—it gave us the chance to show we more than deserved a seat at the table."

In a televised address from the Roosevelt Room, President Joe Biden stated that he "strongly, strongly disagree[d] with the Court's decision," as it threatened to thrust the nation "backwards." Biden, speaking with discernible passion, argued that *SFFA* contravened fundamental American values and aspirations. "America is an idea—an idea—unique in the world," Biden stated. "An idea of hope and opportunity, of possibilities, of giving everyone a fair shot, of leaving no one behind. We have never fully lived up to it, but we've never walked away from it either. We will not walk away from it now." After concluding his formal remarks, when preparing to exit the Roosevelt Room, a reporter shouted: "Is this a rogue Court?" As he approached the door, Biden paused for a moment, turned to the reporter, and responded: "This is not a normal Court."

At Harvard, President Lawrence Bacow, Provost Alan Garber, and the leaders of its various schools signed a highly unusual joint letter criticizing the Supreme Court's ruling. While pledging "[w]e will certainly comply with the Court's decision," Harvard's leadership also insisted that much would remain unchanged. "We write today to reaffirm the fundamental principle that deep and transformative teaching, learning, and research depend upon a community comprising people of many backgrounds, perspectives, and lived experiences," Harvard's leaders vowed. "That principle is as true and important today as it was yesterday."

Claudine Gay, who would officially become the first Black President of Harvard University two days after *SFFA*, issued her own statement mourning the opinion. "Today is a hard day," she stated, "and if you are feeling the gravity of that, I want you to know you're not alone." Ultimately, questions regarding affirmative action shadowed what would turn out to be Gay's vanishingly brief presidency. Right-wing activists dismissed Gay as a "DEI hire," and wielded plagiarism accusations against her to dislodge her from Harvard's helm after only six months. In retrospect, it seems clear that Gay's targeting and eventual ouster telegraphed the right's growing plans for transforming both elite higher education and DEI programs into all-purpose boogeymen.

Racial Revanchism

Edward Blum is a most improbable man to have become the legal architect of the Roberts Court's embrace of colorblind

172   constitutionalism. Most blatantly, this legal architect is not, by training, a lawyer at all; instead, Blum dedicated the early portion of his career at PaineWebber to amassing considerable wealth. In addition, Blum did not grow up in a conservative household, where William F. Buckley Jr.'s *National Review* was required reading. To the contrary, he was raised in a left-wing home in Benton Harbor, Michigan, by parents who worshipped President Franklin Roosevelt's New Deal. Even as an undergraduate attending the University of Texas in the early 1970s, Blum continued to conceive of himself as a committed liberal. By 1992, Blum had drifted far enough rightward that he ran as a Republican for a House of Representatives seat based in Houston. But that congressional race became Blum's radicalizing moment, one that transformed him into an ardent colorblind constitutionalist. Blum's personal road to Damascus ran precisely along the zigzagging boundaries of Texas's eighteenth congressional district. When Blum set out to knock on thousands of constituents' doors, he was alarmed to find it "was impossible to follow the contours of the district." The eighteenth district, in Blum's view, had been impermissibly drawn along racial lines in what he deemed a misguided, illegal effort to foster Black political representation.

        After losing the congressional race to a Black Democratic incumbent, Blum—flashing the convert's zeal—set his mind to destroying not only the Voting Rights Act, but any other programs that bucked his preferred mode of colorblind constitutionalism. Four years after his failed congressional bid, Blum prevailed as a plaintiff in a Supreme Court case asserting that some Texas congressional districts constituted unlawful racial gerrymandering. That victory served as a mere appetizer for Blum's main course: the dismantling of a key pro-vision of the Voting Rights Act. In 2007, Blum wrote a short book—published by the American Enterprise Institute—laying out his vision, not-so-imaginatively titled *The Unintended Consequences of Section 5 of the Voting Rights Act*. Whatever the title lacked in imagination, the book more than compen-sated for with influence, as the book provided the Roberts Court with an intellectual blueprint for destroying the Voting Rights Act. Section 5, often referred to as "the crown jewel" of the Civil Rights Movement, required jurisdictions (mostly in the South) to clear electoral changes before adopting them to make sure that they would not adversely affect racial minorities' voting rights. In 2013, in a lawsuit initiated by Blum, the Supreme Court in *Shelby County v. Holder* effectively invalidated Section 5, and mirrored the reasoning that Blum offered in his book.

Blum then turned his attention toward ending affirma-tive action. Although he encountered a few setbacks along the way, his victory in *SFFA* is without question Blum's master-piece. One of Blum's maxims holds: "You cannot remedy past discrimination with new discrimination." Blum, who describes himself as "an inveterate newspaper reader," arises at 4:30 a.m. every morning and then dedicates numerous hours to "noo-dl[ing] [his] way through [assorted articles] for about three hours looking around for misdeeds by various actors who are discriminating on the basis of race." Blum has called himself the legal equivalent of "Yenta the matchmaker": "I find the plaintiff, I find the lawyer, and I put them together, and then I worry about it for four years."

Yet it must not escape notice that, over the course of more than three decades, Blum has, evidently, *never* used his

174 significant power to fight racial discrimination directed against Black people. Thus, in a world beset by anti-Black racism, Blum has consistently and steadfastly declined to use his formidable matchmaking talents to help challenge such racism. The only racism that seems to make it onto Blum's radar is what was once deemed reverse racism. Indeed, SFFA's spotlighting of Asian American students appears to have stemmed less from any deep-seated outrage about alleged racial discrimination targeting that particular group, and more from tactical considerations about who would make for the most effective plaintiffs to fulfill his ambition of ending affirmative action. Ten years ago, Blum delivered a speech where he bluntly asserted, "I needed Asian plaintiffs." Many of Blum's critics have suggested that SFFA's litigation position does not genuinely speak on behalf of Asian Americans—deeming the organization less grassroots than AstroTurf.

When stepping back to appraise Blum's larger litigation pattern, the mosaic is a disturbing one. Many neutral observers would believe that the American elementary and secondary education system is rife with discrimination against Black students. The only discrimination regarding African Americans in that realm that Blum appears to see, however, benefits Black students. Thus, in the 1990s, Blum filed a lawsuit against the Houston Independent School District because he thought that the gifted and talented programs impermissibly used race to advantage Black students.

Many other neutral observers would detect discrimination in the economic sphere directed against Black people in general, and Black women in particular. But the only such discrimination that Blum seizes upon involves the supposedly illegal measures that seek, even in a modest way, to close large economic gaps. Thus, Blum's American Alliance for Equal Rights recently sued an organization—called the Fearless Fund—that sought to aid Black women entrepreneurs in their efforts to access venture capital. Given this litigation, one might suppose that Black women have become dominant players in the VC domain. But in fact reliable data establishes that VC organizations distribute far less than half of 1 percent to entities founded by Black women.

Blum's profound inattentiveness to anti-Black discrimination leaves the disconcerting impression that his primary motivation is not to end *all* racial discrimination in America, but instead to turn back the clock to a time when Black people knew their place—and stayed in it. His successful attack on affirmative action should be understood as but one part of today's larger, overarching anti-Black and anti-brown agenda that has amassed a disturbing amount of cultural and political influence.

It is critical to understand, then, that Edward Blum is in no sense a one-man movement. He is, rather, an unusually polished, camera-ready spokesperson for a much larger campaign that is predicated on mobilizing and capitalizing upon white grievance. That movement includes Jeremy Carl, author of *The Unprotected Class: How Anti-White Racism Is Tearing America Apart,* published by Regnery in 2024. (Read that title again.) This volume, written by an official from the first Trump administration who now serves as a senior fellow at the Claremont Institute, has gained a wide readership, and has been lauded by Donald Trump Jr., Christopher Rufo, and Tucker Carlson—among other right-wing royalty.

176 *The Unprotected Class* is an unvarnished apologia for white grievance politics, asserting that "anti-white racism is the predominant and most politically powerful form of racism in America today." Carl fears that his fellow white Americans living in rural areas "are in denial about the degree to which they have been replaced as the dominant ethnic group across much of America," and warns them that "a combination of the civil rights revolution and a flood of immigrants over the last sixty years, many from places with thin-to-nonexistent ties to America's core ethnic communities and cultural and social traditions, now wield tremendous political power, which they are using to advantage their groups over whites." In addition to the obligatory broadsides against affirmative action, *The Unprotected Class* catalogues what it portrays as an unrelenting scourge of hostility directed toward Caucasians that pervades America. "Anti-white animus isn't just confined to the silver screen," Carl explained, after criticizing *Black Panther*. "Racial mythmaking is also present in modern commercials, which, in service of an ideological agenda, consistently show higher levels of interracial relationships and friendships than exist in real life." Carl, a graduate of Yale College and Harvard's Kennedy School of Government, may sound like a card-carrying member of the lunatic fringe, but his ideas have now become thoroughly mainstream.

Surveying the plummeting Black enrollments that *SFFA* inflicted upon many premier universities, Carl nevertheless felt a keen sense of dismay. For Carl, the stable Black enrollment at some top colleges revealed that "America's anti-white regime will not just go away because of Court rulings." Carl, writing in *The American Mind*, called for a scorched-earth campaign to vindicate *SFFA*: "If we are going to change the status quo, we will need to ruthlessly enforce the Court's rulings, including massive fines, loss of jobs, revocation of federal funding, potential revocation of legal status for institutions, and punishment *including possible prison terms* for individuals who defy the law." Carl asserted: "[O]ur elite class, epitomized by the Ivy League, will do what it wants regardless of what the peasants decide (including the right-wing 'peasants' on the Supreme Court)."

Today, Blum and Carl have a spirited, ultrapowerful ally in the form of President Donald Trump, who has dedicated considerable effort early in his White House return to promoting the cause of colorblind constitutionalism. In his second inaugural address, delivered on the Martin Luther King Jr. federal holiday in January 2025, President Trump declared: "We will forge a society that is colorblind. . . ." This rhetoric was not aimless chatter. Within the first hours of his presidency, Trump in rapid succession: revoked Executive Order 11246, a six-decade-old measure from the Lyndon Johnson administration that prohibited racial discrimination by entities doing business with the government; placed government officials whose jobs were predicated on pursuing racial justice on leave; and instructed the federal government to investigate racial justice initiatives in the private and nonprofit sectors. The upshot of this blizzard of activity touting colorblindness in the first few days of the second Trump administration was readily apparent. As Professor Kenji Yoshino explained, the actions demonstrated unmistakably that "Trump is putting the muscle of the executive branch" behind *SFFA*. When historians reflect on the period that will one day be called the Age of

178   Trump, his racial revanchism will form a defining part of this dreadful epoch.*

The drawbacks of *SFFA* are considerable and clear: a stark diminution of the Black student bodies—in both literal and metaphorical senses of that term—at the nation's leading universities that will eventually yield a similar reduction within the professional sphere. But will *SFFA* realize its hopes of producing a society where skin color is of no greater significance than eye color? SFFA's founder Edward Blum has suggested that if universities actually adhere to the decision, then some of the nation's racial problems will be alleviated. After M.I.T. announced a massive decline in Black enrollment, Blum stated: "Every student admitted to the class of 2028 at M.I.T. will know that they were accepted only based upon their outstanding academic and extracurricular achievements, not the color of their skin."

The experiences in states that long ago eliminated affirmative action, however, suggest that we should not expect our post-racial nirvana to arrive anytime soon. Consider, for example, the travails of Kyra Abrams, a Black undergraduate at UC Berkeley in 2018. Given that Black students accounted for a small percentage of Berkeley's student population and that affirmative action was outlawed at California's public universities

---

*Darren Beattie, who occupies a senior position in the second Trump administration's State Department, offers a vivid avatar of racial revanchism. In 2024, he wrote that "competent white men must be in charge if you want things to work." Beattie also has an extensive history telling Black citizens to bend "a knee to MAGA," and that they "must learn their place" in American society. Andrew Kaczynski, Jennifer Hansler & Em Steck, "Trump Appoints Speechwriter Fired for Attending Conference with White Nationalists to Top State Department Role," *CNN*, February 3, 2025.

more than two decades prior, one might have thought that any
lingering anti-Black stigma about racial preferences would
have long since been extinguished. But Abrams repeatedly—
and painfully—found that was not the case. One of Abrams's
classmates nakedly informed her that she must have gained
admission to Berkeley exclusively due to her Blackness. When
Abrams's classmates formed computer science study groups,
she noticed that, somehow, she consistently failed to receive
invitations. "They don't think Black students are smart enough
to be in their clubs," Abrams explained. Black students were so
rare on Berkeley's campus that when Abrams walked through
the bustling Sproul Plaza, she noticed that students distributing
flyers did not even attempt to give her one—evidently presuming she was not a student. This phenomenon was sufficiently
commonplace that it had a darkly comic name: "Sprouling while
Black." If these Berkeley experiences augur the nation's post-
SFFA racial future, some might be forgiven for wanting to maintain the pre-*SFFA* status quo.

The Supreme Court as a Hollow Hope?
SFFA also sheds light on a long-standing debate in legal circles that focuses on the Supreme Court's capacity for issuing
decisions that change American society. The most important book in this debate—now in its third edition—is Professor
Gerald Rosenberg's *The Hollow Hope: Can Courts Bring About
Social Change?* Rosenberg answered the question posed in his
subtitle with a resounding, emphatic: "No!" Rosenberg's prime
example of a feckless Supreme Court opinion is *Brown v. Board
of Education*. It may be appealing to believe that *Brown* changed
everything and caused widespread school desegregation in the

180   South, Rosenberg noted, but that belief is erroneous. Rosenberg argued that the Supreme Court ordered school desegregation to occur and very little school desegregation in fact occurred, at least in the Deep South. Meaningful desegregation emerged in the South, Rosenberg added, only after Congress in effect endorsed the Supreme Court's opinion in *Brown* by threatening to withhold federal funding from jurisdictions that maintained Jim Crow schools. For Rosenberg, this lesson from *Brown* is unmistakable: when the Supreme Court acts alone in attempting to challenge a deeply held view, it is powerless to do so. For a judicial opinion to be effective in the face of fierce opposition, Rosenberg posited, the Supreme Court needs help from other governmental actors. "In explaining the changes that occurred in civil rights in the years after *Brown*," Rosenberg argued, "it is clear that paradigms based on court efficacy are simply wrong."

When Rosenberg first floated this vision of *Brown*—and of an anemic Supreme Court—in the early 1990s, it was widely deemed heretical. Over time, however, Rosenberg's view became ascendant and then dominant. In a 2004 law review article titled "What *Brown* Teaches Us About Constitutional Theory," Professor Jack Balkin of Yale Law School paid tribute to Rosenberg's theory. "The political history surrounding *Brown* suggests that, by themselves, courts are relatively slow to act and ineffective when social movements ask them to vindicate their rights," Balkin wrote. "When they work in tandem with other branches of government, however, their contributions in shaping legal doctrine are amplified by the work of others and often become quite important." Balkin proceeded to offer an evocative metaphor, capturing the notion that the Supreme Court is an enfeebled branch of government:

Judges are sort of like place kickers in football. Most place kickers are pretty bad at making an open-field tackle to stop a speedy running back returning a kickoff. But place kickers can help pile on after the other players have tackled or slowed down a runner. That is sometimes how I imagine courts and their relationship to social change: They see the running back lying on the ground, groaning under the weight of a huge pile of linebackers. The judges say to themselves, 'It's time for us to do some justice!' and they throw themselves on the pile.

The Supreme Court's decision in *SFFA*, however, complicates the notion that litigants err when they place their faith in courts to produce social change. Conservatives have, of course, long detested affirmative action. But they consistently failed to gain traction in convincing universities to abandon the consideration of race in university admissions. Rather, university administrators have deeply, consistently, and overwhelmingly pledged allegiance to the racial diversity ethos. Rosenberg's theory thus suggests that a judicial opinion invalidating affirmative action should have proven spectacularly ineffectual without assistance from other governmental actors.

SFFA contradicted the firmly held views of elite university leaders, many of whom issued statements expressing profound disagreement with the Supreme Court's decision, and reaffirming their commitment to racial diversity. President Christina Paxson of Brown University, for instance, issued a statement only hours after *SFFA* appeared, calling herself "deeply disappointed in the Supreme Court ruling," and "underscor[ing] that Brown is and will remain firmly committed to advancing the diversity that is central to achieving the highest standards of academic excellence and preparing our students to grow and lead in a complex world." Brown is not, of course, primarily known as a hotbed of conservatism, and some of Paxson's signature initiatives prior to *SFFA* extolled diversity's importance. Nevertheless, when the Supreme Court issued that opinion, the liberal leader of that famously liberal campus felt sufficiently constrained by the decision that Black enrollment plunged by 40 percent. That change—one that was experienced at many leading universities—is a testament to the Supreme Court's ample capacity for issuing efficacious decisions, even when they contravene powerful actors' foundational commitments.

M.I.T.'s Dean of Admissions Stu Schmill offered an unusually vivid account of how the Court's decision in *SFFA* thwarted and frustrated an academic vision that many university leaders cherish. After M.I.T. saw its Black enrollment fall 66 percent due to *SFFA*, Schmill complained in 2024: "[T]here are now fewer African-American first-years enrolling at M.I.T. than when *I* was a freshman more than forty years ago." Schmill continued, "[T]hat cannot *possibly* be the right outcome for our community; not in a country as large and increasingly diverse as ours, and not at an institution with our history and our values." M.I.T. President Sally Kornbluth issued her own anguished statement, making clear that she "care[s] so deeply" about her institution's declining "racial and ethnic diversity," and attributing the decline to a "consequence of last year's Supreme Court decision." Schmill and Kornbluth palpably wanted to maintain a robust Black enrollment at M.I.T., but the adverse Supreme Court decision prevented them and their colleagues from reaching their preferred destination.

In diminishing the Black enrollment at the nation's eminent universities, conservative litigants achieved a nationwide victory that would have been unthinkable without prevailing in Supreme Court litigation. In *SFFA*, then, conservatives' hope in the federal judiciary proved anything but hollow.

Roberts's Radicalism

Chief Justice Roberts enjoys a reputation as both an institutionalist and an incrementalist, a jurist who is dedicated to ensuring that the Supreme Court serves as a stabilizing force in American society. That reputation has certainly not been invented out of whole cloth. Indeed, Roberts is far less willing to rethink entire legal doctrines from the ground up than, say, Justice Thomas, who believes that original public meaning must be vindicated though the heavens may fall. Juxtaposing the two jurists, Chief Justice Roberts's desire to preserve the existing legal order can mark him as a constitutional conservative; whereas Justice Thomas's refusal to follow precedent if it does not accord with his preferred methodology can mark him not as a constitutional conservative, but instead as a constitutional radical.

The sharply divergent positions that Chief Justice Roberts and Justice Thomas recently adopted in *Dobbs v. Jackson Women's Health Organization* exemplify this dichotomy. For his part, Roberts's concurring opinion preferred to uphold Mississippi's fifteen-week ban on abortions, but nevertheless sought to avoid overruling *Roe v. Wade* and *Planned Parenthood v. Casey* "all the way down to the studs," by finding that the ban did not pose an undue burden on the right to an abortion. In contrast, Justice Thomas's concurrence in *Dobbs* not only advocated gutting *Roe* and *Casey*, but further encouraged his colleagues to

184   rethink other landmark opinions in that line of cases, including the constitutional right to same-sex marriage that the Court recognized in 2015.

SFFA unmistakably reveals, however, that the dominant portrait of Chief Justice Roberts as an incremental institutionalist is overdrawn, at least when it comes to race. When push met shove in the arena of race-conscious decision-making—a core jurisprudential project for Roberts—he shed institutionalism in favor of radicalism. Seeing Roberts—and thus the Court that bears his name—with clarity means understanding that, if he feels sufficient passion about the underlying issue, he is all-too-willing to embrace his inner Justice Thomas.

At first blush, this account may sound utterly intuitive. But it nonetheless bears emphasizing because *SFFA*'s radicalism fails the very models that Chief Justice Roberts himself has pledged to follow. Measuring *SFFA* by his own jurisprudential standards, then, Roberts's opinion comes up short.

Following the completion of his first term on the Court in 2006, Chief Justice Roberts gave a remarkable extended interview to *The Atlantic*'s Jeffrey Rosen. The Chief Justice articulated something like a juridical mission statement that could be used for evaluating his tenure at the Court. "I think judicial temperament is a willingness to step back from your own committed views of the correct jurisprudential approach and evaluate those views in terms of your role as a judge," he stated. "It's the difference between being a judge and being a law professor." While law professors might understandably value holding a consistent *personal* position over time, Roberts suggested, jurists should instead focus on the Court holding a consistent *institutional* position over time. Roberts expressly extolled judges who

were willing to "factor in the Court's institutional role," which
Rosen summed up as "a willingness . . . to suppress his or her
ideological agenda in the interest of achieving . . . stability."

Chief Justice Roberts commended one of his predecessors
for elevating the Court's institutional role above his own ideological commitments in a hotly disputed field for the purpose
of promoting stability. When then-Justice William Rehnquist
joined the Court in the early 1970s and when Roberts clerked
for him in October Term 1980, Rehnquist was the Court's foremost critic of *Miranda v. Arizona*. Nevertheless, in 2000, when
the Court had an opportunity to overrule the *Miranda* warnings
it extended to criminal suspects, Chief Justice Rehnquist wrote
the Court's opinion fundamentally affirming the decision's
continued vitality. Chief Justice Roberts deemed this turnabout
laudable, and consistent with his vision of judging that emphasizes continuity: "[Rehnquist] appreciated that [*Miranda*] had
become part of the law—that it would do more harm to uproot
it—and he wrote that opinion as chief for the good of the institution." Relatedly, he acknowledged that, when new justices
join the Court, concerns heighten about longstanding precedents being jettisoned, as the institution "seem[s] to be lurching around because of changes in personnel."

It is admirable that Chief Justice Roberts dedicated energy
to contemplating and articulating his vision of judging at the
outset of his time leading the Court. One way to understand
this gesture is that Roberts sought to bind himself to the mast,
publicly extolling a judicial vision that prioritizes stability and
institutionalism and therefore eschews ideologically driven
careening because of new justices' arrivals. On this theory, the
public proclamation of judicial humility offered early in his

186   tenure would diminish temptations to embrace a more ideological approach down the line.

But Roberts's opinion in *SFFA* managed to violate virtually every tenet of the judicial approach that he announced two decades ago. The opinion evinced no willingness whatsoever to relinquish his own ideological priors in order to embrace the larger institutional considerations, as Rehnquist had in his latter-day affirmation of *Miranda*. Indeed, it is difficult to understand *SFFA*'s swift disavowal of affirmative action as anything other than a "lurch[] . . . because of changes in personnel." Between the Court's decisions in *Fisher II* and *SFFA*, Justice Kavanaugh replaced Justice Kennedy, and Justice Barrett replaced Justice Ruth Bader Ginsburg; those two replacements effectively signed affirmative action's death warrant. Moreover, if ever there were a time when institutional considerations prizing stability may have been thought to eclipse an individual Justice's ideological commitments, it would have been 2023, as the nation reeled from *Dobbs*'s recent repudiation of *Roe v. Wade*. But these weighty considerations all proved insufficient to cause Roberts to swerve from his pursuit of constitutional colorblindness.

Roberts's *SFFA* opinion also fails the standard that he attributed to Judge Henry J. Friendly, the towering jurist for whom a young Roberts clerked on the US Court of Appeals for the Second Circuit. Even accounting for the generous amounts of adulation that law clerks routinely shower upon "their" judges, Roberts revered Judge Friendly to an unusual degree. During his time on the DC Circuit, then-Judge Roberts managed to cite Judge Friendly in six opinions, even though he published fewer than fifty opinions total during his two years on that court. Consistent with this high esteem, then-Judge Roberts noted during his Supreme Court confirmation hearings in 2005 that Friendly "ha[d] an essential humility about him. He was an absolute genius." Judge Friendly's fundamental humility figured prominently in then-Judge Roberts's conception of the qualities that made for a model jurist. Roberts pressed this point in his 2005 opening statement: "Judges have to have the humility to recognize that they operate within a system of precedent shaped by other judges equally striving to live up to the judicial oath." But Roberts's *SFFA* opinion, by effectively overturning decades of accumulated precedents, exhibited little of the humility that he identified as one of Judge Friendly's primary virtues.*

SFFA betrayed core tenets of constitutional conservatism. In the 1960s, roughly contemporaneous with the rise of affirmative action, constitutional conservatism "meant embracing

---

*Intriguingly, Chief Justice Roberts's substantive position on affirmative action clashed with Judge Friendly's vision. *SFFA* derided Justice Powell's controlling opinion in *Bakke* as being driven by the "pernicious stereotype that 'a black student can usually bring something that a white person cannot offer.'" Students for Fair Admissions, Inc. v. Pres. & Fellows of Harv. Coll. (*SFFA*), 600 U.S. 181, 220 (2023) (quoting *Regents of the Univ. of Cal. v. Bakke*, 438 U.S. 265, 316 (1978) (opinion of Powell, J.)). But Judge Friendly viewed Justice Powell's *Bakke* opinion in a far more flattering light, deeming it a tour de force. Indeed, Judge Friendly so thoroughly admired *Bakke* that he sent Powell a fan letter celebrating the opinion. Friendly, a man who was notoriously stinting with praise, thanked Powell "for the great service you have rendered the nation. This case had the potential of being another *Dred Scott*. . . . Your moderation and statesmanship saved us from that. . . . It reminds one of Mark Twain's remark that God protects children, drunkards, and the United States of America." David M. Dorsen, *Henry Friendly: Greatest Judge of His Era* 204 (2012) (quoting Letter from Henry J. Friendly to Lewis F. Powell Jr., July 1, 1978, quoted in John C. Jeffries Jr., *Justice Lewis F. Powell Jr.*, 498 (1994).

188   a few closely related concepts: venerating precedent; resisting sharp breaks with the past; [and] conceiving of the judicial role as modest." During the Warren Court era, the constitutional conservative beau ideal was Justice John Marshall Harlan II, whose jurisprudence was defined by "a profound respect for precedent," and who exhibited "distrust[] of abrupt change, comfort[] with accustomed rules and practices, and . . . reluctan[ce] to revise the judgments of predecessors." While the Supreme Court has allowed that following precedent "is not an inexorable command," constitutional conservatives of yesteryear particularly valued following prior decisions because it fostered respect for the notion that legal "principles are founded in the law rather than in the proclivities of individuals, and thereby contributes to the integrity of our constitutional system of government."

An honest appraisal of *SFFA* requires acknowledging (with Justice Thomas) that it overturned decades of precedent, perhaps most glaringly in its assessment that the universities had failed to provide even a compelling government interest for affirmative action. That determination represented nothing less than an abrupt volte-face not just from *Bakke* and *Grutter*, but from *Fisher II*, which had been decided only seven years before *SFFA*. In 2016, *Fisher II* underscored that "deference must be given to the University's conclusion, based on its experience and expertise, that a diverse student body would serve its educational goals." With *SFFA*, though, the Supreme Court broke sharply with this era of judicial deference, instead aggrandizing its authority over admissions offices throughout the land in a manner that would make traditional constitutional conservatives wince.

The strained judicial efforts to contend that ending affirmative action in 2023 somehow honored the twenty-five-year timeline that *Grutter* issued in 2003 only highlights the Supreme Court's severe rupture with traditional tenets of constitutional conservatism. SFFA's brief acknowledged that *Grutter* afforded affirmative action a quarter-century "grace period" in 2003, but also requested that the Court overturn *Grutter*. Chief Justice Roberts's majority opinion and Justice Kavanaugh's concurrence claimed both to honor that grace period and to avoid overturning that provision of *Grutter*.

The twenty-five-year timeframe in *Grutter* has generated a firestorm of criticism, and some lawyers have sought to construe it as merely a casual aside. Like the *SFFA* majority and Justice Kavanaugh's concurrence, though, I believe that *Grutter*'s twenty-five-year sunset should be construed as possessing legal authority, as I argued in a *New York Times* essay published on the eve of *SFFA*'s oral argument.

But the way that *SFFA* and Justice Kavanaugh's concurrence in *SFFA* sought to claim that the twenty-five-year period had in effect already run in twenty years beggars belief. The majority and Justice Kavanaugh—recall—suggested that prohibiting admissions offices from engaging in affirmative action immediately accorded with *Grutter* because students admitted to the class of 2028 (and beyond) would have their applications reviewed in a post—affirmative action world.

This method of counting, however, would cause the most unscrupulous politician seasoned in the dark art of fuzzy math to blush with embarrassment. Upon even limited reflection, it becomes plain that if 2028 holds any significance, it matters for the timing of admissions decisions, not the timing of

190   when one's college graduating class is admitted. Set aside for the moment the obvious point that many, many college students take longer than four years to graduate from college—if they end up graduating at all. The Court's decision in *SFFA* governs—at a minimum—all of American higher education, not only undergraduate admissions. But reputable universities, of course, offer degree programs that typically take fewer than four years to complete—including a juris doctor degree (which typically takes three years to complete) and a master of business administration (which typically takes two years to complete). Implementing the Class-of-2028 argument, therefore, would mean allowing law schools to use affirmative action in admitting JD candidates for one additional year, and business schools to use affirmative action in admitting MBA candidates for two additional years. That cannot be right. Or if it is, *SFFA* should have stated as much.

    The fact that *SFFA* felt compelled to pull the plug on affirmative action five years before it could have claimed (with a straight face) that *Grutter*'s twenty-five-year window had in fact actually closed reveals how completely the opinion rejected old-school constitutional conservatism. Whereas constitutional conservatives once disdained repudiating the considered judgments of their predecessors and detested sharp breaks with the past, *SFFA* revealed that the Roberts Court has limited time for such niceties. Legendary legal scholar Alexander Bickel once waxed eloquent about "the [judiciary's] marvelous mystery of time," but *SFFA* shows unmistakably that the Roberts Court is in a hurry.

SFFA's Legacy for Legacy Admissions

The demise of affirmative action has sparked the public to train renewed scrutiny on another form of college admissions preferences: those afforded to the children, or in some instances, the grandchildren, nieces, and nephews of alumni. These legacy preferences have routinely been called "Affirmative Action for White People."

Immediately after *SFFA*, President Michael Roth announced that Wesleyan University would no longer offer legacy preferences. With that move, Wesleyan joined Johns Hopkins, M.I.T., and Amherst College as one of the relatively small number of institutions who voluntarily eliminated legacy preferences. But Stanford University and the University of Southern California *involuntarily* joined their ranks last year—in September 2024—when Governor Gavin Newsom of California signed legislation banning legacy preferences at all private universities.

Prior to *SFFA* only one state—Colorado—had banned legacy preferences. After *SFFA*, however, four additional states—California, Maryland, Illinois, and Virginia—have followed suit. This timing is no accident. Phil Ting, the San Francisco state representative who spearheaded California's anti-legacy measure, allowed that the legislative environment was far more receptive to such measures in the post–affirmative action era. "The timing is much better than it was five years ago," Ting contended. "The fact that universities now cannot look at race as a factor in admissions really underscores the need to make sure that universities shouldn't be taking into account wealth or alumni status, traditions that really close off admissions for a whole host of students." Several more states are currently

192   entertaining anti-legacy legislation, so the bans could become widespread.

Critics of legacy preferences who hope that bans will necessarily redound to the benefit of Black applicants ought to temper those expectations. Even though Amherst, Johns Hopkins, and M.I.T. had already banned legacy admissions prior to *SFFA*, all three of those elite institutions nevertheless suffered steep declines in Black enrollment following affirmative action's demise. Those experiences do not mean, of course, that universities ought to retain legacy preferences. They should assuredly abandon them, as legacy preferences reward privileged students for demonstrating wisdom in selecting their parents. But we must be clear-eyed about the relationship between legacy preferences and Black enrollment. And there is little reason to believe that ending legacy admissions means that many underrepresented students will claim the newly vacated slots.

One fascinating wrinkle is that some Black graduates of elite universities have in recent years become improbable but staunch defenders of legacy preferences. While legacy preferences may have once served to aid overwhelmingly white graduates' children, these defenders argue, the college applicants of today include nontrivial numbers of Black students whose parents attended elite universities. On this theory, eliminating legacy preferences means eliminating a potential source of racial diversity. As one Black alumnus of the University of Virginia who favored retaining legacy admissions put the matter: "We have tons of [Black] friends whose kids are starting [college]. They think, 'Why is it every time we get a chance to do something, the rug is pulled out from under us?'"

In my view, though, such objections hardly suffice to rescue the larger injustice of legacy preferences. Supporting legacy admissions, I have long maintained, is perverse—a little like rooting for Elon Musk to purchase the winning lottery ticket. The perversity of legacy preferences does not magically disappear when it is Black children who select their parents wisely.*

The Rise of Racial Non-Disclosure, or Boxes Unchecked
One of *SFFA*'s clearest legacies is that the decision—and the surrounding controversy—has initiated a dramatic increase in the number of high school seniors who decline to disclose their racial identities by checking a box on their college applications. Prior to *SFFA*, this phenomenon was unusual, but it has now become relatively widespread. At Harvard, before the Court decided *SFFA*, only 4 percent of admitted applicants left the racial boxes unchecked, but 8 percent of such applicants did so following *SFFA*. Similarly, at Georgetown, 9 percent of enrolled first-year students did not disclose their racial identities during the 2023–2024 admissions cycle. Those percentages might not seem large, but solid evidence suggests that racial nondisclosure is not spread among all racial groups equally.

---

*In *SFFA*'s wake, many leading universities—including Brown, Cornell, Dartmouth, Duke, Emory, the University of Pennsylvania, Vanderbilt, and Yale—made clear that they intended to retain legacy admission preferences. One year after *SFFA*, students from approximately twenty elite colleges convened on Brown's campus to contemplate ways that they might encourage their universities to abandon legacy preferences. The inter-collegiate Brown conference met under the auspices of an umbrella organization fittingly called Class Action. See Nick Anderson, "Will Top Schools Continue 'Legacy' Admission Preferences? Many Say Yes," *Washington Post* (September 29, 2023); Aina Marzia, "The Elite College Students Fighting to End Legacy Admissions," *Nation* (November 20, 2024).

194 Rather, the phenomenon seems to have been concentrated among Asian American applicants. The Court's decision in *SFFA* and the abundant media coverage thus appear to have succeeded in increasing the salience of the notion that disclosing an Asian American identity diminishes one's chance of admission.

In anticipation of *SFFA*, the Common Application announced a new feature that would make it possible for universities to conceal their access to racial boxes that applicants may check. Universities have consistently interpreted *SFFA* to prohibit them from accessing applicants' racial boxes during any part of the admissions process—including decisions about whom to admit from the waitlist. After the admissions process is completed, however, universities may then turn to the boxes to determine the racial composition of their entering classes. When admissions offices started announcing the racial composition of their entering classes in the fall of 2024—the first class to be admitted under the new *SFFA* regime—some colleges announced surprising statistics involving Asian American students. *SFFA* was, of course, filed in the name of Asian American applicants, and many observers believed that the opinion would yield increased Asian American enrollments. Princeton College and Yale College, however, reported *decreased* Asian American enrollments, as Princeton fell from 26 percent to 23.8 percent and Yale fell from 30 percent to 24 percent. It was these declining Asian American enrollments that inspired SFFA to threaten additional lawsuits.

Yet, evidence suggests that those percentages in fact understate actual Asian American enrollment. Both Princeton and Yale, like Harvard, almost certainly witnessed a surge in students who left racial boxes unchecked. At Princeton, for example, we know that nearly 8 percent of enrolled students declined to check a racial box after *SFFA*, whereas less than 2 percent declined to do so before *SFFA*. (Yale has not yet released this data.) If a significant percentage of non-racially disclosing students were Asian American, as seems likely, then Princeton and Yale may not have experienced meaningful declines in Asian American students. The rise of racial nondisclosure in elite college admissions almost certainly explains why Harvard, which released its data after its closest competitors, decided to change the way that it calculated its racial composition after *SFFA*. In the fall of 2024, rather than calculating the racial percentages *of the entire matriculated class*, as it had previously done, Harvard decided instead to calculate the racial percentages *of the students who disclosed their racial identities*. This new method of calculation enabled Harvard to report a stable percentage of Asian American enrollment pre- and post-*SFFA*. It also enabled Harvard—for the time being, at least—to avoid receiving a new litigation hold letter from Edward Blum.

Is this increase in racial nondisclosure among some college applicants desirable? Some observers—largely conservatives—will applaud this development as indicating that the significance of race is waning in the United States. On this view, what may have begun as a phenomenon concentrated among Asian American college applicants might eventually be embraced by other races in other contexts, and that development would hasten the demise of America's stubborn racial preoccupations. Other observers—mostly liberals—will view the rise of racial nondisclosure in a negative light, bemoaning that the process of applying to college encourages applicants to engage in acts of racial erasure. These observers would find college applications

196   to be a major, constitutive moment in one's life, and lament that
applicants of Asian descent feel unable to define their identities however they wish. Still other observers will view the development as more symbolic than substantive. On this account,
it seems improbable in the extreme that applicants with para-
digmatic names of Asian descent—say, Xu Jiakang or Kanishka
Ratnayaka—would effectively conceal their racial identities
simply because they decline to check a racial box. However one
assesses the rise of racial nondisclosure, though, this phenomenon merits careful monitoring in the brave new post-*SFFA* world.

Destabilization of Higher Education
SFFA severely destabilizes American higher education. Over the
last several decades, leading universities had honed their admissions systems—through trial and error—to produce classes
of students who would be able to flourish. While affirmative
action's opponents deeply disliked the race consciousness of
these systems, those critics may soon find that universities
adapt in ways that harm vulnerable students.

Affirmative action has been a pillar of elite education for
the last several decades. It is certainly possible to view *SFFA*'s
removal of that pillar through rose-tinted spectacles, as it may
spur universities to reappraise preferences—most prominently
for legacies, donors, recruited athletes, and children of faculty—
that are in desperate need of reappraisal. But this moment of
possibility also contains tremendous possibility for peril.

The volatility created by *SFFA* could yield truly disastrous
consequences, not least for Black and brown students. The peril
of this new post-*SFFA* moment is perhaps best captured by
recalling the profound difficulties that beset some universities

when affirmative action was in its infancy. Consider only two
examples, both from law schools. Professor Graglia's early article exploring affirmative action in 1970 recalled: "At New York
University Law School . . . a special admissions program was
first adopted in 1966. . . . After two years, twelve of fifteen specially admitted students were not maintaining a passing average." Similarly, the class that entered Yale Law School in the
fall of 1969 included more than thirty Black students—a much
larger cohort than had ever previously matriculated. But one
year later, more than half of those students had received sufficiently low marks that they were forced to withdraw.*

The goal here is not to rap 1960s administrators on the
knuckles for having erred. They were doubtless doing their
level best to adapt in a vastly transformed admissions landscape. And that, of course, is precisely the point. Enormous,
life-altering mistakes are likely to occur when a policy is in its
earliest days, and that treacherous state is the one into which
SFFA has now thrust applicants and admissions officers around
the nation. *SFFA* will not eliminate universities' desire to enroll
significant numbers of Black and brown students. But those
universities will not have the benefit of more than five decades
of pertinent trial and error as they attempt to traverse this new,

---

*Justice Thomas, who entered Yale Law School in 1971, recalled many years
later: "When I went to Yale Law School, they had reduced black admissions
from 40 to 12. We were all there on our own merit." Joan Biskupic, "Thomas
Caught Up in Conflict," *Washington Post* (June 6, 1996). It is well known,
of course, that Justice Thomas has vehemently rejected any notion that
his application to Yale Law School benefited from affirmative action. It is
far less appreciated, however, that Justice Thomas entered Yale at a time
of tremendous internal upheaval, when the institution must have still been
reeling from the mass Black exodus that occurred a few years prior.

198   rocky terrain. I fervently hope that the floundering of the late 1960s does not portend the future of universities after *SFFA*. In debates about affirmative action, critics of the policy have often expressed concerns about ensuring that Black and brown students realize their full academic potential. Taking them at their word, though, the uncertainty created by *SFFA* could imperil those students' prospects.

SFFA has struck at the very heart of elite American higher education. Only nine years ago, in *Fisher II*, the Supreme Court reasoned: "A university is in large part defined by those intangible qualities which are incapable of objective measurement but which make for greatness. Considerable deference is owed to a university in defining those intangible characteristics, like student body diversity, that are central to its identity and educational mission." *SFFA* can therefore be viewed as consciously inflicting a mortal blow to something that has long been central to universities' educational mission, hampering their ability to pursue that ineffable quality that produces greatness. For generations, American higher education has been the envy of the world; let us hope that *SFFA* does not spark a sequence of events that transforms it into a laughingstock.

SFFA's Effects in the Business World

The racial legacy of *SFFA* has been far from confined to the campus quadrangle, quickly making its way into many realms—including the C-suite. In *SFFA*'s wake, many companies of various shapes and sizes that had previously established programs designed to foster diversity, equity, and inclusion announced that they were abandoning those efforts. In 2024, for example, Brown-Forman—a renowned, prosperous liquor

distiller—announced that it was shuttering its racial diversity
initiatives because "the world has evolved . . . and the legal and
external landscape has shifted dramatically, particularly within
the United States." Brown-Forman's announcement occurred on
the heels of similar announcements from Lowe's, Ford Motors,
Harley-Davidson, and John Deere. Other iconic American companies that have recently retreated from their commitments to
DEI initiatives include: Amazon, Goldman Sachs, Google, Meta,
McDonald's, and Walmart. These companies did not, of course,
spontaneously decide that racial diversity had ceased to be relevant. Rather, they acted in response to a coordinated right-wing
crusade that has harnessed *SFFA* to threaten legal action against
corporations that avowedly pursue racial diversity. While private companies' policies were not addressed in *SFFA*, some conservative litigators and the second Trump administration have
brandished the opinion to suggest that corporate racial diversity programs violate federal law.

Stephen Miller—the architect of numerous race-baiting
policies during Trump 1.0, who is now exercising even greater
clout during Trump 2.0—successfully weaponized *SFFA* to
intimidate pro-diversity businesses when he ran America First
Legal. Neal Katyal, a leading Washington lawyer in private practice, has witnessed some companies rapidly relenting under
what he terms "the business model for Stephen Miller," which
involves "go[ing] around the country, threaten[ing] to sue
these . . . businesses . . . and get[ting] them to just unilaterally
disarm." Katyal has found that "business after business is [cav-
ing]," and "throw[ing] in the towel because they're afraid."

Katyal maintained that Miller, in his desire to rid the corporate world of programs seeking racial diversity, had betrayed

200   core conservative principles. "It used to be a central libertarian Republican [tenet] that businesses should be able to do what they want," Katyal argued. "But when businesses didn't do what Stephen Miller wanted, he decided to sue them." Katyal further explained that the anti-diversity litigators are highly strategic in timing their lawsuits, "set[ting] their sights on private business" to maximize leverage. "Some of these [Stephen] Miller-types are attacking companies where they know that the companies are at a vulnerable point in their funding," Katyal contended. "They may be seeking a venture capital round. They may be seeking equity loans or something like that. And many lenders have rules like, you can't have a class-action lawsuit coming against you when you're seeking funding. So Stephen Miller styles all of these as class actions."

The parade of anti-diversity executive orders issued at the dawn of the second Trump administration in January 2025 made it abundantly clear that the GOP aimed to brandish *SFFA* in an effort to police private corporations. Even if the Trump administration does not ultimately pursue any particular company, the high-profile maneuvers have nevertheless succeeded in sending a chill through the hallways of corporate America. One lawyer who regularly counsels blue chip companies stated that the Trump orders worked effectively by "striking fear into organizations' hearts."

Modern corporate America is, alas, not replete with Black executives. Although Black people make up 14 percent of the United States, they account for less than 2 percent of the top executives at the nation's largest companies. Stephen Miller, Donald Trump, and their compatriots are dedicated to ensuring that *SFFA* further suppresses those already paltry figures.

An Elegy for Affirmative Action

On university campuses today, the air of uncertainty that *SFFA* introduced has been overwhelmed by a sense of widespread panic for the very future of American higher education. The second Trump administration in early 2025 threatened to withhold massive amounts of federal funding from some leading academic institutions—including Columbia University, Harvard University, and the University of Pennsylvania. That funding has become the modern university's lifeblood, and leaders at other institutions have no doubt lost much sleep fearing that their own will become the next to draw President Trump's ire. These developments are a grievous manifestation of the widely held belief among Trump administration officials that universities are the enemy. If that statement sounds hyperbolic, consider that now—Vice President Vance in 2021 delivered a speech subtly titled: "The Universities Are the Enemy." According to Vance, universities merit attack not only when they espouse progressive politics, but even when they go about the ordinary business of conducting research and educating students.

Against this agonizing backdrop, some readers may well believe that exploring action after affirmative action today misreads the room in an astounding display of tone deafness, or—viewed more charitably—presents a problem best reserved for another day. On this account, the soundest course for university leaders is to keep their heads down, waiting until the much-discussed American political and cultural "vibe shift" shifts yet again, this time in a more palatable direction. Given the existential threat now confronting American universities, such tactics are entirely understandable, in my view. Understandable, but also misguided.

It is precisely when universities are most under siege that they must safeguard their core commitments. Powerful arguments can and should be made to counteract the Trump administration's ongoing assault on university autonomy. University genuflection and acquiescence in the face of President Trump's diktats, moreover, seem less likely to placate than to embolden. Compromising with the Trump administration's distorted vision for higher education could succeed in compromising academic freedom, a core aspect of the university's modern educational mission. In the wake of *SFFA*, Harvard's leadership issued a statement reaffirming that its own educational mission was shaped by the understanding that "[b]ecause the teaching, learning, research, and creativity that bring progress and change require debate and disagreement, diversity and difference are essential to academic excellence." Harvard was, of course, far from alone in reaffirming such beliefs about that critical mission for American higher education. And that academic quest remains vital even in the face of President Trump's attacks on central pillars of American society. If anything, that project and its inextricable connections to our multiracial democracy seem more essential still as President Trump embraces racial revanchism and attempts to remake America in his own image.

The nation's current racial milieu renders the severe decline in Black enrollment that occurred at many eminent universities after *SFFA* cause for even greater distress. Affirmative action—as we have long known it—is dead. And if affirmative action has died, as I noted at the outset, we must not permit it to pass from the scene without honoring and, indeed, celebrating its remarkable life. We turn now to that crucial task.

Although the point long ago became obscured, affirmative action played an indispensable role in creating and bolstering the Black middle- and upper-middle classes, and we should salute it for that indispensable work. Affirmative action, viewed clearly, served as an engine of mobility that shaped and improved modern America, and it should therefore be placed in the same lofty company as other transformational programs, including the GI Bill.

Not all that long ago—at a time that many Americans alive today can still vividly recollect—the nation's premier universities had an infinitesimal number of Black students. Consider the racial composition of some elite college classes that entered in the fall of 1960: Harvard boasted a bumper crop of 9 Black students (in a class of more than 1,200); Yale had 5 Black students (in a class of 1,000); and Princeton—the southernmost Ivy, spiritually if not geographically—claimed a grand total of precisely 1 Black student (in a class of more than 820).

Those figures mean that in January 1961—when President John F. Kennedy proclaimed in his inaugural address that "the torch has been passed to a new generation of Americans"—Black students accounted for only 15 of the more than 3,000 students who entered the nation's most prestigious colleges, a little less than half of 1 percent. Flashing forward just one decade, Black enrollment in ultra-elite colleges had skyrocketed, and—in the process—changed the very face of higher education. In 1970, the number of Black freshmen entering Harvard grew to 98, Yale increased to 83, and Princeton swelled to 103—giving those three colleges 284 African American students in all. In the span of merely ten years, the Black student presence at these and other esteemed universities went from the foreign to the familiar, a sea change that affirmative action indisputably nurtured.

This racial revolution that began on college campuses soon made its way into the nation's foremost professions. In the two-decade period stretching from 1970 to 1990, Black professionals—once a curiosity—became a comparatively common sight: the number of Black lawyers increased by more than a factor of six; Black doctors tripled; and the Black professoriate more than doubled. It is hard to overstate the significance of this radical assault on American pigmentocracy, as—for the first time in our nation's history—meaningful numbers of Black citizens exercised authority within elite corridors. In 1998, William Bowen and Derek Bok—who had served as presidents of Princeton and Harvard, respectively—published a sophisticated, comprehensive book evaluating affirmative action. They found that the program had already produced remarkable rewards in changing the complexion of the American workforce's upper echelon: "If, at the end of the day, the question is whether the most selective colleges and universities have succeeded in educating sizable numbers of minority students who have already achieved considerable success . . . , we have no problem in answering the question. Absolutely."

It may be attractive to believe that this professional overhaul was driven less by the proliferation of affirmative action programs, and more by the widespread adoption of nondiscrimination policies. At times, the nation's most prominent, most acerbic critic of affirmative action—Justice Clarence Thomas, who began attending Yale Law School in 1971—has voiced a version of this argument. In 1987, when Thomas served as a senior official in the Reagan administration, he stated: "This thing about how they let me into Yale [via affirmative action]—that kind of stuff offends me. All they did was stop stopping us."

While this narrative holds obvious appeal, facts on the ground simply do not support it. Setting aside the particularities of Thomas's admission (which Yale officials have flatly stated affirmative action aided), evidence suggests that the policy ushered in the bulk of Black students at Yale Law School during the era the program was adopted. In 1970, the *Public Interest* published a startlingly candid exchange, titled: "The Black Quota at Yale Law School." There, Justice Macklin Fleming of the California judicial system, an alumnus of Yale Law School, wrote a letter to the law school's dean, Louis Pollak. Referencing remarks that Pollak delivered at an alumni event trumpeting Yale's newly adopted affirmative action program, Fleming took exception to many facets of the program, including its scope. "I understand that 43 black students have been admitted to next fall's class, of whom 5 qualified under the regular standards and 38 did not," Fleming wrote. "You anticipate that half this group will actually enroll, thus furnishing 22 black students in the first

206   year class of 165, of whom perhaps 3 will have qualified under
       the regular standards and 19 will not." Fleming further criti-
       cized Yale's commitment to admitting 10 percent of future law
       school cohorts under the auspices of its affirmative action pro-
       gram. Dean Pollak's response to Justice Fleming defended the
       aims of the policy, but he in no way contradicted the central role
       that racial considerations played in admitting the vast majority
       of Black law students to Yale.

       Affirmative action's dramatic import was hardly confined
       to Yale; instead, the policy played a pivotal role in increasing
       the number of Black attorneys across the nation. Indeed, a few
       years after affirmative action became widespread in the 1970s,
       the Educational Testing Service found that if the policy were
       abandoned, the percentage of Black law students would decline
       precipitously, falling from 5.3 percent to hovering somewhere
       between a mere 1 and 2 percent. Affirmative action, then, has
       played a prominent role in diversifying the nation's profes-
       sional classes, and the nation is better for it.

       SFFA compromises those decades of progress. Apart from
       the staggering declines in Black enrollment that many under-
       graduate institutions experienced post-*SFFA*, some influential
       graduate school programs have followed suit. In one particu-
       larly graphic example, the number of incoming Black students
       at Harvard Law School dropped by more than half to 19—
       making it the smallest number of Black Harvard 1Ls since
       1965, and accounting for only 3 percent of the class. Harvard
       Law School has proudly graduated more Black lawyers than
       any American law school other than Howard, and its graduates
       include luminaries like President Barack Obama and Justice

Ketanji Brown Jackson. *SFFA* has now succeeded in tarnishing
that admirable record.

Such declines were entirely foreseeable before *SFFA*, given
the grim experiences of various states where affirmative action
had previously been banned. In 2006, ten years after California
banned affirmative action, UCLA's entering class of under-
graduates numbered around 5,000, but only 96 of them were
Black—the smallest Black freshman enrollment in Westwood
since 1973. The meager number of Black UCLA freshmen proved
so scandalous that the group became known as the "Infamous
96." In Michigan, when affirmative action ended in 2006, Black
enrollment at the University of Michigan stood a little higher
than 7 percent; fifteen years later, that figure had fallen below
4 percent. These dreary figures did not, evidently, make the
Roberts Court flinch, as it pursued colorblind constitutionalism in a headlong fashion.

It is not too much to say that due to *SFFA* the United States
is now seeing—or perhaps more accurately, not seeing—a lost
generation of Black students at elite educational institutions.
And that most unwelcome development means those of us who
spend significant time on university campuses will be forced
to ask, once again, the question that confounded President
Charles Odegaard in Seattle on that brilliant Saturday afternoon, more than six decades ago now: "Where are the black students? Where are the black students?"

ACKNOWLEDGMENTS

This work represents the culmination of many years that I have dedicated to exploring the three-way intersection where race, education, and the Fourteenth Amendment's Equal Protection Clause all converge. While I deeply regret the Supreme Court decision that served as the immediate impetus for this volume, I am delighted to have this opportunity to thank some of the people who helped place me in a stronger position to illuminate its contours.

Justice Stephen Breyer deserves the first mention on this score because he extended my earliest professional opportunity to examine this charged three-way intersection when I served as his law clerk during the 2006–2007 Term. At the end of that Term, Justice Breyer issued a celebrated dissenting opinion in a case called *Parents Involved in Community Schools v. Seattle School District No. 1*. That opinion can be viewed as attempting to avert the constitutional vision that found its ultimate moment of triumph in *SFFA v. Harvard* some sixteen years later. By his example, Justice Breyer imparted the value of registering dissent to confront a misguided majority opinion in this constitutional domain. And Justice Breyer further conveyed that the duty of dissidence extends well beyond those who wear fine black robes.

I completed this book as a member of the faculty at Yale Law School. Dean Heather K. Gerken is an exemplary leader, and she has ensured that I have the space and time to pursue whatever intellectual projects I deem worthy. American legal education would be considerably stronger were there more deans in her mold. Several Yale colleagues have provided valuable feedback on this project: Akhil Reed Amar, Jack Balkin,

Owen Fiss, James Forman Jr., Tracey Meares, Samuel Moyn, Cristina Rodríguez, David Schleicher, Reva Siegel, and John Fabian Witt. Several Yale students helped me with indispensable research and editorial assistance, including Keerthana Annamaneni, Matthew Beattie-Callahan, Kishore Chundi, Rosemary Coskrey, Liam Gennari, Emma Gray, Remington Hill, Joshua Hochman, Alexandra Johnson, Paloma O'Connor, Jamie Piltch, Claire Potter, Sarah Shapiro, Jeremy Thomas, Julia Udell, and Logan Wren.

Beyond Yale, numerous colleagues at other institutions engaged with aspects of this work in various settings. I am especially grateful to the following: Kate Andrias, William Baude, John Q. Barrett, Samantha Bensinger, Gregory Briker, Adam Chilton, Adam Davidson, Rosalind Dixon, Jonathan Entin, Richard Thompson Ford, John Friedman, Pratheepan Gulasekaram, Richard Kahlenberg, Emma Kaufman, Randall Kennedy, Michael Klarman, Randy Kozel, Sanford Levinson, Jonathan Masur, Lucas Powe, Darrell Miller, Kerrel Murray, Saikrishna Prakash, Richard Primus, John Rappaport, Kyle Rozema, Brad Snyder, David Strauss, and Melvin Urofsky.

Several close friends have discussed this topic with me over the years: Jessica Ring Amunson, Noah Biklen, Thabiti Brown, Kerwin Charles, William Edwards, Abelardo Fernández, Tacy Flint, Chad Golder, Danielle Gray, Jonathan Kravis, Matthew McGuire, Brian Nelson, Adam Orlov, Nicola Orlov, Elizabeth Oyer, Daniel Oppenheimer, James T. Patterson, Mike Pyle, Noam Scheiber, Jake Sullivan, Tali Farhadian Weinstein, Kweli Washington, Geoffrey Wyatt, and Mark Yohalem. Their engagement on this topic, and many others besides, has enhanced my life immeasurably.

210   My literary agent, Melissa Flashman of Janklow & Nesbit, provided friendship, encouragement, and excellent insight into the book publishing world. I am particularly grateful that she found a happy home for this project with the formidable Nicholas Lemann of Columbia Global Reports. Nick brought to this project both deep knowledge of the subject matter and shrewd editorial suggestions for improving the manuscript. I am overjoyed to have collaborated on this project with not only Nick but the all-star team he has assembled at CGR—including Jaime Leifer, Jimmy So, Allison Finkel, and Courtney Knights.

I have enjoyed the opportunity to deliver addresses about *SFFA v. Harvard* on several occasions. I received valuable feedback from colleagues and audience members at the following venues: the Chautauqua Institution (where I delivered the Robert H. Jackson Lecture), Harvard Law School (where I participated in the Belinda Sutton Symposium), Princeton University (where I delivered a talk titled "The Affirmative Action Wars"), the US Court of Appeals for the Fourth Circuit Judicial Conference (where I participated on a Supreme Court review panel), Vanderbilt Law School (where I delivered the Victor S. Johnson Lecture), and Yale Law School (where I participated in a conference on the future of constitutionalism).

In various places, this volume draws upon some arguments and formulations that I initially ventured elsewhere: "The Strange Career of Antisubordination," 91 *University of Chicago Law Review* 651 (2024); "The Cure as Disease: The Conservative Case against *SFFA v. Harvard*," 2023 *Supreme Court Review* 1 (2024); and "Assessing Affirmative Action's Diversity Rationale," 122 *Columbia Law Review* 331 (2022) (with Adam Chilton, Jonathan S. Masur, and Kyle Rozema). I appreciate

these journals permitting me to reprise parts of those publi-
cations in this context. In drawing upon these articles here, I
extensively reworked and refined that material to render it suit-
able for this setting. I also appreciate my generous coauthors
on the *Columbia Law Review* article for permitting me to use our
work here.

My daughters, Claire and Darcy, have endured my droning
on about the Supreme Court since long before they can remember. They have done so overwhelmingly with good cheer, and I
am grateful that they have delivered far fewer eye rolls than I
could have any right reasonably to expect. Their inquisitiveness
about this project, and the much larger world, brings me consistent joy.

My biggest debts by far are to my wife, Laura. I can still
recall nervously striking up a conversation with Laura in August
2001 as we toured Harvard Law School's Langdell Hall during
the first day of orientation for new students. More than two
decades later, those nerves have mercifully subsided, but that
first conversation is still going strong—richer, deeper, and live-
lier than ever before. Fortune has smiled on me many times, but
never more so than when she agreed to spend her life with me.
Laura is my companion on all journeys, in all things, and this
book is dedicated to her.

March 2025

TIMELINE OF KEY SUPREME COURT OPINIONS

1896
Plessy v. Ferguson
The Court validates a Louisiana statute that required "equal, but separate" railcar accommodations, holding that racial segregation does not violate the Equal Protection Clause. Justice Harlan alone dissents.

1954
Brown v. Board of Education
The Court unanimously strikes down statutes that explicitly permit or require racial segregation in public schools, determining that "in the field of public education, the doctrine of [*Plessy v. Ferguson*] has no place."

1974
DeFunis v. Odegaard
In weighing the University of Washington School of Law's affirmative action program, the Court declines to issue a decision on the merits, finding that the case is moot. Justice Douglas, writing only for himself, issues a momentous opinion.

1978
Regents of the University of California v. Bakke
The Court strikes down UC Davis Medical School's affirmative action program, which set aside 16 slots for racial minorities in a class of 100, as an unconstitutional quota. Nevertheless, the Court also holds that universities may consider race in admissions for purposes of increasing diversity on campus. In a case decided by a 4−1−4 split, Justice Powell writes the decisive opinion.

2003
Grutter v. Bollinger
The Court upholds the University of Michigan Law School's affirmative action policy. In doing so, Justice O'Connor's opinion for the Court determines that the Law School's program adhered to the guidelines approved in *Bakke*. Noting that twenty-five years had elapsed since *Bakke*, O'Connor further announced the Court's expectation that affirmative action would no longer be practiced twenty-five years hence, or in 2028.

2003
Gratz v. Bollinger
Decided the same day as *Grutter*, the Court invalidates the University of Michigan's undergraduate admissions program because it too closely resembled the unduly rigid approach of UC Davis's Medical School that was outlawed in *Bakke*.

2013
Fisher v. University of Texas (Fisher I)
The Court determines that a lower appellate court had applied the wrong constitutional standard to evaluate a portion of UT's undergraduate admissions program that involved explicit racial classifications.

2016
Fisher v. University of Texas (Fisher II)
The Court, in a 4–3 opinion, upholds UT's undergraduate admissions program in its entirety. Justice Kennedy's opinion emphasizes that universities must continually assess whether admissions relying upon express racial classifications are justified. The case was resolved by only seven Justices because Justice Scalia had recently died and Justice Kagan recused herself from addressing the matter.

2023
Students for Fair Admissions v. Harvard
Students for Fair Admissions v. University of North Carolina
The Court invalidates affirmative action programs throughout the nation, in effect overturning *Bakke*, *Grutter*, and *Fisher II*. Chief Justice Roberts's opinion for the Court determines that universities may positively consider applicants' race if discussed in their personal statements, and refrains from invalidating affirmative action programs at the nation's military academies.

For a panoramic overview of the subject, readers should turn first to Melvin I. Urofsky's *The Affirmative Action Puzzle: A Living History from Reconstruction to Today* (2020). Urofsky does an admirable job of placing the affirmative action controversy into its larger social, political, and legal contexts. Similar virtues can be found in J. Harvie Wilkinson III's *From Brown to Bakke: The Supreme Court and School Integration, 1954–1978* (1979). Although Wilkinson's book was published only one year after the Court decided *Bakke*, he somehow managed to see that recent legal dispute with clear eyes.

Numerous scholars have mounted sophisticated defenses of affirmative action over the years. Stephen L. Carter's *Reflections of an Affirmative Action Baby* (1991) blends personal narrative and analytical rigor in a powerful fashion. While he supports affirmative action, he also refuses to ignore its frailties. A similarly evenhanded, nuanced defense of affirmative action can be found in Randall Kennedy's *For Discrimination: Race, Affirmative Action, and the Law* (2013). For an impassioned and elegant defense of affirmative action that was published on the eve of the Court's decision in *SFFA v. Harvard*, readers should consult Lee C. Bollinger and Geoffrey R. Stone's *A Legacy of Discrimination: The Essential Constitutionality of Affirmative Action* (2023). A comprehensive empirical defense of affirmative action appears in William G. Bowen and Derek Bok's *The Shape of the River: Long-Term Consequences of Considering Race in College and University Admissions* (1998).

Many authors have expressed profound misgivings about affirmative action. Perhaps the most prominent attack on affirmative action to emerge in recent years is Richard H. Sander and Stuart Taylor Jr.'s *Mismatch: How Affirmative Action Hurts Students It's Intended to Help, and Why Universities Won't Admit It* (2012). For earlier books that contain notable denunciations of affirmative action, readers should turn to Shelby Steele's *The Content of Our Character: A New Vision of Race in America* (1990), and John H. McWhorter's *Losing the Race: Self-Sabotage in Black America* (2000).

Some writers have suggested that universities should offer admissions boosts not on the basis of race, but instead on the basis of class disadvantage. This approach, supporters urge, would in effect assist many Black students because Black families are disproportionately poor, and it would avoid raising hackles because indigent white students would also benefit. Two leading efforts in this vein are: Richard D. Kahlenberg's *The Remedy: Class, Race, and Affirmative Action* (1996) and Sheryll Cashin's *Place, Not Race: A New Vision of Opportunity in America* (2014).

Legal scholarship examining affirmative action is ubiquitous. For important, early criticisms of affirmative action, see Lino A. Graglia's "Special Admission of the 'Culturally Deprived' to Law School," 119 *University of Pennsylvania Law Review* 351 (1970), and Antonin Scalia's "The Disease as Cure: 'In Order to Get Beyond Racism, We Must First Take Account of Race,'" (1979) *Washington University Law Quarterly* 147. For only three of the major articles defending affirmative action, see Owen M. Fiss's "Groups and the Equal Protection Clause," 5 *Philosophy & Public Affairs* 107 (1976); Jack M. Balkin and Reva B. Siegel's "The American Civil Rights Tradition: Anticlassification or Antisubordination?," 58 *University of Miami Law Review* (2003); and David A. Strauss's "*Fisher v. University of Texas* and the Conservative Case for Affirmative Action," 2016 *Supreme Court Review* 1 (2017).

The most contentious exchange in legal scholarship about affirmative action in many years was sparked by the publication of Richard Sander's "A Systemic Analysis of Affirmative Action in American Law Schools," 57 *Stanford Law Review* 367 (2004). Sander's article—which formed the basis for his coauthored book titled *Mismatch*—argued that affirmative action unintentionally *decreased* the overall number of Black lawyers. That decline occurred, Sander asserted, because underprepared Black students who were placed in academic environments for which they were ill-equipped subsequently failed the bar exam at greater rates than they would have if they attended less elite law schools. This explosive claim generated powerful empirical rebuttals, including Ian Ayres and Richard Brooks's "Does Affirmative Action Reduce the Number of Black Lawyers?," 57 *Stanford Law Review* 1807 (2005), and Daniel E. Ho's "Affirmative Action's Affirmative Actions: A Reply to Sander," 114 *Yale Law Journal* 2011 (2005).

Finally, readers interested in better understanding how the Supreme Court works as a general proposition can consult several sources. For the best single volume treatment of the Supreme Court's entire history, see Stuart Banner's *The Most Powerful Court in the World: A History of the Supreme Court of the United States* (2024). Readers who wish to understand the major affirmative action opinions within the Supreme Court's last five decades would do well to consult the following: Michael J. Graetz and Linda Greenhouse's *The Burger Court and the Rise of the Judicial Right* (2016); Mark Tushnet's *A Court Divided: The Rehnquist Court and the Future of Constitutional Law* (2005); and Mark Tushnet's *In the Balance: Law and Politics on the Roberts Court* (2013).

INTRODUCTION

12   **"[b]rilliant sunlight matched exactly life's golden vista [for] graduates":** Robert Heilman, *Sunny Day Is All Gold for Graduating U.W. Seniors*, SEATTLE TIMES, June 16, 1963, at 29.

12   **attracted dazzling professors and generous funding:** Carole Beers, *Former President of UW Dies at 88—Known as Key Leader in University's History,* SEATTLE TIMES (November 17, 1999), https://archive.seattletimes.com/archive/?date=19991117&slug=2995736.

13   **virtually all of them had one thing in common: white skin:** *See* J. Harvie Wilkinson III, FROM *BROWN* TO *BAKKE*: THE SUPREME COURT AND SCHOOL INTEGRATION, 1954–1978, at 281 (1979) (noting Odegaard "watching the long white columns at the University of Washington's commencement exercises in 1963").

13   **"Where are the black students? Where are the black students?":** Brief for Respondents at 39 n.26, DeFunis v. Odegaard, 416 U.S. 312 (1974) (No. 73-235); *see also* Wilkinson, FROM *BROWN* TO *BAKKE*, at 281.

13   **"Wisdom is revealed in action":** Heilman, *Sunny Day Is All Gold for Graduating U.W. Seniors,* at 29.

14   **"solely on the basis of merit of the applicants without regard to race, creed, or color":** Dennis Deslippe, PROTESTING AFFIRMATIVE ACTION: THE STRUGGLE OVER EQUALITY AFTER THE CIVIL RIGHTS REVOLUTION 116 (2012).

14   **to ensure that the university educated more than a trivial number of Black students:** Brief for Respondents at 39 n.26, DeFunis v. Odegaard, 416 U.S. 312 (1974) (No. 73-235).

14   **"will have to be matched by at least some years of separate and unequal treatment the other way":** Marty Loken, *Odegaard: Radicals' Charges Untrue,* SEATTLE TIMES, November 10, 1968, at 23.

14   **"*[E]quality was not enough*":** Brief for Respondents at 39 n.26, DeFunis v. Odegaard, 416 U.S. 312 (1974) (No. 73-235).

14   **"to contribute to the solution of the [racial] problem":** *DeFunis v. Odegaard*, 416 U.S. 312, 346–47 (1974).

15   **"approximately 15 to 20 percent is . . . a reasonable proportion":** *DeFunis,* 416 U.S. at 347.

15   **the Supreme Court's earliest encounter with the legality of affirmative action:** 416 U.S. 312 (1974).

16 **the Supreme Court of the United States killed affirmative action:** 600 U.S. 181 (2023).

17 **"[A]ffirmative action will remain a substantial presence in American life":** Randall Kennedy, FOR DISCRIMINATION: RACE, AFFIRMATIVE ACTION, AND THE LAW 240 (2013).

17 **"it does not seem that, whatever the Supreme Court may say [in SFFA], they will go away":** Melvin I. Urofksy, THE AFFIRMATIVE ACTION PUZZLE: A COMPREHENSIVE AND HONEST EXPLORATION OF ONE OF THE MOST CONTROVERSIAL LEGAL AND SOCIAL ISSUES IN U.S. HISTORY 485 (2022).

17 **"a symbolic victory for affirmative action's conservative opponents":** Peter N. Salib & Guha Krishnamurthi, *The Goose and the Gander: How Conservative Precedents Will Save Campus Affirmative Action*, 102 TEX. L. REV. 123, 124 (2023).

18 **"will serve only to highlight the Court's own impotence":** Students for Fair Admissions, Inc. v. President & Fellows of Harvard Coll., 600 U.S. 181, 384 (2023) (Sotomayor, J., dissenting).

18 **"The chances of an individual school getting sued are low":** Anemona Hartocollis, *With Supreme Court Decision, College Admissions Could Become More Subjective*, N.Y. TIMES (July 7, 2023), https://www.nytimes.com /2023/06/29/us/affirmative -action-college-admissions -future.html. For some of Sander's work assailing affirmative action, *see, e.g.,* Richard Sander, *A Systemic Analysis of Affirmative Action in American Law Schools*, 57 STAN. L. REV. 367 (2004).

18 **"I should dread a lawsuit beyond almost anything else short of sickness and of death":** Learned Hand, THE DEFICIENCIES OF TRIALS TO REACH THE HEART OF THE MATTER, Address before the Association of the Bar of the City of New York (November 17, 1921), *in* 3 LECTURES ON LEGAL TOPICS, 1921–1922, 89, 105 (1926).

19 **"I'm going through this trouble because this is a bi-racial (black/white) male":** 600 U.S. 181, 303 n.8 (2023) (Gorsuch, J., concurring).

19 **"should universities defiantly flout this clear ruling":** Anemona Hartocollis, *With Supreme Court Decision, College Admissions Could Become More Subjective*, N.Y. TIMES (July 7, 2023), https://www.nytimes .com/2023/06/29/us/affirmative -action-college-admissions -future.html.

19 **sent a letter to every single law school accredited by the American Bar Association:** Jack Crittenden, *Goodbye Diversity*, NAT'L JURIST, November 20, 2023, at 23.

218

20   "**and all other aspects of student, academic, and campus life**": "Dear Colleague" Letter from Craig Trainor, Acting Secretary for Civil Rights, Department of Education, February 14, 2025.

21   **threatens to create a lost generation of Black students:** *See* Anemona Hartocollis and Stephanie Saul, *At M.I.T., Black and Latino Enrollment Drops Sharply After Affirmative Action Ban*, N.Y. TIMES (August 21, 2024); Anemona Hartocollis and Stephanie Saul, *At 2 Elite Colleges, Shifts in Racial Makeup After Affirmative Action Ban*, N.Y. TIMES (August 30, 2024); Sofia Williams, *Preliminary Admissions Data for Class of 2028 Shows Drop in Black, Latino Enrollment*, STANFORD DAILY (October 2, 2024); James Murphy, *Tracking the Impact of the SFFA Decision on College Admissions*, EDUC. REFORM NOW (September 9, 2024).

21   "**it is necessary that the path to leadership be visibly open to talented and qualified individuals of every race and ethnicity**": *Grutter v. Bollinger*, 539 U.S. 306, 332 (2003).

21   "**so that all members of our heterogeneous society may participate**": *Grutter*, 539 U.S. at 332–33.

22   "**justly and lawfully reduced to slavery for [their] benefit**":

Dred Scott v. Sandford, 60 U.S. 393, 407 (1857).

22   "**it changed the way we thought about where Black people could be**": Gerald Early, *Black Americans Have Always Had Mixed Feelings About Affirmative Action*, CHRON. OF HIGHER EDUC. (July 19, 2023), https://www.chronicle.com /article/black-americans-have -always-had-mixed-feelings -about-affirmative-action.

23   "**it is hard to find a program that has brought so much gain to so many at so little cost**": Orlando Patterson, THE ORDEAL OF INTEGRATION: PROGRESS AND RESENTMENT IN AMERICA'S RACIAL CRISIS 150 (1997).

CHAPTER ONE

25   **one year after the Supreme Court issued *Regents of the University of California v. Bakke*:** 438 U.S. 265 (1978).

25   **published a short article with a long title excoriating the decision:** Antonin Scalia, *The Disease as Cure: "In Order to Get Beyond Racism, We Must First Take Account of Race*,*"* 1979 WASH. U. L.Q. 147. The quotation in Scalia's subtitle is drawn from Justice Harry Blackmun's concurring opinion in *Bakke*. *See* 438 U.S. at 407 (Blackmun, J. concurring).

25   **presented an unconstitutional malady in cases**

like *Brown v. Board of Education*: 347 U.S. 483 (1954).

25 **how could admissions policies that explicitly use racial categories:** Scalia, *The Disease as Cure,* at 150.

25 **"From racist principles flow racist results":** Scalia, *The Disease as Cure,* at 157.

26 *SFFA v. Harvard:* 600 U.S. 181 (2023).

26 **"the son of a prosperous and well-educated black doctor or lawyer":** Scalia, *The Disease as Cure,* at 153–54.

26 **blamed affirmative action for promoting Black students with mediocre academic records:** Scalia, *The Disease as Cure,* at 155–56.

26 **as compensation for a racial debt that long predated their arrival:** Scalia, *The Disease as Cure,* at 152.

26 **"Not only had he never profited from the sweat of any black man's brow":** Scalia, *The Disease as Cure,* at 152.

26 **"that the diversity value of New York City oboists has not been accorded its proper weight":** Scalia, *The Disease as Cure,* at 148.

27 **"one of [the Supreme Court's] finest hours":** Editorial, *A Landmark for Racial Equality*, WALL ST. J., June 30, 2023, at A14.

27 **"the restoration of the colorblind legal covenant":** Michelle N. Amponsah & Emma H. Haidar, *Students for Fair Admissions, Allies Celebrate End of Affirmative Action,* HARV. CRIMSON (June 30, 2023), https://www.thecrimson.com/article/2023/6/30/sffa-decision-reaction.

27 **"greatest opinion in his eighteen years on the Court":** Ed Whelan, *The Chief Justice's Greatest Opinion*, NAT'L REV. (June 29, 2023), https://www.nationalreview.com/bench-memos/the-chief-justices-greatest-opinion.

28 **"recognize the limitations of minority admissions programs":** Derrick A. Bell Jr., Bakke, *Minority Admissions, and the Usual Price of Racial Remedies*, 67 CALIF. L. REV. 3, 19 (1979).

28 **"argue as if affirmative action poses no costs, entails no risks, involves no dangers":** Kennedy, FOR DISCRIMINATION, at 115; *see also* Randall Kennedy, *Persuasion and Distrust: A Comment on the Affirmative Action Debate*, 99 HARV. L. REV. 1327, 1327 n.1 (1986) ("On all too many occasions . . . proponents of affirmative action have hurt their own cause by evading the difficulties posed and costs incurred by the policy they advance.").

220

28 **may soon recognize that the opinion is actually a glorious defeat:** *Cf.* Kenneth B. Clark, *Racial Progress and Retreat: A Personal Memoir, in* RACE IN AMERICA: THE STRUGGLE FOR EQUALITY 3, 18 (Herbert Hill & James E. Jones, Jr. eds., 1993) (reflecting upon his pivotal role in the *Brown v. Board* litigation psychologist Kenneth Clark wrote: "I look back and I shudder at how naïve we all were in our belief in the steady progress racial minorities would make through programs of litigation and education, . . . I am forced to recognize that my life has, in fact, been a series of glorious defeats."). I do not share Clark's grim assessment of *Brown*'s significance. For my own views of *Brown* and its legacy, see Justin Driver, THE SCHOOLHOUSE GATE: PUBLIC EDUCATION, THE SUPREME COURT, AND THE BATTLE FOR THE AMERICAN MIND 242–314 (2018).

28 **attempting to forestall an outcome very much like the one the Supreme Court announced in** *SFFA*: *See, e.g.*, Adam Chilton, Justin Driver, Jonathan S. Masur & Kyle Rozema, *Assessing Affirmative Action's Diversity Rationale*, 122 COLUM. L. REV. 331, 381–88 (2022) (offering empirical evidence supporting affirmative action); Justin Driver, *Think Affirmative Action Is Dead? Think Again.*, N.Y. TIMES, October 31, 2022, at A18.

29 **"involv[ing] whether a university may make admissions decisions that turn on an applicant's race":** Students for Fair Admissions, Inc. v. Pres. & Fellows of Harv. Coll. (*SFFA*), 600 U.S. 181, 208 (2023).

29 **"Eliminating racial discrimination means eliminating all of it":** *SFFA*, 600 U.S. at 206.

29 **the importance of affirmative action policies to the nation's military academies:** *SFFA*, 600 U.S. at 213 n.4.

30 **"in light of the potentially distinct interests that military academies may present":** *SFFA*, 600 U.S. at 213 n.4. In early 2024, the Supreme Court rejected an additional effort to require one of the nation's military academies to comply with *SFFA*'s holding. *See* Abbie VanSickle, *Supreme Court Won't Block Use of Race in West Point Admissions for Now*, N.Y. TIMES (February 2, 2024), https://www .nytimes.com/2024/02/02/us /politics/scotus-admissions-west -point.html.

30 **"an applicant's discussion of how race affected his or her life":** *SFFA*, 600 U.S. at 230.

30 **"may not simply establish through application essays or other means":** *SFFA*, 600 U.S. at 230.

30 **"must be tied to** *that student's* **courage and**

determination": *SFFA*, 600 U.S. at 230–31 (emphasis in original).

30 **"the touchstone of an individual's identity is not challenges bested":** *SFFA*, 600 U.S. at 230–31.

30 **"in race for race's sake":** *SFFA*, 600 U.S. at 220.

30 **"the pernicious stereotype that 'a black student can usually bring something that a white person cannot offer'":** *SFFA*, 600 U.S. at 220 (quoting *Regents of the Univ. of Cal. v. Bakke*, 438 U.S. 265, 316 (1978) (opinion of Powell, J.) (describing Harvard College's admissions program)).

30 **"race in itself 'says [something] about who you are'":** *SFFA*, 600 U.S. at 220 (alteration in original) (quoting Transcript of Oral Argument at 97–98, Students for Fair Admissions v. Univ. of N.C., 600 U.S. 181 (2023) (No. 21-707)).

31 **"it is unclear how courts are supposed to measure [the universities'] goals":** *SFFA*, 600 U.S. at 214; *see id.* at 215 (emphasizing the "elusive nature" of the universities' asserted interests).

31 **"diversity value[s]" received their "proper weight":** Scalia, *The Disease as Cure*, at 148.

31 **he savored this moment:** *SFFA*, 600 U.S. at 287 (Thomas, J., concurring).

31 **"prosperous and well-educated black" physicians and attorneys:** Scalia, *The Disease as Cure*, at 153–54.

31 **"both [applicants] are black, after all":** *SFFA*, 600 U.S. at 282 (Thomas, J., concurring).

32 **"without meaningfully assisting those who struggle with real hardship":** *SFFA*, 600 U.S. at 271.

32 **into settings in which they are ill-equipped to succeed:** For prominent articulations of this idea, see Richard H. Sander, *A Systematic Analysis of Affirmative Action in American Law Schools*, 57 STAN. L. REV. 367 (2004); and Richard H. Sander & Stuart Taylor Jr., MISMATCH: HOW AFFIRMATIVE ACTION HURTS STUDENTS IT'S INTENDED TO HELP, AND WHY UNIVERSITIES WON'T ADMIT IT (2012). Several scholars have offered potent challenges to Professor Sander's arguments.

32 **"simply redistribute individuals among institutions of higher learning":** *SFFA*, 600 U.S. at 268–69 (2023) (Thomas, J., concurring) (internal citation omitted).

32 **"they are less academically prepared than the white and Asian students":** *SFFA*, 600 U.S. at 269 (internal quotation marks omitted).

222

32 "that their race was responsible for their failure to attain a life-long dream": *SFFA*, 600 U.S. at 275.

33 "*exactly* the kind of factionalism that the Constitution was meant to safeguard against": *SFFA*, 600 U.S. at 276 (emphasis in original) (citing THE FEDERALIST NO. 10 (James Madison)).

33 "self-defeating" attitude that prioritizes racial "victimization": *SFFA*, 600 U.S. at 283.

33 "label[ing] all blacks as victims": *SFFA*, 600 U.S. at 279.

33 "their race is not to blame for everything—good or bad": *SFFA*, 600 U.S. at 279–80.

33 "cancerous to young minds seeking to push through barriers": *SFFA*, 600 U.S. at 280.

33 "affirmative action highlights our racial differences with pernicious effect": *SFFA*, 600 U.S. at 274.

33 "sorting by race does not stop at the admissions office": *SFFA*, 600 U.S. at 274.

34 "strident demands for *yet more* racially oriented solutions": *SFFA*, 600 U.S. at 274 (emphasis in original).

34 "prompted to tick one or more boxes to explain 'how you identify yourself'": *SFFA*, 600 U.S. at 291 (Gorsuch, J., concurring).

34 "devised this scheme of [racial] classifications in the 1970s": *SFFA*, 600 U.S. at 291.

34 "helped Asian American students attempt to conceal their racial identities": *SFFA*, 600 U.S. at 293.

34 "with no chance of hiring the kind of consultants who know how to play this game": *SFFA*, 600 U.S. at 294.

35 "an important part of [a] nuanced opinion for the Court": *SFFA*, 600 U.S. at 315; *see SFFA*, 600 U.S. at 312–13 (noting Justice Thomas referred to *Grutter*'s twenty-five-year expectation as a "holding," and Justice Kennedy called it a "pronouncement").

35 "for the college class of 2028": *SFFA*, 600 U.S. at 316 & n.1.

35 which would be a full twenty-nine years post-*Grutter*: *SFFA*, 600 U.S. at 316 n.1.

35 "a lot of pretense or self-delusion (you can take your choice) in all that pertains to affirmative action": Scalia, *The Disease as Cure*, at 148.

36 based on their policy preferences about what race in America should be like, but is not: *SFFA*, 600 U.S. at 353 (Sotomayor, J., dissenting). Justices Kagan and

Jackson joined Justice Sotomayor's dissent. *Id.* at 317.

36 **"Equality requires acknowledgment of inequality":** *SFFA*, 600 U.S. at 334.

36 **but from *Brown v. Board of Education* itself:** *SFFA*, 600 U.S. at 318 (citing 347 U.S. 483 (1954)) (Sotomayor, J., dissenting).

36 **"promot[ing] *Brown*'s vision of a Nation with more inclusive schools":** *SFFA*, 600 U.S. at 318 (Sotomayor, J., dissenting).

36 **"an attempt to put lipstick on a pig":** *SFFA*, 600 U.S. at 363.

36 **"[D]eeming race irrelevant in law does not make it so in life":** *SFFA*, 600 U.S. at 407 (Jackson, J., dissenting); *see also SFFA*, 600 U.S. at 385 ("Our country has never been colorblind.").

36 **"[U]ltimately, ignoring race just makes it matter more":** *SFFA*, 600 U.S. at 407–08.

36 **"[g]ulf-sized race-based gaps [that] exist [regarding] health, wealth, and well-being of American citizens":** *SFFA*, 600 U.S. at 384.

36 **"the well-documented intergenerational transmission of inequality":** *SFFA*, 600 U.S. at 385 (internal quotation marks omitted).

37 **"be it through discrimination, inspiration, or otherwise":** *SFFA*, 600 U.S. at 230.

38 **a "self-defeating" belief in Black "victimhood":** *SFFA*, 600 U.S. at 280, 283 (Thomas, J., concurring).

38 **Shelby Steele's bestselling book from 1990:** *See* Shelby Steele, The Content of Our Character: A New Vision of Race in America (1990).

38 **"encourages blacks to exploit their own past victimization as a source of power and privilege":** Steele, The Content of Our Character, at 118.

39 **"nurtures a victim-focused identity in blacks":** Steele, The Content of Our Character, at 118.

39 **"blacks are encouraged to expand the boundaries of what qualifies as racial oppression":** Steele, The Content of Our Character, at 118.

39 **"who can feel the pea of victimization under twenty mattresses":** Steele, The Content of Our Character, at 118.

39 **"displaying an exceptional ability to discern and protest supposed racial slights":** Lino A. Graglia, *Affirmative Action: Today and Tomorrow*, 22 Ohio N.U. L. Rev. 1353, 1356 (1996).

224

39 **openly acknowledged his debt to Steele:** *See* John McWhorter, Losing the Race: Self-Sabotage in Black America 28 (2000) ("My debt . . . to Shelby Steele's *The Content of Our Character* is obvious.").

39 **"has become a keystone of cultural blackness":** McWhorter, Losing the Race, at xi.

39 **"But thinking you're a victim is a lousy way to get ahead":** Linda Chavez, *Affirmative Action Needs to End*, Columbus Dispatch, (August 9, 2010), https://www.dispatch.com /story/opinion/cartoons/2010/08 /09/linda-chavez-affirmative -action-needs/23662199007.

40 **"Black students discussed their pain":** Aya M. Waller-Bey, *The "T" Word: Resisting Expectations To Share Trauma In College Essays*, Forbes (December 10, 2021), https: //www.forbes.com/sites /civicnation/2021/12/10/the-t -word-resisting-expectations-to -share-trauma-in-college-essays.

40 **caused her to "'just feel a bit lost'":** Cheung, *Affirmative Action Is Over*.

40 **"now that the race box is gone, she feels she should at least mention it":** Cheung, *Affirmative Action Is Over; see also id.* (noting that Rivera-Forbes feared that if she did not write her essay about race her potential would not "be properly recognized").

40 **"put onto the student to display all the struggles that they went through and relive that trauma":** Melissa Korn, *College Applicants Ask: Can I Mention My Race, or Not?*, Wall St. J. (July 31, 2023), https://www.wsj.com /articles/college-applicants-ask -can-i-mention-my-race-or-not -833fa774; *see also* Bernard Mokam, *Highlighting Their Race in Essays for College*, N.Y. Times (January 21, 2024), at 11 (noting several college applicants who had initially drafted essays that omitted discussing race, but after *SFFA* they "decided to rethink their essays to emphasize one key element: their racial identities").

41 **"rather than just about how my parents came here [to America]":** Breanna Ferreira, *Freshmen Reflect on First Admissions Cycle Post Affirmative Action*, Cornell Daily Sun (September 30, 2024), https://cornellsun.com /2024/09/30/freshmen-reflect -on-first-admissions-cycle-post -affirmative-action.

41 **"could mention other aspects of [themselves in] their application[s]":** Ferreira, *Freshmen Reflect on First Admissions Cycle Post Affirmative Action*.

41 **"it's not fair because that takes away from the uniqueness of the applicant":** Rikki Schlott, Opinion, *How Colleges Brazenly Get Around Supreme Court's Affirmative*

Action Ruling, N.Y. Post (September 30, 2023), https: //nypost.com/2023/09/30 /how-colleges-are-skirting -supreme-couts-affirmative -action-ruling.

42   **"this fad of trauma dumping" in college applications:** Anemona Hartocollis, *After the Affirmative Action Ruling, Asian Americans Ask What Happens Next,* N.Y. Times (July 8, 2023), https://www. nytimes.com/2023/07/08/us /affirmative-action-asian -american-students.html.

42   **"ranking themselves against their peers in a form of trauma Olympics":** Claire Hodgdon, *College Essays and Trauma: Students Are Being Pushed to Write About Their Worst Experiences,* Teen Vogue (September 21, 2023), https://www .teenvogue.com/story/college -essays-trauma-students.

42   **"[T]his pressure to package adversity into a palatable narrative can be toxic":** Editorial, *College Essays and the Trauma Sweetspot,* Harv. Crimson (October 21, 2022), https://www .thecrimson.com/article/2022 /10/21/editorial-college -admissions-essay; *see* Mokam, *Highlighting Their Race In Essays For College,* at 11 (noting that some college applicants resented feeling compelled to write their college essays about race, as *SFFA* "made them feel like they were not writing for themselves, but for someone else").

42   **"and now you get to struggle with traumatized-imposter syndrome":** Editorial, *College Essays and the Trauma Sweetspot.*

43   **believing that they secured their spots only because of their brushes with misfortune:** Elijah Megginson, Opinion, *When I Applied to College, I Didn't Want to "Sell My Pain,"* N.Y. Times (May 9, 2021), https://www.nytimes.com /2021/05/09/opinion/college -admissions-essays-trauma.html (recounting a student who felt that her slot at NYU had been illegitimately secured due to her trauma).

43   **groping for that elusive "pea of victimization":** Steele, The Content of Our Character, at 118.

43   **the song "Happy":** Pharrell Williams, Happy (Columbia Records 2013).

43   **essays intoning "Nobody Knows the Trouble I've Seen":** Louis Armstrong, Nobody Knows the Trouble I've Seen (Verve Records 1960).

43   **be superseded by the Microaggression Olympics:** *Cf.* Peggy C. Davis, *Law As Microaggression,* 98 Yale L.J. 1559 (1989).

43   **once emphasized "the *permanence* of racism":** Derrick

226 Bell, FACES AT THE BOTTOM OF THE WELL: THE PERMANENCE OF RACISM (1992) (emphasis added).

43 **what McWhorter labeled the "remnants of racism":** McWhorter, LOSING THE RACE, at xi.

44 **animated the Roberts Court's decision in *Shelby County v. Holder*:** 570 U.S. 529 (2013).

44 **"employed extraordinary measures to address an extraordinary problem":** *Shelby County*, 570 U.S. at 534.

44 **"history did not end in 1965":** *Shelby County*, 570 U.S. at 552.

44 **"there is no denying that . . . our Nation has made great strides":** *Shelby County*, 570 U.S. at 549. For an extended examination of how the Roberts Court's narrative of racial progress shapes its jurisprudence, see Khiara M. Bridges, *Race in the Roberts Court*, 136 HARV. L. REV. 23 (2022).

45 **"through discrimination, inspiration, or otherwise":** Students for Fair Admissions, Inc. v. Pres. & Fellows of Harv. Coll. (*SFFA*), 600 U.S. 181, 230 (2023).

45 **"an essay about how integral their racial identity was to them as a source of pride":** Transcript of Oral Argument at 9–10, *SFFA v. Harvard*, 600 U.S. 181 (No. 20-1199).

45 **obstacles overcome, or, as *SFFA* itself put it, "challenges bested":** *SFFA*, 600 U.S. at 231.

45 **including then-Professor Scalia:** *See* Scalia, *The Disease as Cure*, at 153–54.

45 **Chief Justice John Roberts:** During oral argument in *SFFA*, Chief Justice Roberts expressed profound skepticism that a Black applicant who "grew up in Grosse Point . . . had a great upbringing, . . . his parents went to Harvard, he's a legacy" should be eligible to receive an admissions boost. Transcript of Oral Argument at 62, *SFFA v. Harvard*, 600 U.S. 181 (No. 20-1199).

45 **Justice Samuel Alito:** Fisher v. University of Texas (*Fisher II*), 579 U.S. 365, 419 (2016) (Alito, J., dissenting) (referring to a race-conscious admissions program that provided a boost to students from comparatively "fortunate" backgrounds as "affirmative action gone wild").

45 **Justice Clarence Thomas:** *See SFFA*, 600 U.S. at 271, 282 (Thomas, J., concurring).

47 **this dynamic would harm students who could not pay the freight:** *SFFA*, 600 U.S. at 293–94.

47 **"because it disproved assumptions about who he could be and what he could achieve":** Hannah Natanson, *After Affirmative*

Action, a White Teen's Ivy Hopes Rose. A Black Teen's Sank, WASH. POST (November 18, 2023), https://www.washingtonpost.com/education/interactive/2023/affirmative-action-race-teen-college-applications.

48   **"collection of flag lapel pins":** Natanson, *After Affirmative Action*.

48   **whose college plans suffered from the more complex admissions world created by SFFA:** *See* Cheung, *Affirmative Action Is Over* (chronicling the college application process of Francesco Macias of the Bronx who expressed hesitation about exploring race in his college applications).

48   **was not the only conservative voice in SFFA who blamed affirmative action:** *SFFA*, 600 U.S. at 274–75 (Thomas, J., concurring).

48   **"in our belief . . . have increased racial consciousness":** Transcript of Oral Argument at 21, *SFFA v. Harvard*, 600 U.S. 181 (2023) (No. 20-1199).

48   **made a closely related remark during oral argument:** *See* Transcript of Oral Argument at 5, Students for Fair Admissions, Inc. v. Univ. of N.C., 600 U.S. 181 (2023) (No. 21-707) ("[T]here is no evidence that after two decades[,] *Grutter* has somehow reduced the role of race on campus.").

48   **"saying we ought to take race into account [with] whatever we're doing":** *See* Transcript of Oral Argument at 130, *SFFA v. UNC*, 600 U.S. 181 (2023) (No. 21-707).

48   **"race permeates a lot of what happens at the university":** *See* Transcript of Oral Argument at 129, *SFFA v. UNC*, 600 U.S. 181 (2023) (No. 21-707).

49   **"is a prescription for racial conflict and animosity":** Graglia, *Affirmative Action: Today and Tomorrow*, at 1358.

49   **delayed the day when skin color possessed no greater significance than eye color:** *But see* Toni Morrison, THE BLUEST EYE (1970).

49   **"Race becomes the irritant underlying almost every public issue":** Carl Cohen & James P. Sterba, AFFIRMATIVE ACTION AND RACIAL PREFERENCE: A DEBATE 179 (2003).

49   **"You are an American, yes—but an American of *which kind?*":** Cohen & Sterba, AFFIRMATIVE ACTION AND RACIAL PREFERENCE 178 (emphasis in original).

50   **"in the words of a Harvard prompt, 'shaped who you are'":** Anemona Hartocollis & Colbi Edmonds, *Colleges Want to Know More About You and Your "Identity,"* N.Y. TIMES (August 14, 2023),

228

https://www.nytimes.com/2023/08/14/us/college-applications-admissions-essay.html.

50 **overtly instruct applicants to write about race if they so wish:** *See, e.g.*, Hartocollis & Edmonds, *Colleges Want to Know More About You and Your "Identity*," (noting that Johns Hopkins's post-*SFFA* application states: "Any part of your background, including but not limited to your race, may be discussed in your response to this essay if you so choose.").

50 **"How has difference been a part of your life":** Nick Anderson, *After Supreme Court Ruling, College Applicants Still Write About Race*, Wash. Post (November 27, 2023), https://www.washingtonpost.com/education/2023/11/27/college-applications-race-affirmative-action.

50 **"'says [something] about who you are'":** Students for Fair Admissions, Inc. v. Pres. & Fellows of Harv. Coll. (*SFFA*), 600 U.S. 181, 220 (2023) (quoting Transcript of Oral Argument at 98, Students for Fair Admissions, Inc. v. Univ. of N.C., 600 U.S. 181 (2023) (No. 21-707)).

51 **"that race must be the most important thing about me":** Henry Louis Gates Jr., Colored People: A Memoir, at xv (1994).

51 **"Is that what I want on my gravestone: Here lies an African American?":** Gates Jr., Colored People, at xv.

51 **"that unrelieved suffering is the only 'real' Negro experience":** Ralph Ellison, *The World and the Jug*, *in* Shadow and Act 107, 111 (1964).

51 **"abhors as obscene any trading on one's own anguish":** Ellison, *The World and the Jug*, at 111.

51 **including then-Professor Scalia:** *See* Scalia, *The Disease as Cure*, at 155–56.

51 **and Justice Thomas:** *See SFFA*, 600 U.S. 181, 268–70 (2023) (Thomas, J., concurring).

52 **eight years before *Bakke*:** 438 U.S. 265 (1978).

52 **"[e]nsure that students are placed in schools for which they are not qualified":** Lino A. Graglia, *Special Admission of the "Culturally Deprived" to Law School*, 119 U. Pa. L. Rev. 351, 360 (1970).

52 **who has profoundly influenced Justice Thomas's thought:** *See* Bill Kauffman, *Freedom Now II: Interview with Clarence Thomas*, Reason (November 1987), https://reason.com/1987/11/01/clarence-thomas (identifying Sowell's influence on Thomas's thinking).

52 **"are instead enrolled in famous institutions where they fail":** Thomas Sowell, *Are Quotas*

Good for Blacks?, COMMENTARY, June 1, 1978, at 39, 41.

52   **have challenged the empirical basis for mismatch theory in recent years:** *See, e.g.,* Ian Ayres & Richard Brooks, *Does Affirmative Action Reduce the Number of Black Lawyers?*, 57 STAN L. REV. 1807, 1809 (2005); Daniel E. Ho, *Affirmative Action's Affirmative Actions: A Reply to Sander,* 114 YALE L.J. 2011, 2011–12 (2005); *see also SFFA,* 600 U.S. at 371 (Sotomayor, J., dissenting) (contending that mismatch theory had been "debunked long ago").

52   **Justice Thomas's *SFFA* concurrence:** *SFFA,* 600 U.S. 181, 268–70 (Thomas, J., concurring); *see also Grutter,* 539 U.S. 306, 372 (Thomas, J., concurring in part and dissenting in part) (arguing that affirmative action prompts "overmatched students [to] take the bait, only to find that they cannot succeed in the cauldron of competition").

52   **over the vociferous objections of Justice Sotomayor:** *SFFA,* 600 U.S. at 371–72 (Sotomayor, J., dissenting).

54   **in racially diverse—rather than only monoracial—settings:** 579 U.S. 365 (2016) (*Fisher II*).

55   **"[t]he black student with high grades from Andover":** *Fisher II,* 579 U.S. at 391 (Alito, J., dissenting) (quoting Brief for Respondents at 34, Fisher v. Univ.

of Tex. (*Fisher I*), 570 U.S. 297 (2013) (No. 11-345)); *id.* at 41–18 (quoting Brief for Respondents at 33, *Fisher II* (No. 14-981)).

55   **issued a narrow, technical decision in *Fisher I*:** *Fisher I,* 570 U.S. 297.

55   **no longer foregrounded its Andover defense:** *Fisher II,* 579 U.S. at 417–18 (Alito, J., dissenting).

55   **the *wrong kind* of African-American and Hispanic students:** *Fisher II,* 579 U.S. at 391 (Alito, J., dissenting) (emphasis in original).

55   **"turn[ed] affirmative action on its head":** *Fisher II,* 579 U.S. at 391.

56   **"because it does not work to the advantage of those who are more fortunate":** *Fisher II,* 579 U.S. at 419. For his part, Justice Alito contends that empirical evidence belies the notion that students admitted under the Top Ten Percent plan suffer more academically than students admitted through the race-conscious model. *See Fisher II,* 579 U.S. at 410–16. This empirical conclusion, like many empirical matters, is hotly disputed. For a claim that Top Ten Percent students do in fact encounter greater difficulties, see Eric Furstenberg, *Academic Outcomes and Texas's Top Ten Percent Law,* 627 AM. ACAD. POL. SOC. SCI. 167 (2010).

229

230

56 **including then-Professor Scalia in his post-*Bakke* article:** *See* Scalia, *The Disease as Cure*, at 153–54.

56 **Justice Thomas in his *SFFA* concurrence:** *See* Students for Fair Admissions v. Pres. & Fellows of Harv. Coll. (*SFFA*), 600 U.S. 181, 268–70 (2023) (Thomas, J., concurring).

56 **"Negroes may be specially admitted [under affirmative action] even though they are of middle class background":** Graglia, *Special Admission of the "Culturally Deprived" to Law School,* at 351.

56 **"they are in large part battling over what skin colors the rich kids have":** Walter Benn Michaels, *The Way We Live Now*, N.Y. TIMES, April 11, 2004, at 12.

57 **"would . . . disqualify by definition many of the ablest minority students":** J. Harvie Wilkinson III, FROM *BROWN* TO *BAKKE*: THE SUPREME COURT AND SCHOOL INTEGRATION: 1954–1978, at 288–89 (1979).

57 **"are likely to be overmatched at ultracompetitive universities":** *See, e.g.*, STEPHEN L. CARTER, REFLECTIONS OF AN AFFIRMATIVE ACTION BABY 80 (1991) (noting that "the truly disadvantaged are not likely to succeed in college").

57 **"[t]he most troubled and violent school in the blighted southeast corner of Washington, D.C.":** Ron Suskind, A HOPE IN THE UNSEEN: AN AMERICAN ODYSSEY FROM THE INNER CITY TO THE IVY LEAGUE 1 (1998).

57 **Ballou educated a student body that was almost entirely Black:** Suskind, A HOPE IN THE UNSEEN, at 2.

58 **"I'm not sure if I would have selected an Ivy League school":** Suskind, A HOPE IN THE UNSEEN, at 120.

58 **"suddenly finds himself among almost all whites":** Suskind, A HOPE IN THE UNSEEN, at 120. Justice Thomas's private advice to Jennings about the perils of attending an all-Black high school stands in some contrast with his public opinions that have attested to the greatness of some all-Black high schools. *See* Missouri v. Jenkins, 515 U.S. 70, 114 (1995) (Thomas, J., concurring) ("It never ceases to amaze me that the courts are so willing to assume that anything that is predominantly black must be inferior.").

58 **"ended up getting addicted to drugs and dropping out":** Suskind, A HOPE IN THE UNSEEN, at 120.

59 **"would have made it easier for them to leave the comfort zone of segregation":** Clarence Thomas,

My Grandfather's Son: A Memoir 54 (2007).

59 **"Why, I asked, were these gifted young people being sacrificed on the altar of an abstract theory of social justice":** Thomas, My Grandfather's Son, at 54.

60 **which declined to require the nation's military academies to comply with the decision:** See SFFA, 600 U.S. 181, 213 n.4 (2023).

60 **a dynamic that infamously emerged during the Vietnam War:** "In Vietnam, racial tensions reached a point where there was an inability to fight." David Maraniss, U.S. Military Struggles to Make Equality Work, Wash. Post (March 5, 1990), https://www.washington post.com/archive/politics/1990 /03/06/us-military-struggles-to -make-equality-work/e43bfbf9 -e170-4f3f-b6c5-ff74cade07f4 (quoting Lt. Gen. Frank Petersen, Jr.).

60 **the necessity of a diverse officer corps for the military's ability to function effectively:** See Grutter v. Bollinger, 539 U.S. 306, 331 (2003) (citing Consolidated Brief of Julius W. Becton, Jr., et al. as Amici Curiae Supporting Respondents, Grutter, 539 U.S. 306 (No. 02-241)).

61 **military academies produce only 19 percent of the active-duty officers:** Office of the Under Sec'y of Def., Personnel & Readiness, Dep't of Def., Active Component Commissioned Officer Corps, FY18: By Source of Commission, Service, Gender, and Race/Ethnicity (2018), App. B, Tbl. B-33, at 96, https://www.cna.org/pop-rep/2018 /appendixb/appendixb.pdf.

62 **continues to be plagued by an unvarnished racism:** See Racism Plagues U.S. Military Academies Despite Diversity Gains, Associated Press (December 3, 2021) https://www.nbcnews.com/news/nbcblk /racism-plagues-us-military -academies-diversity-gains -rcna7523.

62 **including then-Professor Scalia in 1979:** See Scalia, The Disease as Cure, at 154–55.

62 **and Justice Thomas in SFFA:** See SFFA, 600 U.S. 181, 270 (2023) (Thomas, J., concurring).

62 **"unhappy consequence will be to perpetuate the hostilities":** Grutter v. Bollinger, 539 U.S. 306, 394-95 (2003) (Kennedy, J., dissenting).

63 **Black and brown racial aggrievement can also merit judicial solicitude:** See Reva B. Siegel, From Colorblindness to Antibalkanization: An Emerging Ground of Decision in Race Equality Cases, 120 Yale L.J. 1278, 1359 (2011) (contending antibalkanization "should be enforced in ways that are at least as responsive to practices

232   and conditions of concern to minority as to majority communities").

63   **"Why did I serve if I'm only looked at as cannon fodder?":** *See The Supreme Court Banned Affirmative Action—Except at Military Service Academies*, NPR, September 20, 2023, https://www .npr.org/transcripts/1197953097.

63   **Racism in the US military has a lengthy, sordid history:** Formal racial segregation existed in the US military until 1948. *See* Maraniss, *U.S. Military Struggles to Make Equality Work.*

64   **"they did not soon forget this unequal distribution of harm":** Naima Green-Riley & Andrew Leber, *Whose War Is It Anyway? Explaining the Black-White Gap in Support for the Use of Force Abroad,* 32 SECURITY STUDS. 811, 836 (2023).

64   **"We want all Black men to be exempt from military service":** *The Black Panther Party's Ten-Point Program*, UC PRESS BLOG (February 7, 2017), https://www.ucpress.edu /blog/25139/the-black-panther -partys-ten-point-program. Explaining their position, the Black Panthers reasoned: "We believe that Black people should not be forced to fight in the military service to defend a racist government that does not protect us. We will not fight and kill other people of color in the world who, like Black people, are being

victimized by the White racist government of America." *Id.*

64   **teems with instances of racial mistreatment:** Wallace Terry, BLOODS: BLACK VETERANS OF THE VIETNAM WAR: AN ORAL HISTORY (1984).

64   **"the armed forces suffered increased racial polarization":** Consolidated Brief of Julius W. Becton, Jr., et al. as Amici Curiae Supporting Respondents at 6, *Grutter*, 539 U.S. 306 (No. 02-241).

64   **"[T]hey could not understand that I'm a Black man / and I could never be a veteran":** Public Enemy, BLACK STEEL IN THE HOUR OF CHAOS (Columbia Records 1988).

64   **"stifle [the] success [of racial minorities]" in the military disproportionately:** Zoe Kreitenberg, *Affirmative Action Is Banned—Except at Military Academies? Why That Won't Help Students,* L.A. TIMES (July 17, 2023), https://www.latimes.com/opinion /story/2023-07-17/military -exception-supreme-court -affirmative-action.

65   **"they had seen examples of white nationalism or ideologically driven racism among their fellow troops":** Helene Cooper, *African-Americans Are Highly Visible in the Military, but Almost Invisible at the Top*, N.Y. TIMES (October 18, 2021) https://www.nytimes.com/2020

/05/25/us/politics/military -minorities-leadership.html. For a book contending America's military has served as an incubator of white nationalism, see Kathleen Belew, BRING THE WAR HOME: THE WHITE POWER MOVEMENT AND PARAMILITARY AMERICA (2018).

65   **only two of those were Black:** *See* Cooper, *African-Americans Are Highly Visible in the Military, But Almost Invisible at the Top.*

65   **"[y]ou would have thought it was 1950":** Cooper, *African-Americans Are Highly Visible in the Military, but Almost Invisible at the Top.* Another Black retired military official stated that if "[i]t's America's military," then "[w]hy doesn't this photo look like America?" *Id.*

65   **"[t]he African-Americans who do become officers are often steered to specialize in logistics and transportation":** Cooper, *African-Americans Are Highly Visible in the Military, but Almost Invisible at the Top.*

65   **"would be less likely to heed instructions coming directly from a Black man":** *See* Helene Cooper, *Lloyd Austin Confronts the Perils of Being a Private Man in a Public Job,* N.Y. TIMES (January 13, 2024), https://www.nytimes.com/2024 /01/13/us/politics/lloyd-austin -private-public.html.

65   **featured an acronym that originated in the Aryan Brotherhood:** *See* Cooper, *African-Americans Are Highly Visible in the Military, but Almost Invisible at the Top.*

65   **routinely refer to their Black colleagues as "nonswimmer[s]":** Cooper, *African-Americans Are Highly Visible in the Military, but Almost Invisible at the Top.*

66   **their colleagues have referred to them collectively as "eggplants":** Cooper, *African-Americans Are Highly Visible in the Military, but Almost Invisible at the Top.*

66   **"an embarrassment to teach":** Scalia, *The Disease as Cure,* at 147.

66   **"difficult to pretend to one's students that the decisions of the Supreme Court are tied together by threads of logic and analysis":** Scalia, *The Disease as Cure,* at 147.

CHAPTER TWO

67   **deny[ing] any person within its jurisdiction the equal protection of the laws":** U.S. CONST. amend. XIV, § 1.

67   **"the usual last resort of constitutional arguments":** *Buck v. Bell,* 274 U.S. 200, 208 (1927).

68   **prohibiting the government from engaging in racial classification:** *See, e.g.,* Owen M.

234   Fiss, *Groups and the Equal Protection Clause*, 5 PHIL. & PUB. AFFAIRS 107, 108–09, 147 (1976) (identifying two competing Equal Protection Clause visions while generally employing different terminology).

68   **prohibiting the government from perpetuating racial subordination:** Fiss, *Groups and the Equal Protection Clause*, at 155–57.

68   ***Brown v. Board of Education:*** 347 U.S. 483 (1954).

68   **perpetuated racism by suggesting that Black people were inferior:** *See* 347 U.S. at 494.

68   **they form the very axis upon which the Equal Protection Clause turns:** *See, e.g.,* Sanford Levinson, Jack M. Balkin, Akhil Reed Amar, Reva B. Siegel & Cristina M. Rodríguez, PROCESSES OF CONSTITUTIONAL DECISIONMAKING: CASES AND MATERIALS 1110 (8th ed. 2022) (explaining the difference between "the *antisubordination* principle and . . . the *anticlassification* principle" (emphasis in original)); *id.* at 1149–54 (elaborating upon this distinction).

68   **because it held quite tangible consequences for assessing the constitutionality of affirmative action:** Melvin I. Urofsky, THE AFFIRMATIVE ACTION PUZZLE: A LIVING HISTORY FROM RECONSTRUCTION TO TODAY xvi (2020) ("The literature on affirmative action is immense, and continues to grow, because, as some scholars argue, no other issue divides Americans more.").

68   **anticlassification school— associated overwhelmingly with constitutional conservatives:** *See, e.g.,* Scalia, *The Disease as Cure*, 153–54; Adarand Constructors, Inc. v. Peña, 515 U.S. 200, 239 (1995) (Scalia, J., concurring in part):

> To pursue the concept of racial entitlement—even for the most admirable and benign of purposes—is to reinforce and preserve for future mischief the way of thinking that produced race slavery, race privilege and race hatred. In the eyes of government, we are just one race here. It is American.

See also Students for Fair Admissions, Inc. (SFFA) v. President and Fellows of Harvard Coll., 600 U.S. 181, 206 (2023) ("Eliminating racial discrimination means eliminating all of it.").

69   **antisubordination school— identified predominantly with legal liberals:** *See* Fiss, *Groups and the Equal Protection Clause*, at 160–61.

69   **published the foundational article advancing what came to be termed the antisubordination theory:** Fiss, *Groups and the Equal Protection Clause,* at 147 (introducing the "group-disadvantaging principle"); Jack M.

Balkin & Reva B. Siegel, *The American Civil Rights Tradition: Anticlassification or Antisubordination?*, 58 U. MIAMI L. REV. 9, 9 (2003) (contending "Fiss inaugurated the antisubordination tradition in legal scholarship"); Pamela S. Karlan, *What Can Brown® Do for You?: Neutral Principles and the Struggle Over the Equal Protection Clause*, 58 DUKE L.J. 1049, 1061 (calling Fiss's article "foundational").

69   "the state law or practice [that] aggravates . . . or perpetuates": *See* Fiss, *Groups and the Equal Protection Clause*, at 157.

69   the Supreme Court's first, inconclusive brush with affirmative action: *See DeFunis v. Odegaard*, 416 U.S. 312, 319–20 (1974) (declining to reach the merits due to mootness).

69   *Regents of the University of California v. Bakke*: 438 U.S. 265 (1978).

69   did not invoke the anticlassification theory to invalidate the then-fledgling affirmative action programs: *See* Fiss, *Groups and the Equal Protection Clause*, at 159–60.

69   Laurence Tribe offered "an antisubjugation principle": Laurence H. Tribe, AMERICAN CONSTITUTIONAL LAW §§ 1514–15 (2d ed. 1988).

69   **Cass Sunstein advanced "the anticaste principle":** Cass R. Sunstein, *The Anticaste Principle*, 92 MICH. L. REV. 2410 (1994).

70   "that enforce the inferior social status of historically oppressed groups": Reva B. Siegel, *Equality Talk: Antisubordination and Anticlassification Values in Constitutional Struggles over Brown*, 117 HARV. L. REV. 1470, 1472–73 (2004).

70   emphasizing antisubordination values means viewing affirmative action as constitutionally permissible: *See, e.g.*, Sunstein, *The Anticaste Principle*, at 2452 ("If a basic goal is opposition to caste, affirmative action policies are ordinarily permissible.").

71   "I doubt whether anyone believes that preferential admissions to law schools for blacks impairs the status of the group": Fiss, *Groups and the Equal Protection Clause*, at 160.

71   managed to shoo away the objection in a single sentence or buried it in a footnote: *See, e.g.*, Paul Brest, *Foreword: In Defense of the Antidiscrimination Principle*, 90 HARV. L. REV. 1, 18 (1976) ("It is conceivable, but not likely, that . . . preferential . . . admissions policies might reflect assumptions that minorities are innately inferior and therefore in need of special aid."); Charles R. Lawrence III, *The*

235

236 *Id, the Ego, and Equal Protection: Reckoning with Unconscious Racism,* 39 Stan. L. Rev. 317, 379–80 n.294 (1987) (burying the question of whether affirmative action programs flunk his own "racial meaning" test).

71 **conveyed "stigma and caste," and placed "a stamp of inferiority":** *DeFunis,* 416 U.S. at 343 (Douglas, J., dissenting).

71 **Antisubordination, it seems, is a coat of many colors:** *Cf.* Bd. Of Educ. v. Allen, 392 U.S. 236, 249 (1968) (Harlan, J., concurring) ("Neutrality is . . . a coat of many colors.").

71 **Supreme Court's decision in *SFFA v. Harvard*:** 600 U.S. 181 (2023).

72 ***Strauder v. West Virginia*:** 100 U.S. 303 (1880).

73 ***Loving v. Virginia*:** 388 U.S. 1 (1967).

73 **invalidated a statute that prohibited Black people from serving on juries:** *Strauder,* 100 U.S. at 310–12.

73 **"an assertion of their inferiority, and a stimulant to that race prejudice":** *Strauder,* 100 U.S. at 308.

73 **"legal discriminations, implying [their] inferiority":** *Strauder,* 100 U.S. at 308.

73 **highlight the iconic decision's language condemning school segregation because it perpetuated notions of Black inferiority:** *See, e.g.,* Siegel, *Equality Talk,* at 1480–89.

73 **"may affect their hearts and minds in a way unlikely ever to be undone":** *Brown,* 347 U.S. at 494.

73 **invalidation of state bans on interracial marriage:** *See* David A. Strauss, *Discriminatory Intent and the Taming of* Brown, 56 U. Chi. L. Rev. 935, 941 (1989).

73 **"[t]he fact that Virginia prohibits only interracial marriages involving white persons":** *Loving,* 388 U.S. at 11.

74 ***Palmer v. Thompson*:** 403 U.S. 217 (1971).

74 **one of the most reviled racial decisions in modern American history:** For a recent repudiation, see generally Randall Kennedy, *Reconsidering* Palmer v. Thompson, 2018 Sup. Ct. Rev. 179 (2019).

74 **"are being denied their constitutional rights when the city has closed the public pools to black and white alike":** *Palmer,* 403 U.S. at 226 (emphasis omitted).

74 **because Jackson had not racially classified residents, it also had not violated:** *Palmer,* 403 U.S. at 226.

74   **were driven by a view of the Black body as undesirable, even contaminated:** *See* Kennedy, *Reconsidering* Palmer, at 189–91. For an examination of the swimming pool as a site of racial conflict, see generally Jeff Wiltse, CONTESTED WATERS: A SOCIAL HISTORY OF SWIMMING POOLS IN AMERICA (2007).

74   **"an . . . official policy that Negroes are unfit to associate with whites":** *Palmer*, 403 U.S. at 240–41 (White, J., dissenting) (describing a hypothetical town's pool closure policy that is "little, if any, different from" Jackson, Mississippi's).

74   **have routinely asserted that affirmative action combats subordination:** *See, e.g.*, Siegel, *Equality Talk,* at 1538–40 (contending that *Grutter* "explicitly embraces antisubordination values").

75   **"and in the end . . . may produce that result despite its contrary intentions":** *DeFunis*, 416 U.S. at 343 (Douglas, J., dissenting).

75   **"a stamp of inferiority that a State is not permitted to place on any lawyer":** *DeFunis*, 416 U.S. at 343.

75   **the dreaded "stamp of inferiority":** *DeFunis*, 416 U.S. at 343.

75   **entertaining how affirmative action could harm Black and brown students:** *Bakke*, 438 U.S. at

297–98, 297 n.37 (Powell, J., writing for the Court).

75   **also prohibited them from implementing the sort of naked quota:** *Bakke*, 438 U.S. at 319–20.

76   **"preferential programs may only reinforce common stereotypes":** *Bakke*, 438 U.S. at 319–20 (citing *DeFunis*, 416 U.S. at 343 (Douglas, J., dissenting)).

76   **but he did concede that they existed:** In *Bakke*, Justice Brennan rejected the notion that UC Davis's admissions "program [can] reasonably be regarded as stigmatizing the program's beneficiaries or their race as inferior." *Bakke*, 438 U.S. at 375 (Brennan, J., concurring in part and dissenting in part). Justice Brennan contended this affirmative action-as-subordinating interpretation would be inaccurate because all of the students admitted to UC Davis Medical School were qualified. *Bakke*, 438 U.S. at 375–76.

76   **his colleagues in the majority believed that Black students needed affirmative action to flourish:** *Grutter*, 539 U.S. at 350 (Thomas, J., concurring in part and dissenting in part).

76   **there was no way to distinguish Black students "who belong[ed]":** *Grutter*, 539 U.S. at 373.

237

238   76   "The majority of blacks are admitted to the Law School because of discrimination": *Grutter*, 539 U.S. at 373.

77   "it is an open question today whether their skin color played a part in their advancement": *Grutter*, 539 U.S. at 373.

77   "asking the question itself unfairly marks those blacks who would succeed without discrimination": *Grutter*, 539 U.S. at 373.

77   "tar[s]," "stigmat[izes]," and "marks" Black people as substandard: *Grutter*, 539 U.S. at 373.

77   *Fisher v. University of Texas (Fisher I)*: 570 U.S. 297 (2013).

77   use explicit racial classifications in rounding out the class: *Fisher I*, 570 U.S. at 306.

77   declined to determine whether Texas's express racial classifications violated the Equal Protection Clause: *Fisher I*, 570 U.S. at 314–15.

77   "insidious consequences" that result from "racial engineering": *Fisher I*, 570 U.S. at 331 (Thomas, J., concurring).

77   "injures . . . Asian applicants who are denied admission because of their race": *Fisher I*, 570 U.S. at 331.

77   the taint applied to every member of those racial groups at Texas: *Fisher I*, 570 U.S. at 333.

78   "no one can distinguish those students from the ones whose race played a role in their admission": *Fisher I*, 570 U.S. at 333.

78   "a badge of inferiority" pinned to their chests solely as a result of their skin color: *Fisher I*, 570 U.S. at 333 (quoting *Adarand*, 515 U.S. at 241 (Thomas, J., concurring in part and concurring in the judgment)).

78   transformed into a booby prize: *See Booby Prize*, Oxford English Dictionary (3d ed. 2010) (defining the term as "[a] prize or reward (frequently consisting of something ridiculous or undesirable) given as a joke to the competitor coming in last place in a contest, race, etc.").

78   *Schuette v. Coalition to Defend Affirmative Action*: 572 U.S. 291 (2014).

78   whether the Equal Protection Clause prohibited states from banning affirmative action in education: *Schuette*, 572 U.S. at 300–301.

78   held that states could do so without running afoul of the Constitution: *Schuette*, 572 U.S. at 310. Justice Kagan recused herself from participating in *Schuette*.

78   **for ignoring that "[r]ace matters" in myriad ways:** *Schuette*, 572 U.S. at 380–81 (Sotomayor, J., dissenting) (internal quotation marks and citations omitted).

79   **"The way to stop discrimination on the basis of race is to stop discriminating on the basis of race":** Parents Involved in Cmty. Schs. v. Seattle Sch. Dist. No. 1, 551 U.S. 701, 748 (2007) (plurality opinion).

79   **"is to speak openly and candidly on the subject of race":** *Schuette*, 572 U.S. at 381 (Sotomayor, J., dissenting).

79   **"that the preferences do more harm than good":** *Schuette*, 572 U.S. at 315 (Roberts, C.J., concurring).

80   **"in the long run reinforce stereotypes of incompetence":** Lino A. Graglia, *Special Admission of the "Culturally Deprived" to Law School*, 119 U. PA. L. REV. 351, 355–56 (1970).

80   **would conclude they needed a white attorney:** Graglia, *Special Admission of the "Culturally Deprived" to Law School*, at 356 (emphasis in original).

80   **whom Justice Thomas has lavishly praised:** Justice Thomas has stated that encountering Sowell's writing "was manna from heaven," and reading his work "was like pouring half a glass of water on

the desert [in that] I just soaked it up." Bill Kauffman, *Freedom Now II: Interview with Clarence Thomas*, REASON (November 1987).

80   **"is that *black people just don't have it*":** Thomas Sowell, BLACK EDUCATION: MYTHS AND TRAGEDIES 292 (1972) (emphasis in original).

80   **"the idea of an 'affirmative action' doctor is particularly troubling":** Richard A. Posner, *The* Bakke *Case and the Future of "Affirmative Action,"* 67 CALIF. L. REV. 171, 187 (1979).

81   **"establish[ing] a second-class, 'minority' degree":** Scalia, *The Disease as Cure*, at 155.

81   **"to eliminate all minority group members?":** Scalia, *The Disease as Cure,* at 154. In this same vein, Scalia contended that affirmative action in effect establishes "a regime reminiscent of major league baseball in the years before Jackie Robinson: a separate 'league' for minority students, which makes it difficult for the true excellence of the minority star to receive his or her deserved acknowledgment." Scalia, *The Disease as Cure*, at 155.

81   **"and if I'm not equal, then I'm inferior":** Nell Perry, *Clarence Thomas: Protecting People's Rights*, MINORITIES & WOMEN IN BUSINESS, September/October 1989, at 26 (cited in *Nomination of Judge*

240 *Clarence Thomas to Be Associate Justice of the Supreme Court of the United States, Hearings Before the S. Comm. on the Judiciary,* 102d Cong. 748 (1991)).

82 **"the presumption was that you were dumb and didn't deserve to be there on merit":** Kevin Merida & Michael A. Fletcher, *Clarence Thomas' Years at Yale Law School,* J. BLACKS IN HIGHER EDUC., no. 56, 2007, at 82, 82.

82 **"like having a monkey jump down on your back from the Gothic arches":** Merida & Fletcher, *Clarence Thomas' Years at Yale Law School.*

82 **a founder of critical race theory:** *See, e.g.,* Fred A. Bernstein, *Derrick Bell, Pioneering Law Professor And Civil Rights Advocate, Dies at 80,* N.Y. TIMES (October 7, 2011), https://www.nytimes.com /2011/10/06/us/derrick-bell -pioneering-harvard-law -professor-dies-at-80.html (labeling Bell "a pioneer of critical race theory"); Jelani Cobb, *The Man Behind Critical Race Theory,* NEW YORKER (September 13, 2021), (contending that Bell's influence extended to "generations of thinkers").

83 **"denied the signal of their competence which students admitted under traditional qualifications receive":** Derrick A. Bell, Jr., *Black Students in White Law Schools: The Ordeal and the*

Opportunity, 2 U. TOL. L. REV. 539, 551 (1970).

83 **"envelop[ed] minority applicants in a cloud of suspected incompetency":** Bell, *Minority Admissions, and the Usual Price of Racial Remedies,* at 8.

83 **"suggests the giving of charity rather than the granting of relief":** Bell, *Minority Admissions, and the Usual Price of Racial Remedies,* at 8 (emphasis in original).

83 **affirmative action programs may contain anti-Black racism:** *See* Bell, *Minority Admissions, and the Usual Price of Racial Remedies,* at 9 ("The presence of racism in policies intended to remedy racism is not generally recognized.").

83 **the policy often has destructive, subordinating effects:** Stephen L. Carter, REFLECTIONS OF AN AFFIRMATIVE ACTION BABY 66–69, 71–72, 84–88 (1991) (expressing support for affirmative action, albeit with major qualifications and reservations).

83 **"on the box [are] label[s], not of my own choosing":** Carter, REFLECTIONS OF AN AFFIRMATIVE ACTION BABY, at 1.

83 **"WARNING! AFFIRMATIVE ACTION BABY!":** Carter, REFLECTIONS OF AN AFFIRMATIVE ACTION BABY, at 2.

84   "black people cannot compete intellectually with white people": Carter, REFLECTIONS OF AN AFFIRMATIVE ACTION BABY, at 47.

84   "stigmatizes its beneficiaries and, indeed, anyone affiliated": Kennedy, FOR DISCRIMINATION, at 115–21 (noting the stigmatic effects of affirmative action).

84   "their sense of being diminished, underestimated, devalued, or condescended to": Kennedy, FOR DISCRIMINATION, at 119.

84   "'I feel like I have AFFIRMATIVE ACTION stamped on my forehead'": Kennedy, FOR DISCRIMINATION, at 120.

85   notion that Asian Americans were the Model Minority: For an insightful overview of the Model Minority concept and its origins, see Philip Lee, *Rejecting Honorary Whiteness: Asian Americans and the Attack on Race-Conscious Admissions*, 70 EMORY L.J. 1475, 1494–98 (2021).

85   being a racial minority in the United States did not invariably yield alienation and impoverishment: *See generally* Elizabeth Hinton, AMERICA ON FIRE: THE UNTOLD HISTORY OF POLICE VIOLENCE AND BLACK REBELLION SINCE THE 1960S (2021) (providing a long history of urban unrest in the United States).

85   overcome racial discrimination by dint of hard work and sound values: *See, e.g.*, William Pettersen, *Success Story, Japanese-American Style*, N.Y. TIMES MAG., January 9, 1966, at 20.

85   "Chinese-Americans are moving ahead on their own—with no help from anyone else": *Success Story of One Minority Group in U.S.*, U.S. NEWS & WORLD REP., December 26, 1966, at 73.

85   "[s]till being taught in Chinatown is the old idea that people should depend on their own efforts": *Success Story of One Minority Group in U.S.*, at 73.

86   "to become a model of self-respect and achievement in today's America": *Success Story of One Minority Group in U.S.*, at 73, 76.

86   "ethnic Asians have been steadily marching into the ranks of the educational elite": Susanna McBee, George White, Joseph L. Galloway, Sarah Peterson, Pat Lynch, & Michael Bosc, *Asian-Americans: Are They Making the Grade?*, U.S. NEWS & WORLD REP., April 2, 1984, at 41.

86   "Nowhere is the strong ambition of Asians more evident than in the classroom": McBee et al., *Asian-Americans: Are They Making the Grade?*, at 41.

242   86   "If I went to any other school, my mother would kill me": McBee et al., *Asian-Americans: Are They Making the Grade?*, at 41.

86   Asian American student stereotyping: *Asian-Americans: The Drive to Excel*, at 4.

86   "They say that Asian Americans behave as a model minority": *Asian-Americans: The Drive to Excel*, at 4.

87   "frighten many other students with their academic interests and prowess": *Asian-Americans: The Drive to Excel*, at 4.

87   "[o]ther students speak of dropping courses if they walk into a classroom and see too many Oriental faces": *Asian-Americans: The Drive to Excel*, at 8; *see also id.* (reporting without rebuking a Stanford senior majoring in mathematics who contended that his Asian Americans classmates were "very nerdy—just very stereotypical").

87   "the willingness of Asian-American students to pay almost any price to get ahead": *Asian-Americans: The Drive to Excel*, at 7.

87   "They aren't out on Saturday night getting drunk—they're hitting the books": *Asian-Americans: The Drive to Excel*, at 7.

87   "more unidimensional than our other students": *Asian-Americans: The Drive to Excel*, at 11.

87   "the concert stage might soon be dominated by Asian-American musicians": *Asian-Americans: The Drive to Excel*, at 8.

87   "Asian students are willing to work harder from a very early age": *Asian-Americans: The Drive to Excel*, at 8.

88   "one-dimensional, technical supermen": Vincent T. Chang & Amy C. Han, *Newsweek's Asian-American Stereotypes*, HARVARD CRIMSON (April 23, 1984).

88   "are not a monolithic group and cannot be characterized by facile, sweeping generalities": Chang & Han, *Newsweek's Asian-American Stereotypes*.

88   "invit[ing] resentment against the supposed domination of universities": Chang & Han, *Newsweek's Asian-American Stereotypes*.

88   "[a]s soon as admissions of Asian students began reaching 10 or 12 percent": Robert Lindsey, *Colleges Accused of Bias to Stem Asians' Gains*, N.Y. TIMES, January 19, 1987, at A10 (emphasis omitted).

88   "and they began to look for ways of slowing down the admissions of Asians": Lindsey, *Colleges Accused of Bias to Stem Asians' Gains* (emphasis omitted).

88   the four leading news networks all contacted Wang for interviews: *See* Jerome Karabel,

THE CHOSEN: THE HIDDEN HISTORY OF
ADMISSION AND EXCLUSION AT HARVARD,
YALE, AND PRINCETON 502 (2005)
(noting the media response to
Wang's claims, and that "[f]or the
first time, allegations of anti-Asian
discrimination were in the mass
media").

89 "one admissions officer
responded that they tend to be
'driven'": John H. Bunzel & Jeffrey
K.D. Au, *Diversity or Discrimination?
Asian Americans in College*, PUB. INT.,
Spring 1987, at 49, 56.

90 "lack an appreciation for a
'well-rounded liberal education'":
Bunzel & Au, *Diversity or
Discrimination?*, at 59; *see also*
James S. Gibney, *The Berkeley
Squeeze: The Future of Affirmative
Action*, NEW REPUBLIC (April 11,
1988), at 15 (noting that "[Asian
Americans] claim that
discrimination is keeping their
number artificially low").

91 "relegating them to an
inferior caste for no reason other
than race": Brief for Respondent
at 3, *SFFA v. Harvard*, 600 U.S. 181
(No. 20-1199).

91 "attempts to equate this case
with *Brown* trivialize the grievous
legal and moral wrongs of
segregation": Brief for the United
States as Amicus Curiae
Supporting Respondent at 5–6,
SFFA v. Harvard, 600 U.S. 181 (No.
20-1199).

91 **contended that university**   243
**admissions policies (especially at
Harvard) subordinated Asian
American applicants:** *See* Brief for
Petitioner at 47, 51, *SFFA v.
Harvard* & *SFFA v. UNC*, 600 U.S.
181 (Nos. 20-1199 & 21-707)
(invoking colorblindness).

91 **that animus directed toward
the group is hardly a thing of the
past:** *See* Brief for Petitioner at
25–26, *SFFA v. Harvard* & *SFFA v.
UNC*, 600 U.S. 181 (Nos. 20-1199 &
21-707) (citing *Yick Wo v. Hopkins*,
118 U.S. 356 (1886), and *Korematsu
v. United States*, 323 U.S. 214 (1944)).

91 **"stereotyped as timid, quiet,
shy, passive":** Brief for Petitioner
at 25, *SFFA v. Harvard* & *SFFA v.
UNC*, 600 U.S. 181 (Nos. 20-1199 &
21-707); *see* Brief for Petitioner at
63, *SFFA v. Harvard* & *SFFA v. UNC*,
600 U.S. 181 (Nos. 20-1199 &
21-707) ("Every day, Asian
Americans are stereotyped as shy,
passive, perpetual foreigners, and
model minorities.").

91 **"are interested only in math
and science":** Brief for Petitioner at
48, 63, *SFFA v. Harvard* & *SFFA v.
UNC*, 600 U.S. 181 (Nos. 20-1199 &
21-707).

92 **"putting the lie to the notion
that this discrimination is
somehow 'benign'":** Brief for
Petitioner at 48, *SFFA v. Harvard* &
SFFA v. UNC, 600 U.S. 181 (Nos.
20-1199 & 21-707) (emphasis in
original).

244 92 "[a]n entire industry . . . help[ing] them appear 'less Asian' on their college applications": Brief for Petitioner at 63, *SFFA v. Harvard & SFFA v. UNC*, 600 U.S. 181 (Nos. 20-1199 & 21-707).

92 **"don't attach a photograph":** Brief for Petitioner at 63–64, *SFFA v. Harvard & SFFA v. UNC*, 600 U.S. 181 (Nos. 20-1199 & 21-707) (quoting Princeton Review, CRACKING COLLEGE ADMISSIONS 174 (2d ed. 2004)).

92 regions that Harvard dubbed **"sparse country":** Brief for Petitioner at 21, *SFFA v. Harvard & SFFA v. UNC*, 600 U.S. 181 (Nos. 20-1199 & 21-707).

92 **"lived [in sparse country] for their entire lives":** Brief for Petitioner at 21, *SFFA v. Harvard & SFFA v. UNC*, 600 U.S. 181 (quoting 2 Joint Appendix at 562, *SFFA v. Harvard*, 143 S. Ct. 2141 (No. 20-1199)).

93 purported to measure applicants' **"self-confidence," "likeability," "leadership,"** and **"kindness":** Brief for Petitioner at 16, 63, *SFFA v. Harvard & SFFA v. UNC*, 600 U.S. 181 (Nos. 20-1199 & 21-707).

93 construing that ethnic group as possessing less appealing **personalities:** Brief for Petitioner at 63, 73, *SFFA v. Harvard & SFFA v. UNC*, 600 U.S. at 181 (Nos. 20-1199 & 21-707).

93 **"Because the first conclusion is racist and false, the second must be true":** Reply Brief for Petitioner at 20, *SFFA v. Harvard*, 600 U.S. 181 (No. 20-1199) (citation omitted). For a law review article anticipating the claim in *SFFA* that affirmative action subordinates Asian Americans, though avoiding "antisubordination" terminology, see Cory K. Liu, *Affirmative Action's Badge of Inferiority on Asian Americans*, 22 TEX. REV. L. & POL. 317, 330 (2018) (contending affirmative action makes "Asians . . . feel like second-class citizens and perpetual foreigners," and that such "stereotyping is incompatible with the logic . . . of *Brown*").

93 **"reinforces negative stereotypes historically used to justify discrimination":** Brief of Amici Curiae the Asian American Coalition for Education et al. in Support of Petitioner at 7, 8, *SFFA v. Harvard*, 600 U.S. 181 (No. 20-1199).

94 **"race is a minus for Asians":** Transcript of Oral Argument at 3, *SFFA v. Harvard*, 600 U.S. 181 (No. 20-1199); *see id.* at 119 (emphasizing the "statistically significant relationship between being Asian and getting a low personal rating").

94 **"[Affirmative action programs] stigmatize their intended beneficiaries":** Transcript of Oral Argument at 117,

SFFA v. Harvard, 600 U.S. 181 (No. 20-1199).

94   "**They should not be the victims of Harvard's racial experimentation**": Transcript of Oral Argument at 120–21, *SFFA v. Harvard*, 600 U.S. 181 (No. 20-1199); *cf.* Thomas K. Nakayama, *"Model Minority" and the Media: Discourse on Asian America*, 12 J. COMMC'N INQUIRY 65, 68 (1988) ("The systematic referral of Asian Americans as 'Asians' reinforces the importance of Asia.").

95   "**and those are the people who are discriminated against**": Transcript of Oral Argument at 29, *SFFA v. UNC*, 600 U.S. 181 (No. 21-707).

95   "**or there has to be something wrong with this personal score**": Transcript of Oral Argument at 53–54, *SFFA v. Harvard*, 600 U.S. 181 (No. 20-1199); *see* Reply Brief for Petitioner at 20, *SFFA v. Harvard*, 600 U.S. 181 (No. 20-1199) (citation omitted) (noting that SFFA's merits brief stated: "Why does Harvard assign Asian-American applicants significantly lower personal ratings? Either Asian Americans really do lack 'integrity,' 'courage,' 'kindness,' and 'empathy.' Or Harvard is discriminating against them.").

96   "**designed to bring individuals of all races together so that they can all learn**": Transcript of Oral Argument at 112, *SFFA v.*

Harvard, 600 U.S. 181 (No. 20-1199).

96   "**It doesn't mean that they're either smarter or people think they're smarter**": Transcript of Oral Argument at 60–61, *SFFA v. Harvard*, 600 U.S. 181 (No. 20-1199).

96   **liked this answer enough to offer a slightly modified version of it elsewhere:** Waxman acknowledged that while "there is a slight numerical disparity with respect to the personal rating of Asian Americans, . . . [there is] also a slight numerical disparity to the advantage of Asian Americans with respect to the extracurricular rating and the academic rating." Transcript of Oral Argument at 55, *SFFA v. Harvard*, 600 U.S. 181 (No. 20-1199).

97   "**You're more likely to be viewed as less academic—as having less academic potential**": Transcript of Oral Argument at 8, *SFFA v. UNC*, 600 U.S. 181(No. 21-707) (emphasis added).

98   "**broadly understood as imposing constitutional colorblindness in college admissions**": *See, e.g.,* Jamelle Bouie, Opinion, *No One Can Stop Talking About Justice John Marshall Harlan*, N.Y. TIMES (July 7, 2023), https://www.nytimes.com/2023/07/07/opinion/harlan-thomas-roberts-affirmative-action.html ("If

246 nothing else, the Supreme Court's decision in [*SFFA*] is a victory for the conservative vision of the so-called colorblind Constitution—a Constitution that does not see or recognize race in any capacity, for any reason."); Noah Feldman, Opinion, *Affirmative Action Is High Court's Latest Casualty*, BLOOMBERG L. (June 29, 2023), https://news.bloomberglaw.com/us-law-week/affirmative-action-is-high-courts-latest-casualty-noah-feldman (attributing *SFFA* to colorblind constitutionalism).

98 "whether a university may make admissions decisions that turn on an applicant's race": *SFFA*, 600 U.S. at 208.

98 "Eliminating racial discrimination means eliminating all of it": *SFFA*, 600 U.S. at 206. For a similar formulation, see *Parents Involved in Cmty. Schs. v. Seattle Sch. Dist. No. 1*, 551 U.S. 701, 748 (2007) (plurality opinion) ("The way to stop discrimination on the basis of race is to stop discriminating on the basis of race.").

98 noted that universities could reward applicants for essays that centered on race: *See SFFA*, 600 U.S. at 213 n.4, 230. Justice Jackson parried that carving out an exception for military academies puts the majority in the "awkward place" of indicating that it was acceptable to "prepare Black

Americans and other underrepresented minorities for success in the bunker, not the boardroom." *Id.* at 411 (Jackson, J., dissenting).

98 "worked to subordinate the afflicted [Black] students": *SFFA*, 600 U.S. at 203.

98 preferred to view themselves as offering a "plus": *SFFA*, 600 U.S. at 196.

99 "may not operate as a stereotype": *SFFA*, 600 U.S. at 218.

99 employed noticeably similar language regarding the Fourteenth Amendment's prohibitions: *See, e.g., SFFA*, 600 U.S. at 230 (contending Harvard and UNC "unavoidably employ race in a negative manner [and] involve racial stereotyping"); *id.* at 213 (stating university admissions offices "may never use race as a stereotype or negative"); *id.* at 219 ("How else but 'negative' can race be described if, in its absence, members of some racial groups would be admitted in greater numbers than they otherwise would have been?").

99 "so long as there is enough of one to compensate for a lack of the other": *SFFA*, 600 U.S. at 216 (emphasis in original).

99 "consideration of race has led to an 11.1% decrease in the number of Asian-Americans

admitted": *SFFA*, 600 U.S. at 218; *see also id.* (observing that the district court acknowledged "that Harvard's policy of considering applicants' race . . . overall results in fewer Asian American . . . students being admitted" (internal quotation marks omitted)).

99 **"has a higher chance of admission (12.8%) than an Asian American in the *top* decile"**: *SFFA*, 600 U.S. at 197 n.1 (alteration and emphasis in original) (internal quotation marks omitted) (quoting Brief for Petitioner at 24, *SFFA v. Harvard* & *SFFA v. UNC*, 600 U.S. 181 (Nos. 20-1199 & 21-707)); *see id.* (noting "black applicants in the top four academic deciles are between four and ten times more likely to be admitted to Harvard than Asian applicants in those deciles") (citing 4 Joint Appendix at 1793, *SFFA v. Harvard*, 600 U.S. 181 (No. 20-1199)).

99 **"[t]he universities' main response . . . is, essentially, 'trust us'"**: *SFFA*, 600 U.S. at 217.

100 **"incoherent," "irrational stereotypes" attached to "the 'Asian' category"**: *SFFA*, 600 U.S. at 291–92 (Gorsuch, J., concurring) (quotation marks in original).

100 **"many colleges consider 'Asians' to be 'overrepresented' in their admission pools"**: *SFFA*, 600 U.S. at 293 (quotation marks in original).

100 **"[t]o suggest otherwise . . . is to deny reality"**: *SFFA*, 600 U.S. at 304 (Gorsuch, J., concurring).

100 **carried water for this misguided understanding of the Fourteenth Amendment**: *SFFA*, 600 U.S. at 250 (Thomas, J., concurring).

100 **he portrayed as providing an impoverished substitute for his beloved colorblind constitutionalism**: *SFFA*, 600 U.S. at 251–52.

101 **"that the Amendment forbids only laws that hurt, but not help, blacks"**: *SFFA*, 600 U.S. at 246 (Thomas, J., concurring).

101 **only the second time that a federal court at any level had done so**: A Westlaw search reveals that, prior to *SFFA*, the only time that a federal court has *ever* used the term "antisubordination"—using the search terms "antisubord!" and "anti-subord!"—occurred in 2020. That year, the Fourth Circuit cited a law review article using that term in its title, and then included an accompanying parenthetical using the words "anticlassification" and "antisubordination." *Grimm v. Gloucester Cnty. Sch. Bd.*, 972 F.3d 586, 607 (4th Cir. 2020). Simply because federal judges have conspicuously eschewed the terminology of antisubordination does not, of course, indicate they have disregarded its theoretical underpinnings.

248

101 **Justice Sotomayor was profoundly mistaken, Justice Thomas insisted:** *SFFA*, 600 U.S. at 250 (citing Fiss, *Groups and the Equal Protection Clause*, at 147; Siegel, *Equality Talk* at 1473 n.8); *see also id.* at 271 (contending that "[t]he antisubordination view . . . has never guided the Court's analysis").

101 **"accomplish positive social goals":** *SFFA*, 600 U.S. at 266.

101 **"what initially seems like aid may in reality be a burden":** *SFFA*, 600 U.S. at 268.

102 **"stamp [Blacks and Hispanics] with a badge of inferiority":** *SFFA*, 600 U.S. at 270 (quoting *Adarand*, 515 U.S. at 241).

102 **"tain[t] the accomplishments of all" such students:** *SFFA*, 600 U.S. at 270 (quoting *Fisher I*, 570 U.S. at 333) (alterations in original) (internal quotation marks and citations omitted).

102 **because those programs were produced by nothing less than racial bigotry:** *SFFA*, 600 U.S. at 284.

102 **"If such a burden would seem difficult to impose on a bright-eyed young person":** *SFFA*, 600 U.S. at 283.

102 **"make sacrifices . . . for this new phase of racial**

subordination": *SFFA*, 600 U.S. at 283.

102 **invoked the Supreme Court's own sordid decisions validating governmental actions that oppressed people of Asian descent:** *SFFA*, 600 U.S. at 273 (citing *Korematsu*, 323 U.S. 214, and Gong Lum v. Rice, 275 U.S. 78, 81–82, 85–87 (1927)).

103 **"[a]bolition alone could not repair centuries of racial subjugation":** *SFFA*, 600 U.S. at 319–20 (Sotomayor, J., dissenting).

103 **"the Fourteenth Amendment was intended to undo the effects of a world":** *SFFA*, 600 U.S. at 329 n.3.

103 **"a racially integrated system of schools where education is available to all on equal terms":** *SFFA*, 600 U.S. at 328 (internal quotation marks omitted).

103 **"*Bakke, Grutter,* and *Fisher* [decisions] . . . exten[d] . . . Brown's legacy":** *SFFA*, 600 U.S. at 332.

103 **"cit[ed] nothing but his own long-held belief":** *SFFA*, 600 U.S. at 372 (alterations in original) (internal quotation marks omitted).

103 **"The three Justices of color on this Court":** *SFFA*, 600 U.S. at 372.

104 **"cit[ed] no evidence . . . suggest[ing] that race-conscious**

admissions programs discriminate against Asian American students": *SFFA*, 600 U.S. at 374.

104 "a lengthy trial to test those allegations [occurred], which SFFA lost": *SFFA*, 600 U.S. at 374.

104 "a facially race-*neutral* component": *SFFA*, 600 U.S. at 374 (emphasis in original).

104 "is critical to improving cross-racial understanding and breaking down racial stereotypes": *SFFA*, 600 U.S. at 375.

104 "deeming race irrelevant in law does not make it so in life": *SFFA*, 600 U.S. at 407 (Jackson, J., dissenting).

105 "intergenerational transmission of inequality that still plagues our citizenry": *SFFA*, 600 U.S. at 385 (Jackson, J., dissenting) (internal quotation marks omitted).

105 "ensuring a diverse student body in higher education helps *everyone*": *SFFA*, 600 U.S. at 405 (emphasis in original).

105 invoked by name no fewer than *twenty-nine* times across five different opinions: *See, e.g.*, *SFFA*, 600 U.S. at 205, 230 (invoking Justice Harlan); *id.* at 230, 244, 264 (Thomas, J., concurring) (same); *id.* at 307–08 (Gorsuch, J., concurring) (same); *id.* at 320–21,

326–28 (Sotomayor, J., dissenting) (same); *id.* at 388, 393 (Jackson, J., dissenting) (same). Justice Kavanaugh alone refrained from invoking Justice Harlan in *SFFA*. *Id.* at 311–17 (Kavanaugh, J., concurring).

106 "Justice Harlan, standing alone in dissent, wrote: 'Our constitution is color-blind . . . .'": *SFFA*, 600 U.S. at 264 (Thomas, J., concurring) (quoting *Plessy*, 163 U.S. at 559 (Harlan, J., dissenting)).

106 "It distorts the dissent in *Plessy* to advance a colorblindness theory": *SFFA*, 600 U.S. at 330 (Sotomayor, J., dissenting).

106 "'colored citizens are so inferior and degraded that they cannot be allowed to sit in public coaches occupied by white citizens'": *SFFA*, 600 U.S. at 326–27 (quoting *Plessy*, 163 U.S. at 559–60 (Harlan, J., dissenting)).

106 "Justice Harlan knew better": *SFFA*, 600 U.S. at 388 (Jackson, J., dissenting).

107 then stated: "Indeed he did": *SFFA*, 600 U.S. at 230.

107 the most misconstrued: *See* Driver, THE SCHOOLHOUSE GATE, at 36.

107 Justice Harlan advanced a comparatively modest claim: *See* Driver, THE SCHOOLHOUSE GATE, at 36–37 (contextualizing Justice Harlan's dissent within the

250 contemporaneous constitutional framework).

107 asserted that white dominance would "continue to be for all time": *Plessy*, 163 U.S. at 559 (Harlan, J., dissenting).

107 "the Chinese race" is "so different from our own": *Plessy*, 163 U.S. at 561.

108 "a Chinaman can ride in the same passenger coach with white citizens of the United States": *Plessy*, 163 U.S. at 561.

108 was invoked even in a case where one of the plaintiff's central claims alleged that Asian Americans are treated as "perpetual foreigners": Brief for Petitioner at 63, *SFFA v. Harvard* & *SFFA v. UNC*, 600 U.S. 181 (Nos. 20-1199 & 21-707).

109 "but as constitutional argument, it leaves you hungry an hour later": Robert H. Bork, *The Unpersuasive Bakke Decision*, WALL ST. J., July 21, 1978, at 8.

109 "strikes me as an excellent compromise between two committees of the American Bar Association on some insignificant legislative proposal": Scalia, *The Disease as Cure*, at 148.

109 "But it is thoroughly unconvincing as an honest, hard-minded, reasoned analysis": Scalia, *The Disease as Cure*, at 148.

109 "use to dignify their use of racial preferences as they . . . engineer . . . a *look* of racial parity": Kennedy, FOR DISCRIMINATION, at 101 (quoting an email from Shelby Steele).

109 "[t]he original, morally incontestable goal of . . . the integration of African-Americans": Orlando Patterson, *Affirmative Action: The Sequel*, N.Y. TIMES (June 22, 2003), https://www .nytimes.com/2003/06/22/opinion /affirmative-action-the-sequel .html.

110 than the archetypal St. Grottlesex product who "earns" 1600: For thoughtful works that have assailed meritocracy in university admissions and beyond, see Lani Guinier, *Admissions Rituals as Political Acts: Guardians at the Gates of Our Democratic Ideals*, 117 HARV. L. REV. 113, 131, 142 (2003); Nicholas Lemann, THE BIG TEST: THE SECRET HISTORY OF THE AMERICAN MERITOCRACY (1999); Daniel Markovits, THE MERITOCRACY TRAP: HOW AMERICA'S FOUNDATIONAL MYTH FEEDS INEQUALITY, DISMANTLES THE MIDDLE CLASS, AND DEVOURS THE ELITE (2019); and Michael J. Sandel, THE TYRANNY OF MERIT: WHAT'S BECOME OF THE COMMON GOOD? (2020).

111 it is impossible to distinguish "merit" admits from "non-merit" admits: *See, e.g.*, *Grutter*, 539 U.S. at 373 (Thomas, J., concurring in part and dissenting in

part); *Fisher I.*, 570 U.S. at 333–34 (Thomas, J., concurring).

112 **"It's not, maybe that person was smart; it's gotta be Affirmative Action":** Urofsky, THE AFFIRMATIVE ACTION PUZZLE, at 408 (emphasis omitted).

112 **this default rule should be inverted:** *See generally* Ian Ayres & Robert Gertner, *Filling Gaps in Incomplete Contracts: An Economic Theory of Default Rules*, 99 YALE L.J. 87 (1989) (exploring the default rule concept).

113 **"the idea that diversity means, specifically, better learning has turned out to be difficult to prove":** John McWhorter, *Harvard, Brown and Other Top Schools Are Thinking About Black Freshmen the Wrong Way*, N.Y. TIMES (September 12, 2024).

113 **"Nothing so epitomizes the politically correct gullibility of our times as the magic word 'diversity.'":** Thomas Sowell, *The 'Diversity' Fraud*, CREATORS (December 20, 2016), https://www.creators.com/read/thomas-sowell/12/16/the-diversity-fraud.

114 **"I remain doubtful about social scientific 'proof' of diversity's values":** Randall Kennedy, FOR DISCRIMINATION: RACE, AFFIRMATIVE ACTION, AND THE LAW 103 (2013).

114 **"How is a court to know whether leaders have been adequately 'train[ed]'":** Students for Fair Admissions, Inc. v. Pres. & Fellows of Harv. Coll. (*SFFA*), 600 U.S. 181, 214 (2023).

114 **"not identif[ied] any metric that would allow a court to":** See Fisher v. Univ. of Tex. at Austin (*Fisher II*), 136 S. Ct. 2198, 2215 (2016) (Alito, J., dissenting).

114 **study published in the *Columbia Law Review*:** *See* Adam Chilton, Justin Driver, Jonathan S. Masur & Kyle Rozema, *Assessing Affirmative Action's Diversity Rationale*, 122 COLUM. L. REV. 331 (2022).

115 **"is the least-cited volume of the *Harvard Law Review* in the last 20 years":** Jeffrey Ressner & Ben Smith, *Obama Kept Law Review Balanced*, POLITICO (June 23, 2008), https://www.politico.com/story/2008/06/obama-kept-law-review-balanced-011257.

115 **"presided over a general 'dumbing down'" of the *Review*'s standards:** Ressner & Smith, *Obama Kept Law Review Balanced* (quoting Ferry Pellwock, Comment to Barack Obama and the *Harvard Law Review*, VOLOKH CONSPIRACY (February 5, 2008), https://web.archive.org/web/20080207110749/http:/volokh.com/posts/1202117776.shtml).

252   115   **"subordinated academic merit to diversity considerations":** Complaint at 6, Fac., Alumni & Students Opposed to Racial Preferences v. N.Y. Univ. L. Rev., No. 1:18-cv-9184 (S.D.N.Y. October 7, 2018), 2018 WL 4899065; Complaint at 6, Fac., Alumni & Students Opposed to Racial Preferences v. Harvard L. Rev., No. 1:18 cv-12105 (D. Mass. October 6, 2018), 2018 WL 5148474.

116   **"harder still to hold an honest conversation about the reasons why it is hard to hold an honest conversation":** Carter, REFLECTIONS OF AN AFFIRMATIVE ACTION BABY, at 2.

CHAPTER THREE

118   *SFFA* **had introduced "tremendous uncertainty":** Cheung, *Affirmative Action Is Over.*

118   **persisted even after President Joe Biden's Department of Justice and Education Department issued guidance:** Julia Goldberg & Izzy Polanco, *College Removes Supplemental Essay from Application, Forms Working Group in Wake of Affirmative Action Ruling,* WILLIAMS RECORD (October 18, 2023), https://williamsrecord.com/464789/news/williams-college-removes-supplemental-essay-working-group-affirmative-action.

118   **"a summer of uncertainty":** Eric Hoover, *A Time to Tear Down, a Time to Build Up,* CHRON. HIGHER EDUC. (October 4, 2023), https://www.chronicle.com/article/a-time-to-tear-down-a-time-to-build-up.

118   **"swirl of uncertainty, confusion and misinformation about an admissions process":** Cheung, *Affirmative Action Is Over.*

119   **"still working on our training and guideline language on how the admissions staff should approach these questions":** Cheung, *Affirmative Action Is Over.*

119   **universities are siloed from one another because they fear that collaboration will expose them to antitrust litigation:** Alert readers may wonder how shifts in university admissions strategies could possibly trigger antitrust concerns. Extending this point, some readers may ask: Given that selective universities are typically nonprofits, does antitrust law apply to educational institutions at all? At one point, the dominant view answered that query in the negative. Indeed, US Senator John Sherman of Ohio—the man for whom the Sherman Antitrust Act is named—is said to have "scoffed" at the very idea that universities were in any sense bound by antitrust law. Jennifer Zimbroff et al., *Antitrust Issues Affecting Colleges and Universities,* NACUA NOTES (2015). But as early as 1985, a leading

scholar of higher education implored administrators to "accord antitrust considerations an important place in their legal planning." William A. Kaplin, THE LAW OF HIGHER EDUCATION 501(2d ed. 1985). In support of this view, universities can be understood as competing on the price of tuition. (Yes, I am aware that this notion may seem farfetched—if not downright laughable—to readers who have recently had the privilege of paying their child's tuition bills.) Several plausible alternatives that universities may adopt after *SFFA*—including a preference for students from low-income areas—could work to raise tuition prices. And that approach could well raise antitrust alarm bells if the universities were viewed as collaborating on the implementation of such a policy.

119   **"[W]e've got plans, but we're not going to broadcast them and put a target on our back":** Eric Hoover, *A Time to Tear Down, a Time to Build Up*, CHRON. HIGHER EDUC. (October 4, 2023), https://www.chronicle.com/article/a-time-to-tear-down-a-time-to-build-up.

120   **"The video statement will allow applicants to provide the Admissions Committee with additional insight into their personal strengths":** Aaron Sibarium, *Columbia Law School Said It Would Require Applicants to*

Submit 'Video Statements' in Wake of Affirmative Action Ban. Then it Backtracked., WASH. FREE BEACON (August 1, 2023), https://freebeacon.com/campus/columbia-law-school-said-it-would-require-applicants-to-submit-video-statements-in-the-wake-of-affirmative-action-ban-then-it-backtracked.

120   **insisting that the video requirement had somehow inadvertently been posted:** David Bernstein, *Columbia Law School Posts, then Retracts, Video Statement Requirement for Applicants*, VOLOKH CONSPIRACY (August 1, 2023).

120   **applicants "who speak multiple languages":** 600 U.S. 181, 365 (2023) (Sotomayor, J., dissenting).

121   **"that is diverse across a range of factors, including race and ethnicity":** *Advance Diversity and Opportunity in Higher Education: Justice and Education Departments Release Resources to Advance Diversity and Opportunity in Higher Education*, U.S. DEP'T OF EDUC. (August 14, 2023), https://www.ed.gov/about/news/press-release/advance-diversity-and-opportunity-higher-education-justice-and-education.

122   **order the "Collection of Demographic Data":** Civil Rights Div. & Office for Civil Rights, *Dear Colleague Letter from Assistant Attorney General Kristen Clarke &*

254   *Assistant Secretary for Civil Rights Catherine E. Lhamon*, U.S. Dep't Educ. & U.S. Dep't Just. (August 14, 2023), https://www.justice.gov/opa/file/1310156/dl?inline.

122   then the college will penalize them for doing so: Natanson, *After Affirmative Action*.

123   "race *qua* race—[or,] race for race's sake": 600 U.S. 181, 220 (2023).

123   "to those who may have little in common with one another but the color of their skin": *SFFA*, 600 U.S. at 220 (internal quotation marks omitted).

123   "is not like treating them differently because they are from a city or from a suburb": *SFFA*, 600 U.S. at 220.

124   "He is the justice who has had the most important impact": *How Antonin Scalia Changed America*, Politico (February 14, 2016), https://www.politico.com/magazine/story/2016/02/antonin-scalia-how-he-changed-america-213631.

124   to have held fast to the teachings of Justice Scalia: *See, e.g.,* Bostock v. Clayton County, 590 U.S. 644, 670, 674 (2020); *see id.* at 685 (Alito, J., dissenting) (contending that Justice Gorsuch's majority opinion "is like a pirate ship. It sails under a textualist flag, but what it actually represents is a

theory of statutory interpretation that Justice Scalia excoriated").

124   a "role model" and even a "hero": Manu Raju & Joan Biskupic, *Trump's Supreme Court Pick Calls Antonin Scalia a "Role Model" and a "Judicial Hero,"* CNN (August 13, 2018), https://www.cnn.com/2018/08/13/politics/brett-kavanaugh-antonin-scalia-role-model-supreme-court/index.html.

125   "selecting or rejecting them *on the basis of their race*": Scalia, *The Disease as Cure*, at 156 (emphasis in original).

125   "But I am not willing to prefer the son of a prosperous and well-educated black doctor or lawyer": Scalia, *The Disease as Cure,* at 153 (emphasis added).

126   "consider[ ] each application in a racially neutral way": *DeFunis v. Odegaard*, 416 U.S. 312, 332, 334 (1974) (Douglas, J., dissenting).

126   "A black applicant who pulled himself out of the ghetto into a junior college": *DeFunis v. Odegaard*, 416 U.S. at 331.

126   "but because as an individual he has shown he has the potential": *DeFunis v. Odegaard*, 416 U.S. at 331.

127   "as a factor in attempting to assess his true potential for a successful legal career": *DeFunis v. Odegaard*, 416 U.S. at 340–41.

127   forbade admissions officers from relying upon "race *per se*": *Hopwood v. Texas,* 78 F.3d 932, 946 (5th Cir. 1996).

127   "may reasonably consider a host of factors—*some of which may have some correlation with race*": *Hopwood v. Texas,* 78 F.3d 932, 946 (emphasis added).

127   "may even consider factors such as whether an applicant's parents attended college": *Hopwood v. Texas,* 78 F.3d 932, 946.

129   it would not violate the Constitution even if *everyone* in a preferred admissions category were Black: *See* Scalia, *The Disease as Cure,* at 156.

130   "applied to *freedmen* (and refugees), a formally race-neutral category, not blacks writ large": 600 U.S. 181, 247 (2023) (Thomas, J., concurring) (internal quotation marks omitted, second emphasis added) (quoting Michael B. Rappaport, *Originalism and the Colorblind Constitution,* 89 Notre Dame L. Rev. 71, 98 (2013)).

131   "everyone knew whom the Freedmen's Bureau Act was meant to assist": Adam Serwer, *The Most Baffling Argument a Supreme Court Justice Has Ever Made,* Atl. (July 7, 2023), https://www.theatlantic .com/ideas/archive/2023/07/freed men-race-neutral-supreme-court -affirmative-action-clarence -thomas/674641.

131   "the most baffling argument a Supreme Court Justice has ever made": Serwer, *The Most Baffling Argument* (capitalization altered).   255

131   "neither is a program that is designed to help slavery's descendants": Some readers may object that the descendants of slavery should be understood as conceptually distinct from those who were themselves enslaved. The trouble with that argument, however, is that Congress also chartered the Freedman's Savings and Trust Company, a federal bank explicitly created to help freed slaves and their descendants. *See* Jack M. Balkin, Living Originalism 417 n.20 (2011).

131   "a benefit to descendants of slaves would not be race-based": Transcript of Oral Argument at 15, Students for Fair Admissions, Inc. v. President & Fellows of Harvard Coll., 600 U.S. 181 (2023) (No. 20-1199).

131   "[Y]ou said . . . that the benefit for former slaves was not race-based": Transcript of Oral Argument at 16, *SFFA v. Harvard,* 600 U.S. 181 (2023) (No. 20-1199).

132   "whom I understand . . . constitute a surprisingly large subset of the Black beneficiaries of affirmative action": Stanford Law School, *Affirmative Action: Stanford Law School Faculty Analyze the Supreme Court's Ruling,* YouTube (June 30, 2023), https://www

256   .youtube.com/watch?v
=J7p0g9eSvMg.

132   **compelling evidence for
originalists because of its
"historical grounding":** Stanford
Law School, *Affirmative Action.*

132   **"retaining the ability to
redress the lingering harms from
state-sponsored racism without
[violating] . . . the 14th
Amendment":** David Bernstein,
*Diversity by Diktat: An Obscure 1977
OMB Memo Forms the Basis for
Today's Affirmative-Action
Programs,* ScotusBlog, October 26,
2022.

132   **"a significant improvement
over [affirmative action]
policies":** Ilya Somin, *Rights and
Wrongs of Replacing Traditional
Affirmative Action with Preferences
for Descendants of Slaves,* Volokh
Conspiracy (February 12, 2022). Not
every legal conservative is
convinced that preferences for
slavery's descendants would pass
constitutional muster. *See, e.g.,*
Josh Blackman, *Review of Oral
Argument in Students for Fair
Admission v. University of North
Carolina,* Volokh Conspiracy
(November 1, 2022).

133   **eked out the impoverished
existence of sharecroppers:** Ruth J.
Simmons, Up Home: One Girl's
Journey 19 (2023).

133   **"who reminded them of a
flock of buzzards, gathering to**

feed on leavings and detritus":
Simmons, Up Home, at 12–13.

134   **"[T]here wasn't a single
peep from another university":**
Jennifer Schuessler, *Confronting
Academia's Slavery Ties,* N.Y. Times
(March 6, 2017), at C1.

134   **"was indirectly a beneficiary
on a very very small scale":** Pam
Belluck, *Brown U. to Examine Debt to
Slave Trade,* N.Y. Times (March 13,
2004).

134   **"It certainly didn't escape
me, my own past in relationship to
[slavery]":** Belluck, *Brown U. to
Examine Debt to Slave Trade.*

134   **"trying to understand as a
descendant of slaves how to feel
good about moving on":** Belluck,
*Brown U. to Examine Debt to Slave
Trade.*

134   **"but there's nothing in
particular they think Brown can
do or should do":** Belluck, *Brown U.
to Examine Debt to Slave Trade.*

135   **exploring how slavery played
a foundational role in shaping
those institutions:** *See, e.g.,* David
W. Blight, Yale and Slavery: A
History (2004); The Princeton &
Slavery Project: An Exploration of
Princeton University's Historical
Ties to the Institution of Slavery
(2024), available at https://slavery
.princeton.edu; Rachel L. Swarns,
*Georgetown Confronts Its Role in
Nation's Slave Trade,* N.Y. Times,

April 17, 2016, at A1; Jennifer Schuessler, *Confronting Academia's Slavery Ties*, N.Y. TIMES, March 6, 2017, at C1.

135 **"Harvard was directly complicit in America's system of racial bondage":** Drew G. Faust, *Recognizing Slavery at Harvard*, HARV. CRIMSON (March 30, 2016).

135 **it stood beside church and state as the third pillar of a civilization built on bondage:** Craig Steven Wilder, EBONY AND IVY: RACE, SLAVERY, AND THE TROUBLED HISTORY OF AMERICA'S UNIVERSITIES 13 (2014).

136 **"killing or maiming him was not a crime":** *Regents of Univ. of Cal. v. Bakke*, 438 U.S. 265, 387–88 (1978) (Marshall, J., concurring).

137 **"historic deficit[s]" and "the effects of societal discrimination":** *Bakke*, 438 U.S. at 306 (plurality opinion).

137 **"amorphous concept[s] of injury that may be ageless":** *Bakke*, 438 U.S. at 307.

137 **applicants who indicated enslaved ancestry did not do so fraudulently:** For criticism along these lines, see Ilya Somin, *Rights and Wrongs of Replacing Traditional Affirmative Action with Preferences for Descendants of Slaves*, VOLOKH CONSPIRACY (February 12, 2022).

137 **would not somehow represent the *creation* of**

verification issues but rather their *continuation*: *See* Brief for Petitioner at 78, Students for Fair Admissions, Inc. v. President & Fellows of Harvard Coll., 600 U.S. 181 (2023) (No. 20-1199) ("Harvard never verifies whether applicants are really the race that they check. . . .").

138 **the descendants of people who profited from slavery are digitizing crucial records:** Amanda Holpuch, *Descendants Trace Histories Linked by Slavery*, N.Y. TIMES, March 26, 2022.

139 **would provide admissions boosts to the descendants of 272 slaves that the institution owned and eventually sold:** *See* Rachel L. Swarns, *Georgetown Plans Steps to Atone for Slave Past*, N.Y. TIMES, September 2, 2016, at A1.

139 **"We live, every day, with the legacies of enslavement":** Jeannie Suk Gersen, *The End of Legacy Admissions Could Transform College Access*, NEW YORKER (August 8, 2023).

141 **"a monochromatic obelisk, with only one racial beneficiary":** Josh Blackman, *Review of Oral Argument in* Students for Fair Admission v. University of North Carolina, VOLOKH CONSPIRACY (November 1, 2022), https://reason .com/volokh/2022/11/01/review -of-oral-argument-in-students -for-fair-admission-v-university -of-north-carolina.

258   **142 a figure that is consistent with a long-term trend:** *See* Abby Budiman, Christine Tamir, Lauren Mora & Luis Noe-Bustamante, *Facts on U.S. Immigrants, 2018,* PEW RESEARCH CENTER (August 20, 2020), https://www.pewresearch.org /hispanic/2020/08/20/facts-on-u -s-immigrants-current-data.

142 first- and second-generation immigrants account for: Stephen Dinan, *Activists Urge Colleges to Use Immigration to Diversify Schools After End of Racial Preferences,* WASH. TIMES (August 2, 2023), https://www.washingtontimes.com /news/2023/aug/2/activists-urge -colleges-use-immigration -diversify-/.

142 "give a plus to applicants whose parents were immigrants to this country?": Transcript of Oral Argument at 45, *SFFA v. UNC,* 600 U.S. 181 (No. 20-707) (2023).

143 Strawbridge registered no objections to such a plan: Transcript of Oral Argument at 45–46, *SFFA v. UNC,* 600 U.S. 181 (No. 20-707) (2023).

143 "I had to find a way of relating to my classmates who came from very different backgrounds": Transcript of Oral Argument at 33, *SFFA v. UNC,* 600 U.S. 181 (No. 20-707) (2023).

143 "not being based upon the race but upon the cultural experiences or the ability to adapt": Transcript of Oral Argument at 33-34, *SFFA v. UNC,* 600 U.S. 181 (No. 20-707) (2023).

144 neo-nativism informed some of the more startling moments of President Trump's second term: *See* Carlos Lozada, *Apparently, America Is Full of the Wrong Kind of People,* N.Y. TIMES (February 11, 2025).

144 purported to eliminate birthright citizenship for certain people: Executive Order, Protecting the Meaning and Value of American Citizenship, January 20, 2025.

144 blamed immigration policies for a terrorist attack in New Orleans: Marianne LeVine & Cat Zakrzewski, *Trump Appears to Blame Biden Border Policy for New Orleans Attack by U.S. Citizen,* WASH. POST (January 2, 2025).

145 "turning affirmative action almost against the group it was originally designed to help": Stephen Dinan, *Activists Urge Colleges to Use Immigration to Diversify Schools After End of Racial Preferences,* WASH. TIMES (August 2, 2023), https://www.washington times.com/news/2023/aug/2 /activists-urge-colleges-use -immigration-diversify-/.

145 eventually dropped Native American enrollment: *See* Brief for the President and Chancellors of the University of California as Amici Curiae Support Respondents at 24, Students for Fair Admissions, Inc. v. President & Fellows of Harvard Coll., 600 U.S. 181 (2023) (No. 20-1199).

145 all reported that their first-year numbers of Native students decreased by approximately 50 percent: Sarah Weissman, *How the End of Affirmative Action Is Affecting Indigenous Students*, INSIDE HIGHER ED (November 8, 2024).

146 "the preference is political rather than racial in nature": *Morton v. Mancari*, 417 U.S. 535, 554 n.24 (1974).

146 that a tribal membership criterion differed from a racial designation: *See* 438 U.S. 265, 304 n.42 (1978).

147 "bedrock principle that [tribal] status is a 'political rather than racial' classification": *Haaland v. Brackeen*, 599 U.S. 255, 310 (2023) (Gorsuch, J., concurring) (quoting *Morton v. Mancari*, 417 U.S. 535, 553, n.24 (1974)). *See also* Matthew L. M. Fletcher, *The Original Understanding of the Political Status of Indian Tribes*, 82 ST. JOHN'S L. REV. 153, 180-81 (2008) ("[O]ne must reach the inescapable conclusion that the relationship between Indian tribes and the federal government is political in character and that federal law relating to Indian tribes does not implicate either the Fifth Amendment or the Fourteenth

Amendment Due Process Clauses or the Equal Protection Clause.").

147 overwhelmingly support the constitutionality of governmental programs that offer preferences for tribal membership: *See, e.g.,* Sarah Krakoff, *They Were Here First: American Indian Tribes, Race, and the Constitutional Minimum*, 69 STAN. L. REV. 491, 502-03 (2017) (contending that *Morton v. Mancari*'s rule "remains sensible").

147 "view classifications based on Indian-tribe membership as not being based on race": Eugene Volokh, *The California Civil Rights Initiative: An Interpretive Guide*, 44 UCLA L. REV. 1335, 1359 (1997).

148 "costing real American Indians access to higher education": Quoted in Sarah Viren, *The Native Scholar Who Wasn't*, N.Y. TIMES (May 25, 2021).

148 solved what they deem the Elizabeth Warren problem: *See* Viren, *The Native Scholar Who Wasn't* (noting that "Senator Elizabeth Warren . . . was listed as Native American by both Harvard and the University of Pennsylvania Law School when she was on the faculty at those institutions and has since apologized for claiming that identity").

148 preferences for students from modest economic backgrounds: Richard Kahlenberg is the most prominent advocate of

260   class-based affirmative action. *See, e.g.*, Richard D. Kahlenberg, *Class-Based Affirmative Action*, 84 CAL. L. REV. 1037, 1037 (1996); Richard D. Kahlenberg, THE REMEDY: CLASS, RACE, AND AFFIRMATIVE ACTION (1996).

149   Horatio Alger's tales continue to exercise a vise grip on the American imagination: *See* Horatio Alger Jr., RAGGED DICK (Hildegard Hoeller ed., W. W. Norton & Co. 2007) (1868).

149   actual upward mobility rates in the United States have been outstripped by some European nations: Jason DeParle, *Harder for Americans to Rise from Lower Rungs*, N.Y. TIMES (January 4, 2012), https://www.nytimes.com/2012 /01/05/us/harder-for-americans -to-rise-from-lower-rungs.html.

149   "would do little more than substitute less-affluent whites for more-affluent whites": Wilkinson, FROM *BROWN* TO *BAKKE*, at 289 (internal quotation marks omitted).

150   who both come from low-SES families and have test scores that are above the threshold: William G. Bowen & Derek Bok, THE SHAPE OF THE RIVER: LONG-TERM CONSEQUENCES OF CONSIDERING RACE IN COLLEGE AND UNIVERSITY ADMISSIONS 51 (1998). *See also* Deborah C. Malamud, *Assessing Class-Based Affirmative Action*, 47 J. LEG. EDUC. 452, 465 (1997) (noting "the beneficiaries of

poverty-based affirmative action will be disproportionately white"); Robert Bruce Slater, *Why Socioeconomic Affirmative Action in College Admissions Works Against African Americans* (1995) J. OF BLACKS IN HIGHER EDUC. 57, 57.

150   evocatively titled *Place, Not Race*: *See* Sheryll Cashin, PLACE, NOT RACE: A NEW VISION OF OPPORTUNITY IN AMERICA (2014); *see also* Sheryll Cashin, *Place, Not Race: Affirmative Action and the Geography of Educational Opportunity*, 47 U. MICH. J. L. REFORM 935, 954 (2014).

151   map onto the Census Bureau's own 2020 estimates of where the American population resides: *See* Michael Ratcliffe, *Redefining Urban Areas Following the 2020 Census*, U.S. CENSUS BUREAU (December 22, 2022), https://www .census.gov/newsroom/blogs /random-samplings/2022/12 /redefining-urban-areas -following-2020-census.html.

152   treating someone differently because of their skin color is *not* like treating them differently because they are from a city or from a suburb: 600 U.S. 181, 220 (2023) (emphasis in original).

152   suggest focusing upon an applicant's postal zip code: *See* Danielle Allen, *Talent Is Everywhere: Using ZIP Codes and Merit to Enhance Diversity, in* THE FUTURE OF AFFIRMATIVE ACTION 154 (Richard D. Kahlenberg ed., 2014) ("Just as bridging ties are beneficial on college campuses, they are also valuable in schools and neighborhoods.").

152 more than 100,000 residents in one five-digit number: *See* Matt Stiles, *The ZIP Code Turns 50 Today; Here Are 9 That Stand Out,* NPR (July 1, 2013), https://www.npr.org/sections/the two-way/2013/07/01/197623129/the-zip-code-turns-50-today -here-are-9-that-stand-out.

152 include approximately 4,000 residents: *See* U.S. Census Bureau, Glossary, https://www.census.gov/programs-surveys /geography/about/glossary.html.

152 "78% of Blacks live in 'high disadvantage' neighborhoods": Sally Chung, *Affirmative Action: Moving Beyond Diversity,* 39 N.Y.U Rev. L. & Soc. Change 387, 399 (2015).

153 where today's racialized American ghettos actually present an opportunity: On American ghettos, *see, e.g.,* Kenneth B. Clark, Dark Ghetto: Dilemmas of Social Power (1965); Tommie Shelby, Dark Ghettos: Injustice, Dissent, and Reform (2016); and Mitchell Duneier, Ghetto: The Invention of a Place, the History of an Idea (2016).

153 "Talent is everywhere, but opportunity is not": Raj Chetty, John Friedman, Nathaniel Hendren,

Maggie R. Jones & Sonya Porter, *The Opportunity Atlas,* U.S. Census Bureau (October 1, 2018), https://www.census.gov/newsroom /blogs/research-matters/2018/09 /the_opportunity_atla.html.

153 in the hopes of identifying the many academic stars hidden in our urban and rural skies: Hailey Talbert, *Could This New Admissions Tool Explain Yale's Post-Affirmative Action Demographics?,* Yale Daily News (October 8, 2024).

154 the average wealth of Black families barely cracked $200,000: *Nine Charts about Wealth Inequality in America,* Urban Inst. (April 25, 2024), https://apps.urban.org /features/wealth-inequality -charts.

154 "an admissions policy that gave extra consideration to a student who grew up in a family with a net worth of less than $30,000": David Leonhardt, *The Hard Question of Affirmative Action and Slavery,* N.Y. Times (May 1, 2023).

154 who have sometimes been tagged with the motto "class not race": Kennedy, For Discrimination, at 92.

154 Even a partial listing of this phenomenon includes: I am grateful to my colleague James Forman Jr., for impressing upon me the close proximity of America's

262   elite universities to underserved educational communities.

155   long sent a fleet of its most able students to Yale College: *See* Karabel, The Chosen, at 116, 204, 211, 225, 330, 355.

155   "There's a joke that Harvard was started a year after our school as a place for our students to go": Meg P. Bernhard, *The Making of a Harvard Feeder School*, Harv. Crimson (December 13, 2013), https://www.thecrimson.com/article/2013/12/13/making-harvard-feeder-schools.

155   graduated from one of just seven high schools: *See* Bernhard, *The Making of a Harvard Feeder School.*

155   roughly 20,000 public and private high schools exist in the United States: *See How Many Schools Are in the U.S.?*, MDR Educ. (March 26, 2024), https://mdreducation.com/how-many-schools-are-in-the-u-s.

156   the largest total in its more than three centuries of existence: *See* Hailey Talbert & Jaela Landowski, *Yale Admitted a Record-High Number of New Haven Public Schools Students*, Yale Daily News (September 13, 2024).

156   students who attended struggling schools seldom even applied to the flagship university: *See* Stephanie Saul, *Five Ways*

College Admissions Could Change, N.Y. Times (June 30, 2023), https://www.nytimes.com/2023/06/30/us/politics/affirmative-action-college-admissions-supreme-court.html.

157   "should get a very significant boost": Stanford Law School, *Affirmative Action: Stanford Law School Faculty Analyze the Supreme Court's Ruling*, YouTube (June 30, 2023), https://www.youtube.com/watch?v=J7p0g9eSvMg.

157   universities would be given the ability to conceal the racial boxes: Anemona Hartocollis, *Colleges Will Be Able to Hide a Student's Race on Admissions Applications*, N.Y. Times (May 26, 2023), https://www.nytimes.com/2023/05/26/us/college-admissions-race-common-app.html.

157   the desire to retain roughly equivalent percentages of male and female students: *See* Susan Dominus, *"There Was Definitely a Thumb on the Scale to Get Boys,"* N.Y. Times (September 26, 2023), https://www.nytimes.com/2023/09/08/magazine/men-college-enrollment.html.

159   who not only have led lives of relative hardship, but also have a Black or brown racial identity: *See, e.g.,* Cashin, *Place, Not Race*, at 954 ("black children are disproportionately disadvantaged by growing up in single-parent households"); *SFFA v. Harvard*, 600

U.S. 181, 394 (2023) (Jackson, J., dissenting) ("Today, as was true 50 years ago, Black home ownership trails White home ownership by approximately 25 percentage points."); Anna Bahney, *The Gulf Between Black Homeowners and White Is Actually Getting Bigger, Not Smaller,* CNN (March 2, 2023), https://www.cnn.com/2023/03/02/homes/race-and-home-buying-nar/index.html; and Lauren E. Glaze & Laura M. Maruschak, U.S. Dep't Just., Parents in Prison and Their Minor Children (2010) ("Black children (6.7%) were seven and a half times more likely than white children (0.9%) to have a parent in prison. Hispanic children (2.4%) were more than two and a half times more likely than white children to have a parent in prison.").

159   ruled that measures requiring racially segregated railcars did not violate equal protection principles: 163 U.S. 537 (1896).

159   declaring the *Plessy* regime "inherently unequal": 347 U.S. 483, 495 (1954).

160   even if those approaches are racially neutral on their faces: *See, e.g.,* Brian T. Fitzpatrick, *The Hidden Question in* Fisher, 10 N.Y.U. J. L. & Liberty 168 (2016).

161   generate enough support at the Supreme Court to even hear the case: For an illuminating appraisal of magnet school

admissions processes, and their implications for equal protection, see Sonja Starr, *The Magnet School Wars and the Future of Colorblindness,* 76 Stan. L. Rev. 161 (2024).

161   "There are race-neutral factors that will be perfectly legal, as well as fair, in admissions decisions": Laura Meckler & Susan Svrluga, *Latest Trump Guidance on Race has Schools Scrambling Amid 'Intense* Fear,' Wash. Post (February 22, 2025). *See also* "Dear Colleague" Letter from Craig Trainor, Acting Assistant Secretary for Civil Rights, Department of Education, February 14, 2025. For thoughtful works exploring the role of standardized testing in American higher education, see Nicholas Lemann, The Big Test: The Secret History of the American Meritocracy (1999); Nicholas Lemann, Higher Admissions: The Rise, Decline, and Return of Standardized Testing (2024).

162   "We are watching people start to cut off their arms": Liam Knox, *A National Summit on a Higher Ed "Low Point,"* Inside Higher Ed (July 27, 2023), https://www.insidehighered.com/news/admissions/traditional-age/2023/07/27/frustration-and-uncertainty-affirmative-action-summit.

163   outright defiance against *Brown* marked a searing

264 **cautionary tale in American history:** For example, Governor Orval Faubus of Arkansas, who in 1957 fought Central High School's desegregation in Little Rock, famously declared *Brown* was "not the law of the land." Numan V. Bartley, THE RISE OF MASSIVE RESISTANCE: RACE AND POLITICS IN THE SOUTH DURING THE 1950'S 273 (1969).

165 **to advocate for systemic improvements to destitute neighborhoods:** *See* Danielle Allen, *Talent Is Everywhere: Using ZIP Codes and Merit to Enhance Diversity, in* THE FUTURE OF AFFIRMATIVE ACTION 154 (Richard D. Kahlenberg ed., 2014) ("Just as bridging ties are beneficial on college campuses, they are also valuable in schools and neighborhoods.").

165 **"'What is the clearest thing we ought to do first'":** Charles L. Black Jr., A NEW BIRTH OF FREEDOM: HUMAN RIGHTS, NAMED AND UNNAMED 137 (1997).

CHAPTER FOUR
167 **"You are now on notice":** Letter from Edward Blum, President, Students for Fair Admissions, to Kim Taylor, Vice President & Gen. Counsel, Duke Univ. (September 17, 2024); Letter from Edward Blum, President, Students for Fair Admissions, to Ramona E. Romero, Vice President & Gen. Counsel, Princeton Univ. (September 17, 2024); Letter from Edward Blum, President, Students for Fair Admissions, to Alexander E. Dreier, Senior Vice President & Gen. Counsel, Yale Univ. (September 17, 2024).

167 **"Racial Preferences on the Sly?":** Editorial Board, *Racial Preferences on the Sly?*, WALL ST. J. (September 18, 2024).

167 **"What they are trying to do is cheat in a way that doesn't get them caught in court":** Jason L. Riley, *Some Elite Colleges Dodge the Affirmative-Action Ruling*, WALL ST. J. (September 24, 2024).

167 **"and they're admitting them under the same criteria they were before":** Josie Reich, Chris Tillen, Hailey Talbert & Karla Cortes, *Could Yale Face Post-Affirmative Action Lawsuits*, YALE DAILY NEWS (September 17, 2024), https://yaledailynews.com/blog/2024/09/17/analysis-could-yale-face-post-affirmative-action-lawsuits.

168 **Blum immediately announced that SFFA would appeal that decision:** *See* Anemona Hartocollis, *Federal Judge Upholds Racial Preferences in Naval Academy Admissions*, N.Y. TIMES (December 6, 2024).

168 **celebrated the decision as "a great day for America":** Julia Manchester, *Trump Praises SCOTUS Ruling on Affirmative Action: "This is a Great Day for America,"* THE HILL (June 29, 2023), https://thehill.com

/homenews/campaign/4073726
-trump-praises-scotus-ruling-on
-affirmative-action-this-is-a
-great-day-for-america.

168 **"Our greatest minds must
be cherished and that's what this
wonderful day has brought":** Julia
Manchester, *Trump Praises SCOTUS
Ruling on Affirmative Action.*

168 **"are finally being rewarded":**
Manchester, *Trump Praises SCOTUS
Ruling on Affirmative Action.*

168 **"made today's historic
decision to end the racist college
admissions process":** Manchester,
*Trump Praises SCOTUS Ruling on
Affirmative Action.*

169 **"intend to initiate litigation
should universities defiantly flout
this clear ruling":** Press Release,
Students for Fair Admissions
Applauds Supreme Court's
Decision to End Racial Preferences
in College Admissions (June 29,
2023), https://www.prnewswire
.com/news-releases/students-for
-fair-admissions-applauds
-supreme-courts-decision-to
-end-racial-preferences-in-college
-admissions-301867088.html.

169 **"These cases mark the end
of the beginning, not the
beginning of the end":** William
McGurn, *Edward Blum, the Man
Who Killed Affirmative Action*, WALL
ST. J. (July 3, 2023).

169 **"[W]e're blessed to have
this Supreme Court opinion":**
Lulu Garcia-Navarro, *He Worked for
Years to Overturn Affirmative Action
and Finally Won. He's Not Done.*, N.Y.
TIMES (July 8, 2023).

169 **Blum leapt from his chair
with unbridled joy:** 600 U.S. 181,
206 (2023); William McGurn,
*Edward Blum, the Man Who Killed
Affirmative Action*, WALL ST. J.
(July 3, 2023).

169 **"the type of history being
made at that moment":** Audra D. S.
Burch, *One Black Family, One
Affirmative Action Ruling, and Lots of
Thoughts*, N.Y. TIMES (July 2, 2023).

170 **"in a country rooted in a
history and current reality of
racial injustice":** Press Release,
Legal Defense Fund, In an Alarming
Departure from Long-Settled
Precedent, U.S. Supreme Court
Holds Harvard and UNC's
Admissions Practices
Unconstitutional (June 29, 2023).

170 **"the Supreme Court has
thrown into question its own
legitimacy":** Press Release,
Congressional Black Caucus,
Congressional Black Caucus Issues
Statement Regarding Supreme
Court Decision on Affirmative
Action (June 23, 2023).

170 **"extremists [seeking] to
turn back the clock on progress":**
Press Release, Congressional Black
Caucus, Congressional Black

266   Caucus Issues Statement Regarding Supreme Court Decision on Affirmative Action (June 23, 2023).

170   "it gave us the chance to show we more than deserved a seat at the table": Christina Pazzanese, *University "Remains Steadfast" in Commitment to Campus that Reflects Wide Range of Backgrounds and Experiences*, Harvard Gazette (June 29, 2023), https://news.harvard.edu/gazette /story/2023/06/harvard-united -in-resolve-in-face-of-supreme -courts-admissions-ruling.

170   "strongly, strongly disagree[d] with the Court's decision": Joe Biden, President, Remarks by President Biden on the Supreme Court's Decision on Affirmative Action (June 29, 2023).

170   "We have never fully lived up to it, but we've never walked away from it either": Joe Biden, President, Remarks by President Biden on the Supreme Court's Decision on Affirmative Action (June 29, 2023).

170   "Is this a rogue Court?": Joe Biden, President, Remarks by President Biden on the Supreme Court's Decision on Affirmative Action (June 29, 2023).

171   "This is not a normal Court": Joe Biden, President, Remarks by President Biden on the Supreme Court's Decision on Affirmative Action (June 29, 2023).

171   Harvard's leadership also insisted that much would remain unchanged: *Supreme Court Decision*, Harvard Univ. (June 29, 2023), https://www.harvard.edu /admissionscase/2023/06/29 /supreme-court-decision.

171   "That principle is as true and important today as it was yesterday": *Supreme Court Decision*, Harvard Univ. (June 29, 2023).

171   "and if you are feeling the gravity of that, I want you to know you're not alone": *A Message from President Claudine Gay*, Harvard Univ. (June 29, 2023), https://www .harvard.edu/admissionscase/2023 /06/29/a-message-from -president-elect-claudine-gay.

171   Right-wing activists dismissed Gay as a "DEI hire": *See* Ilya Shapiro (@ishapiro) X (December 9, 2023), https://x.com /ishapiro/status/17336819627 14353860 ("Claudine Gay was worse than an affirmative action hire; she was a DEI hire."). Claudine Gay's tenure lasted six months and two days. Emma H. Haidar & Cam E. Kettles, *Harvard President Claudine Gay Resigns, Shortest Tenure in University History*, Crimson (January 3, 2024), https://www. thecrimson.com/article/2024/1/3 /claudine-gay-resign-harvard.

172   "was impossible to follow the contours of the district": Morgan Smith, *One Man Standing*

Against Race-Based Laws, N.Y. TIMES (February 23, 2012).

172 what he deemed a misguided, illegal effort to foster Black political representation: The thumbnail sketch of Blum in this paragraph and beyond is drawn from the following sources: Morgan Smith, *One Man Standing Against Race-Based Laws*; Kali Holloway, *Inside the Cynical Campaign to Claim That Affirmative Action Hurts Asian Americans*, THE NATION (August 9, 2023); Lulu Garcia-Navarro, *He Worked for Years to Overturn Affirmative Action and Finally Won. He's Not Done.*; David G. Savage, *Conservative Legal Strategist Has No Office or Staff, Just a Surprising Supreme Court Track Record*, L.A. TIMES (December 22, 2015); Joan Biskupic, *Special Report: Behind U.S. Race Cases, A Little-Known Recruiter*, REUTERS (December 4, 2012); Douglas Belkin, *The Man Behind the Push to End Affirmative Action*, WALL ST. J. (June 29, 2023).

173 "You cannot remedy past discrimination with new discrimination": Belkin, *The Man Behind the Push to End Affirmative Action*; Garcia-Navarro, *He Worked for Years to Overturn Affirmative Action and Finally Won. He's Not Done* (quoting Blum as offering the same analysis).

173 "looking around for misdeeds by various actors who are discriminating on the basis of race": Garcia-Navarro, *He Worked for Years to Overturn Affirmative Action and Finally Won. He's Not Done.*

173 "I put them together, and then I worry about it for four years": Smith, *One Man Standing Against Race-Based Laws*.

174 "I needed Asian plaintiffs": Holloway, *Inside the Cynical Campaign to Claim That Affirmative Action Hurts Asian Americans*.

174 he thought that the gifted and talented programs impermissibly used race to advantage Black students: Smith, *One Man Standing Against Race-Based Laws*.

175 sued an organization—called the Fearless Fund—that sought to aid Black women entrepreneurs: Nikole Hannah-Jones, *The "Colorblindness" Trap: How a Civil Rights Ideal Got Hijacked.*, N.Y. TIMES (March 13, 2024).

175 Edward Blum is in no sense a one-man movement: *See* Jeannie Park & Kristin Penner, *The Absurd, Enduring Myth of the "One-Man" Campaign to Abolish Affirmative Action*, SLATE (October 25, 2022).

176 "anti-white racism is the predominant and most politically powerful form of racism in America today": Jeremy Carl, THE UNPROTECTED CLASS: HOW

268   Anti-White Racism Is Tearing
America Apart xv–xvi (2024).

176   "which they are using to
advantage their groups over
whites": Carl, The Unprotected
Class, at xvii.

176   "Racial mythmaking is also
present in modern commercials":
Carl, The Unprotected Class, at 145.

176   "America's anti-white
regime will not just go away
because of Court rulings": Jeremy
Carl, Combatting Elite Universities'
Admissions Lawlessness, American
Mind (October 9, 2024).

177   "punishment *including
possible prison terms* for
individuals who defy the law":
Carl, Combatting Elite Universities'
Admissions Lawlessness (emphasis
added).

177   "[O]ur elite class,
epitomized by the Ivy League, will
do what it wants": Carl,
Combatting Elite Universities'
Admissions Lawlessness.

177   "We will forge a society that
is colorblind": *See* Donald Trump,
Second Inaugural Speech,
January 20, 2025.

177   Trump in rapid succession:
See Erica L. Green & Hamed Aleaziz,
Federal Workers Ordered to Report on
Colleagues Over D.E.I. Crackdown,
N.Y. Times (January 25, 2025); Emma
Goldberg, Trump's D.E.I. Order
Creates "Fear and Confusion" Among
Corporate Leaders, N.Y. Times
(January 23, 2025).

177   "Trump is putting the
muscle of the executive branch":
See Goldberg, Trump's D.E.I. Order
Creates "Fear and Confusion" Among
Corporate Leaders.

178   "Every student admitted to
the class of 2028 at M.I.T. will
know": Anemona Hartocollis &
Stephanie Saul, At M.I.T., Black and
Latino Enrollment Drops Sharply
After Affirmative Action Ban, N.Y.
Times, (August 21, 2024).

179   "They don't think Black
students are smart enough to be
in their clubs": Amy Harmon, How
It Feels to Have Your Life Changed by
Affirmative Action, N.Y. Times
(June 21, 2023).

179   "Sprouling while Black":
Harmon, How It Feels to Have Your
Life Changed by Affirmative Action.

180   "it is clear that paradigms
based on court efficacy are simply
wrong": Gerald N. Rosenberg, The
Hollow Hope: Can Courts Bring
About Social Change? 105 (1991).

180   "by themselves, courts are
relatively slow to act and
ineffective": Jack M. Balkin, What
Brown Teaches Us About
Constitutional Theory, 90 Va. L. Rev.
1537, 1549 (2004).

181   "'It's time for us to do some
justice!'": Balkin, What Brown

Teaches Us About Constitutional Theory, at 1549.

181 "underscor[ing] that Brown is and will remain firmly committed": Christina H. Paxson, *The Supreme Court's Ruling on Affirmative Action* (June 29, 2023), https://president.brown.edu /president/supreme-courts -ruling-affirmative-action.

182 "fewer African-American first-years enrolling at M.I.T. than when *I* was a freshman more than forty years ago": Stu Schmill, *MIT After SFFA*, MIT ADMISSIONS (August 21, 2024), https: //mitadmissions.org/blogs/entry /mit-after-sffa.

182 "[T]hat cannot *possibly* be the right outcome for our community": Schmill, *MIT After SFFA*.

182 "consequence of last year's Supreme Court decision": Sally Kornbluth, *Undergraduate Admissions Transcript*, MIT OFFICE OF THE PRESIDENT (August 21, 2024), https://president.mit.edu/writing -speeches/undergraduate -admissions-transcript.

183 ensuring that the Supreme Court serves as a stabilizing force in American society: *See, e.g.,* Melvin I. Urofsky, THE AFFIRMATIVE ACTION PUZZLE: A COMPREHENSIVE AND HONEST EXPLORATION OF ONE OF THE MOST CONTROVERSIAL LEGAL AND SOCIAL ISSUES IN US HISTORY 474

(2022) (calling Chief Justice Roberts "an institutionalist").

183 who believes that original public meaning must be vindicated though the heavens may fall: Justice Scalia can be viewed as rebuking Justice Thomas, when he noted that—unlike his fellow originalist, Justice Thomas—he nevertheless believed in at least some role for precedent. "I'm an originalist—I'm not a nut," Justice Scalia said. *See* Strauss, THE LIVING CONSTITUTION, at 17.

183 sharply divergent positions that Chief Justice Roberts and Justice Thomas recently adopted in *Dobbs v. Jackson Women's Health Organization*: 597 U.S. 215 (2022).

183 by finding that the ban did not pose an undue burden on the right to an abortion: 597 U.S. at 353–54 (Roberts, C.J., concurring in the judgment) (referencing Roe v. Wade, 410 U.S. 113 (1973) and Planned Parenthood of Se. Pa. v. Casey, 505 U.S. 833 (1992)).

183 encouraged his colleagues to rethink other landmark opinions in that line of cases: *Dobbs,* 597 U.S. at 332 (Thomas, J., concurring) (referencing Griswold v. Connecticut, 381 U.S. 479 (1965) and Obergefell v. Hodges, 576 U.S. 644 (2015)).

184 "It's the difference between being a judge and being a law

270   **professor"**: Jeffrey Rosen, *Roberts's Rules*, ATL. (January/February 2007), at 113.

185   **"a willingness . . . to suppress his or her ideological agenda in the interest of achieving . . . stability"**: Rosen, *Roberts's Rules*, at 113.

185   **Rehnquist was the Court's foremost critic of *Miranda v. Arizona***: 384 U.S. 436 (1966); *see* Edward Walsh, *High Court Upholds Miranda Rights*, 7-2, WASH. POST, June 26, 2000, at A1 (noting that Rehnquist was a "a frequent and vocal critic of . . . Miranda . . . during his earlier years on the bench").

185   **fundamentally affirming the decision's continued vitality:** *Dickerson v. United States*, 530 U.S. 428 (2000) (upholding *Miranda*).

185   **"he wrote that opinion as chief for the good of the institution"**: Rosen, *Roberts's Rules*, at 112.

185   **"seem[s] to be lurching around because of changes in personnel"**: Rosen, *Roberts's Rules*, at 112.

186   **"lurch . . . because of changes in personnel"**: Rosen, *Roberts's Rules*, at 112.

186   **Roberts revered Judge Friendly to an unusual degree:** Robert Gordon, *Friendly Fire*, SLATE (August 11, 2005), https://slate.com /news-and-politics/2005/08 /friendly-fire.html (noting that one of Roberts's former colleagues stated that Roberts spoke of Friendly "with 'deep reverence' and 'a certain twinkle in his eye'").

186   **managed to cite Judge Friendly in six opinions:** Brad Snyder, *The Judicial Genealogy (and Mythology) of John Roberts: Clerkships from Gray to Brandeis to Friendly to Roberts*, 71 OHIO ST. L.J. 1149, 1230 (2010) (noting the high frequency with which then-Judge Roberts invoked Judge Friendly).

187   **"ha[d] an essential humility about him"**: *Confirmation Hearing on the Nomination of John G. Roberts, Jr. to Be Chief Justice of the United States: Hearing Before the S. Comm. on the Judiciary*, 109th Cong. 1, 202 (2005). Brad Snyder's scholarship examining the relationship between Roberts and Friendly deeply influenced my own thinking on this topic. *See* Snyder, *The Judicial Genealogy (and Mythology) of John Roberts*, at 1215–21, 1231–41.

187   **"Judges have to have the humility to recognize that they operate within a system of precedent"**: *Confirmation Hearing on the Nomination of John G. Roberts, Jr.*, at 55.

187   **"meant embracing a few closely related concepts"**: Justin Driver, *The Constitutional Conservatism of the Warren Court*, 100 CALIF. L. REV. 1101, 1105 (2012).

188   "reluctan[ce] to revise the judgments of predecessors": Norman Dorsen, *The Second Mr. Justice Harlan: A Constitutional Conservative*, 44 N.Y.U. L. REV. 249, 250, 257 (1969).

188   "is not an inexorable command": *Vasquez v. Hillery*, 474 U.S. 254, 266 (1986).

188   "thereby contributes to the integrity of our constitutional system of government": *Vasquez*, 474 U.S. at 265.

188   its assessment that the universities had failed to provide even a compelling government interest for affirmative action: *SFFA*, 600 U.S. 181, 214; *id.* at 232 (Thomas, J., concurring).

188   "that a diverse student body would serve its educational goals": 579 U.S. 365, 376–77 (2016) (internal quotation marks and citations omitted).

189   but also requested that the Court overturn *Grutter*: Brief for Petitioner at 12, 68, *SFFA v. Harvard & SFFA v. UNC*, 600 U.S. 181 (Nos. 20-1199 & 21-707).

189   some lawyers have sought to construe it as merely a casual aside: *See, e.g.,* Lee C. Bollinger & Geoffrey R. Stone, A LEGACY OF DISCRIMINATION: THE ESSENTIAL CONSTITUTIONALITY OF AFFIRMATIVE ACTION 70 (2023) (ridiculing *Grutter*'s "expiration date");

Transcript of Oral Argument at 99, *SFFA v. Harvard*, 600 U.S. 181 (2023) (No. 20-1199) (quoting Solicitor General Prelogar arguing that *Grutter*'s timeline did not provide a firm end date for affirmative action).

189   I believe that *Grutter*'s twenty-five-year sunset should be construed as possessing legal authority: *See* Justin Driver, *Think Affirmative Action Is Dead? Think Again.*, N.Y. TIMES, October 31, 2022, at A18.

190   many college students take longer than four years to graduate from college: *Digest of Education Statistics*, NAT'L CTR. FOR EDUC. STAT. (February 2023), https://nces.ed .gov/programs/digest/d22/tables /dt22_326.10.asp (finding that less than half of the 2011–2015 college entry cohorts graduated within four years of matriculating).

190   "the [judiciary's] marvelous mystery of time": Alexander M. Bickel, THE LEAST DANGEROUS BRANCH: THE SUPREME COURT AT THE BAR OF POLITICS 26 (1962).

191   "really underscores the need to make sure that universities shouldn't be taking into account wealth or alumni status": Blake Jones, *Why Legacy Admissions Bans Have Exploded in the US*, POLITICO (October 2, 2024).

192   "'Why is it every time we get a chance to do something, the rug

272   **is pulled out from under us?'":** Stephanie Saul, *Elite Colleges' Quiet Fight to Favor Alumni Children*, N.Y. TIMES (October 31, 2022).

193   **rooting for Elon Musk to purchase the winning lottery ticket:** Saul, *Elite Colleges' Quiet Fight to Favor Alumni Children* (quoting Justin Driver on legacy admissions).

193   **but 8 percent of such applicants did so following *SFFA*:** *See* Elyse C. Goncalves & Matan H. Josephy, *How the Supreme Court Shaped the Class of 2028 at Harvard*, HARV. CRIMSON (September 13, 2024).

193   **did not disclose their racial identities during the 2023–2024 admissions cycle:** Evie Steele, *GU Admits Fewer Students of Color in First Post-Affirmative Action Class*, THE HOYA (October 18, 2024).

195   **whereas less than 2 percent declined to do so before *SFFA*:** Anemona Hartcollis, *Yale, Princeton and Duke Are Questioned Over Decline in Asian Students*, N.Y. TIMES (September 17, 2024).

195   **Yale has not yet released this data:** Hailey Talbert, *Breaking Down Yale's Class of 2028—What do We Know About Racial Diversity Post-Affirmative Action?*, YALE DAILY NEWS (September 12, 2024).

195   **Harvard decided instead to calculate the racial percentages of the students who disclosed their**

racial identities: *See* Goncalves & Josephy, *How the Supreme Court Shaped the Class of 2028 at Harvard*.

195   **concentrated among Asian American applicants:** Amy Qin, *Applying to College, and Trying to Appear "Less Asian,"* N.Y. TIMES (June 20, 2023).

196   **that are in desperate need of reappraisal:** Anemona Hartocollis & Amy Harmon, *Affirmative Action Ruling Shakes Universities Over More Than Race*, N.Y. TIMES (July 26, 2023), https://www.nytimes.com/2023/07/26/us/affirmative-action-college-admissions-harvard.html.

197   **"After two years, twelve of fifteen specially admitted students were not maintaining a passing average":** Lino Graglia, *Special Admission of the Culturally Deprived to Law School*, 119 U. PA. L. REV. 351, 359 (1970).

197   **"one year later, more than half of those students had received sufficiently low marks that they were forced to withdraw":** *See* Ken Foskett, JUDGING THOMAS: THE LIFE AND TIMES OF CLARENCE THOMAS 119–20 (2004); Macklin Fleming & Louis Pollak, *The Black Quota at Yale Law School*, 1970 PUB. INT. 44, 44–45.

197   **will not eliminate universities' desire to enroll significant numbers of Black and**

brown students: *See* Kennedy, FOR DISCRIMINATION, at 240, 15, 239.

198 have often expressed concerns about ensuring that Black and brown students realize their full academic potential: *See, e.g.,* Sander, *A Systemic Analysis of Affirmative Action in American Law Schools,* at 442–54.

198 "deference is owed to a university in defining those intangible characteristics": *Fisher v. Univ. of Tex.* (*Fisher II*), 579 U.S. 365, 388 (2016) (internal citations and quotation marks omitted).

199 "the legal and external landscape has shifted dramatically, particularly within the United States": Editorial Board, *Business Backs Away from DEI*, WALL ST. J. (August 29, 2024).

199 similar announcements from Lowe's, Ford Motors, Harley-Davidson, and John Deere: Editorial Board, *Business Backs Away from DEI.*

199 iconic American companies that have recently retreated from their commitments to DEI: *See* Neil Vigidor, *What's Next for D.E.I. With Trump Back in Office?*, N.Y. TIMES (January 22, 2025); Rob Copeland, *Fearing Trump, Wall Street Sounds a Retreat on Diversity Efforts*, N.Y. TIMES (February 11, 2025); Nico Grant, *Google Unwinds Employee Diversity Goals, Citing*

Trump's D.E.I. Orders, N.Y. TIMES (February 5, 2025).

273

199 have brandished the opinion to suggest that corporate racial diversity programs violate federal law: Editorial Board, *Business Backs Away from DEI*; Grant, *Google Unwinds Employee Diversity Goals.*

199 to intimidate pro-diversity businesses when he ran America First Legal: Jonathan Swan, Maggie Haberman, David A. Fahrenthold & Charlie Savage, *Stephen Miller, Channeling Trump, Has Built More Power Than Ever*, N.Y. TIMES (January 17, 2025).

199 "and get[ting] them to just unilaterally disarm": AJ Hess, *How Stephen Miller and the Anti-DEI Movement Are Going After Small Businesses*, FAST COMPANY (September 27, 2024), https://www.fastcompany.com/91193116/how-stephen-miller-and-the-anti-dei-movement-are-going-after-small-businesses.

199 "business after business is [caving]": Hess, *How Stephen Miller and the Anti-DEI Movement Are Going After Small Businesses.*

200 "But when businesses didn't do what Stephen Miller wanted, he decided to sue them": Hess, *How Stephen Miller and the Anti-DEI Movement Are Going After Small Businesses.*

274   200   "set[ting] their sights on private businesses" to maximize leverage: Hess, *How Stephen Miller and the Anti-DEI Movement Are Going After Small Businesses.*

200   "So Stephen Miller styles all of these as class actions": Hess, *How Stephen Miller and the Anti-DEI Movement Are Going After Small Businesses.*

200   "striking fear into organizations' hearts": Emma Goldberg, *Trump's D.E.I. Order Creates "Fear and Confusion" Among Corporate Leaders*, N.Y. TIMES (January 23, 2025).

200   less than 2 percent of the top executives at the nation's largest companies: *See* Jessica Guynn & Brent Schrotenboer, *Why Are There Still So Few Black Executives in America*, USA TODAY (August 20, 2020).

CONCLUSION

201   "The Universities Are the Enemy": Eboo Patel, *J.D. Vance Is Coming for Higher Ed*, CHRONICLE OF HIGHER EDUCATION (July 19, 2024).

201   even when they go about the ordinary business of conducting research and educating students: *See* Michelle Goldberg, *Trump Wants to Destroy All Academia, Not Just the Woke Parts*, N.Y. TIMES (February 14, 2025).

202   the Trump administration's ongoing assault on university autonomy: *See, e.g.,* Kate Andrias, Jessica Bulman-Pozen, et al., *A Title VI Demand Letter that Itself Violates Title IV (and the Constitution),* BALKINIZATION (March 15, 2025), https://balkin.blogspot.com/2025/03/a-title-vi-demand-letter-that-itself.html.

202   "diversity and difference are essential to academic excellence": *Supreme Court Decision*, HARVARD UNIV. (June 29, 2023).

203   the racial composition of some elite college classes: *See* Karabel, THE CHOSEN, at 379.

204   accounted for only 15 of the more than 3,000 students who entered the nation's most prestigious colleges: Karabel, THE CHOSEN, at 379. *See* AMERICAN POLITICAL SPEECHES 95 (Terry Golway & Richard Beeman eds., 2012).

204   Black enrollment in ultra-elite colleges had skyrocketed: Karabel, THE CHOSEN, at 379.

204   once a curiosity—became a comparatively common sight: *See* Abigail Thernstrom & Stephan Thernstrom, *Black Progress: How Far We've Come, and How Far We Have to Go*, BROOKINGS INST. (March 1, 1998), https://www.brookings.edu/articles/black-progress-how-far-weve-come-and-how-far-we-have-to-go.

205   "we have no problem in answering the question": William G. Bowen & Derek Bok, THE SHAPE OF THE RIVER: LONG-TERM CONSEQUENCES OF CONSIDERING RACE IN COLLEGE AND UNIVERSITY ADMISSIONS 284 (1998).

205   "All they did was stop stopping us": Juan Williams, *A Question of Fairness*, ATL. (February 1, 1987), https://www.theatlantic.com/magazine/archive/1987/02/a-question-of-fairness/306370.

205   "The Black Quota at Yale Law School": *The Black Quota at Yale Law School*, PUBLIC INTEREST, June 23, 1969, at 44.

205   "You anticipate that half this group will actually enroll": *The Black Quota at Yale Law School*, at 44.

206   criticized Yale's commitment to admitting 10 percent of future law school cohorts: *See The Black Quota at Yale Law School*, at 45.

206   in no way contradicted the central role that racial considerations played: *See The Black Quota at Yale Law School*, at 50–52.

206   if the policy were abandoned, the percentage of Black law students would decline precipitously: *See* Wilkinson, FROM BROWN TO BAKKE, at 288–89.

206   making it the smallest number of Black Harvard 1Ls since 1965: Stephanie Saul & Anemona Hartocollis, *Black Student Enrollment at Harvard Law Drops by More Than Half*, N.Y. TIMES (December 16, 2024).

207   smallest Black freshman enrollment in Westwood since 1973: *See* Stephanie Saul, *Top Colleges Where Affirmative Action Was Banned Say It's Needed*, N.Y. TIMES (August 27, 2022); Erika Hayasaki, *A Voice for Diversity at UCLA*, L.A. TIMES (December 3, 2006), https://www.latimes.com/archives/la-xpm-2006-dec-03-me-freshman3-story.html.

207   so scandalous that the group became known as the "Infamous 96": NPR Staff, *What Happens Without Affirmative Action: The Story of UCLA*, NPR (June 23, 2013), https://www.npr.org/2013/06/23/194656555/what-happens-without-affirmative-action-the-story-of-ucla.

207   fifteen years later, that figure had fallen below 4 percent: *See* Brief for the University of Michigan as Amicus Curiae at 22, Students for Fair Admissions, Inc. v. President & Fellows of Harvard Coll., 600 U.S. 181 (2023) (No. 20-1199).

207   a lost generation of Black students at elite educational institutions: *Cf.* Stephanie Saul, *If Affirmative Action Ends, College*

276   *Admissions May Be Changed Forever*, N.Y. TIMES (January 26, 2023), https://www.nytimes.com/2023/01/15/us/affirmative-action-admissions-scotus.html (quoting Angel Pérez, the chief executive of the National Association for College Admission Counseling as stating that, because of *SFFA*, "We will see a decline in students of color attending college . . . ," and "We will be missing an entire generation.").

207   **"Where are the black students? Where are the black students?":** Brief for Respondents at 39 n.26, DeFunis v. Odegaard, 416 U.S. 312 (1974) (No. 73-235); *see also* Wilkinson, FROM *BROWN* TO *BAKKE*, at 281.

Columbia Global Reports is a nonprofit publishing imprint from Columbia University that commissions authors to produce works of original thinking and on-site reporting from all over the world, on a wide range of topics. Our books are short—novella-length, and readable in a few hours—but ambitious. They offer new ways of looking at and understanding the major issues of our time. Most readers are curious and busy. Our books are for them.

If this book changed the way you look at the world, and if you would like to support our mission, consider making a gift to Columbia Global Reports to help us share new ideas and stories.

Visit globalreports.columbia.edu to support our upcoming books, subscribe to our newsletter, and learn more about Columbia Global Reports. Thank you for being part of our community of readers and supporters.